G000167958

THE DOMESTIC, MORAL AND POLITICAL ECONOMIES OF POST-CELTIC TIGER IRELAND

Manchester University Press

IRISH SOCIETY

The Irish Society series provides a critical, interdisciplinary and in-depth analysis of Ireland that reveals the processes and forces shaping social, economic, cultural and political life, and their outcomes for communities and social groups. The books seek to understand the evolution of social, economic and spatial relations from a broad range of perspectives, and explore the challenges facing Irish society in the future given present conditions and policy instruments.

SERIES EDITOR
Rob Kitchin

ALREADY PUBLISHED

Public private partnerships in Ireland: Failed experiment or the way forward for the state? *Rory Hearne*

Migrations: Ireland in a global world
Edited by Mary Gilmartin and Allen White

THE DOMESTIC, MORAL AND POLITICAL ECONOMIES OF POST-CELTIC TIGER IRELAND

What rough beast?

Kieran Keohane and Carmen Kuhling

MANCHESTER UNIVERSITY PRESS
Manchester and New York

*distributed in the United States exclusively
by Palgrave Macmillan*

Copyright © Kieran Keohane and Carmen Kuhling 2014

The rights of Kieran Keohane and Carmen Kuhling
to be identified as the authors of this work have been asserted by them in accordance
with the Copyright, Designs and Patents Act 1988.

Published by Manchester University Press
Oxford Road, Manchester M13 9NR, UK
and Room 400, 175 Fifth Avenue, New York, NY 10010, USA
www.manchesteruniversitypress.co.uk

Distributed in the United States exclusively by
Palgrave Macmillan, 175 Fifth Avenue, New York,
NY 10010, USA

Distributed in Canada exclusively by
UBC Press, University of British Columbia, 2029 West Mall,
Vancouver, BC, Canada V6T 1Z2

British Library Cataloguing-in-Publication Data
A catalogue record for this book is available from the British Library

Library of Congress Cataloging-in-Publication Data applied for

ISBN 978 07190 8482 9 hardback

First published 2014

The publisher has no responsibility for the persistence or accuracy of URLs for any
external or third-party internet websites referred to in this book, and does not guarantee
that any content on such websites is, or will remain, accurate or appropriate.

Typeset in Minion
by Action Publishing Technology Ltd, Gloucester
Printed in Great Britain
by CPI Antony Rowe Ltd, Chippenham, Wiltshire

Series editor's foreword

Over the past twenty years Ireland has undergone enormous social, cultural and economic change. From a poor, peripheral country on the edge of Europe with a conservative culture dominated by tradition and Church, Ireland transformed into a global, cosmopolitan country with a dynamic economy. At the heart of the processes of change was a new kind of political economic model of development that ushered in the so-called Celtic Tiger years, accompanied by renewed optimism in the wake of the ceasefires in Northern Ireland and the peace dividend of the Good Friday Agreement. As Ireland emerged from decades of economic stagnation and The Troubles came to a peaceful end, the island became the focus of attention for countries seeking to emulate its economic and political miracles. Every other country, it seemed, wanted to be the next Tiger, modelled on Ireland's successes. And then came the financial collapse of 2008, the bursting of the property bubble, bank bailouts, austerity plans, rising unemployment and a return to emigration. From being the paradigm case of successful economic transformation, Ireland has become an internationally important case study of what happens when an economic model goes disastrously wrong.

The Irish Society series provides a critical, interdisciplinary and in-depth analysis of Ireland that reveals the processes and forces shaping social, economic, cultural and political life, and their outcomes for communities and social groups. The books seek to understand the evolution of social, economic and spatial relations from a broad range of perspectives, and explore the challenges facing Irish society in the future given present conditions and policy instruments. The series examines all aspects of Irish society including, but not limited to: social exclusion, identity, health, welfare, life cycle, family life and structures, labour and work cultures, spatial and sectoral economy, local and regional development, politics and the political system, government and governance, environment, migration and spatial planning. The series is supported by the Irish Social Sciences Platform (ISSP), an all-island platform of integrated social science research and graduate education focusing on the social, cultural and economic transformations shaping Ireland in the twenty-first century. Funded by the Programme for Research in Third Level Institutions, the ISSP brings together leading social science academics from all of Ireland's universities and other third-level institutions.

Given the marked changes in Ireland's fortunes over the past two decades it is important that rigorous scholarship is applied to understand the forces at work, how they have affected different people and places in uneven and unequal ways, and what needs to happen to create a fairer and prosperous society. The Irish Society series provides such scholarship.

Rob Kitchin

Contents

Preface: Our methods of theorizing Ireland's domestic, moral and political economies   *page* ix

Introduction: 'What rough beast?' Monsters of post-Celtic Tiger Ireland   1

Part I: Domestic economy

1   Ireland's haunted houses   19
2   The value of house and home   33
3   Foundations of Europe's collective household   51

Part II: Moral economy

4   Fair trade and free market   69
5   Political theologies in the wake of the Celtic Tiger   87
6   Conversion: Turning towards a radiant ideal   107

Part III: Political economy

7   Pleonexic tyranny in Plato's *Republic* and in the Irish republic   125
8   Anamnesis for a new Ireland   142
9   Conclusion: omen of a post-republic: the demon child of neoliberalism   158

Bibliography   170
Index   189

Preface: Our methods of theorizing Ireland's domestic, moral and political economies

We are trapped within the horizons of the present crisis, stuck in a moment that we cannot see our way out of, seeking return to growth, return to competitiveness, return to the Markets, repeating the same patterns over and over again, 'like a fly trapped in bottle', Wittgenstein (1994: 309) says. Media commentary as well as what is conventionally taken to be social science – 'policy relevant', 'evidence based', 'rational', 'progressive', even 'critical' social science – are fully implicated in this problem – bouncing from side to side, from one moment of crisis to the next, banging against glass walls. To understand what is going on by following the news and keeping up with events is like trying to tell the time by looking only at the second hand on a clock, for the news is the 'now', the instantaneous, and the media is the 'in-between', in the middle of instants, buzzing furiously but going around in circles.[1] Social science and conventional sociology are little better. Empiricism, historicism, positivism, economism, rationalism – the various 'isms', buzz-words of modern social science – seldom get beyond the spatio-temporal limits of the European and Western parameters of Enlightenment and Modernity (Elias, 1985; Delanty, 2006), as though there have been no other civilizations, no other forms of life from which that we can learn, and that our problems are uniquely ours and entirely new. Modern social science is fully in the grip of the very thing that it imagines itself to be the master of. This contemporary 'conceit of scholars', as Vico (1999) called it in his day, is greatly exacerbated by disciplinary differentiation and specialization on the one hand, and, especially in places such as Ireland, by the particularism of national historicity on the other, what Vico (ibid) calls 'the conceit of nations'. The task, Wittgenstein says, is 'to show the fly the way out of the bottle', by 'changing the aspect under which things are viewed' (Wittgenstein, 1994, 309: 195–196). How can we get a perspective on our situation by virtue of which we may be able to imagine alternatives?

Sociological imagination, C. Wright Mills (1959) says, is a way of seeing the world as through a lens or a prism with various facets through which our present reality may be viewed and refracted. As well as working with the reper-toire of often contrasting perspectives within the sociological tradition one should actively seek historical perspectives, anthropological perspectives, philosophical – that is to say, Ideal perspectives, literary and aesthetic perspec-tives, mythological perspectives, theological perspectives, biographical and autobiographical self-reflective and psychoanalytical perspectives, philological comparative linguistic and semiotic perspectives, and others too. 'Try to think in terms of a variety of viewpoints and in this way to let your mind become a moving prism catching light from as many angles as possible' (Mills, 1959: 214). By this means we can think ourselves away and look back on our own reality from different points of view, see it on the one hand as strange, but also as not so unique as we had thought; that other peoples in other places, and we ourselves in other times, have grappled with similar problems and found ways through them from which we might learn.

Methods of theorizing

Social theory and method are inextricably bound up with one another, despite the convention of their separation and a tendency to differentiate them entirely by emphasizing technical training in particular methods over general education in culture and thinking. But to theorize, whether in Sociology, Philosophy, Politics, Anthropology, Economics or in any cognate field in the arts, humanities and social sciences, means not simply to arrange empirical evidence, but also to seek to clarify ideals by virtue of a way of inquiry that is sustained and methodically pursued, so much so that we may speak of method(s) of theorizing. Methods of theorizing are thus ways of attending to the world so as to bring into view, contemplate and articulate ideal standards of beauty, truth and the good life; radiant ideals that illuminate and make possible an understanding and interpretation of our present practices and institutions, thereby enabling our self-critique and self-transformation in light of such ideals.

According to Durkheim, 'the value of a thing cannot be, and never has been estimated except in relation to some conception of the ideal' (1974: 90) and Weber concurs: 'all historical experience confirms the truth – that man would not have attained the possible unless time and again he had reached out for the impossible' (1978a: 225). Theorizing can thus be conceived of as the methodical reaching out for the impossible ideal so as to guide our actions in the real world. But as *theoria* and *methodus* have become differentiated we lose sight of the ways towards recovering our ideals just at a time when economic crisis, ecological catastrophe and political turmoil threaten to overwhelm us.

Sociology as a vocation

Sociology retreats into the present and loses sight of ideals, relying on the myopic techniques of purportedly positive evidence and empirical analysis because the world ultimately refutes the aspiration of Enlightenment to master it. Despite the claims of modern social science that the world is rational and that it can be mastered by reason, Weber says:

> Not only the whole course of world history, but every frank examination of everyday experience points to the very opposite. The development of religions all over the world is determined by the fact that the opposite is true. The age-old problem of theodicy consists of the very question of how it is that a power which is said to be at once omnipotent and kind could have created such an irrational world of undeserved suffering, unpunished injustice, and hopeless stupidity. Either this power is not omnipotent or not kind, or, entirely different principles of compensation and reward govern our life – principles we may interpret meta-physically, or even principles that forever escape our comprehension. This problem – the experience of the irrationality of the world – has been the driving force of all religious evolution. The Indian doctrine of karma, Persian dualism, the doctrine of original sin, predestination and the *deus absconditus*, all these have grown out of this experience. Also the early Christians knew full well the world is governed by demons and that he who lets himself in for politics, that is, for power and force as means, contracts with diabolical powers and for his action it is not true that good can follow only from good and evil only from evil, but that often the opposite is true. Anyone who fails to see this is, indeed, a political infant. (Weber, 1978: 212)

We take seriously Weber's insight as to the irrational and demonic character of the world in general and modern society in particular – that the world is governed by demons, in that it is and remains ambiguous, ambivalent and paradoxical, so that normatively oriented sociology informed by histori-cal and anthropological critical reflexivity, knowing the naivety of claims to value neutrality and scientific detachment and aspiring to be politically influ-ential – 'policy relevant' in the prevailing jargon – however reasonable it may believe itself to be, it is still vocationally akin to demonology and exorcism. We are always grappling with spirits that possess and animate social and bodies politic, spirits that are sometimes benign but are as often malevolent; and that work of exorcism is accomplished only by virtue of the power of a radiant Idea: Beauty, Truth and the Good, a theosophical trinity conventionally designated in terms of Divinity. It is only by invoking the name of God (or whatever universal Ideal is its placeholder – Reason, the Rational Subject or the Ideal

Speech Community are specifically modern instances) that the beast can be called to identify itself, and then, when named, that it can be subdued and controlled by the divine power of *Agape*, that is by the authority of a political community. But the demon, the 'rough beast', as we shall see has many names: Sphinx, Baal, Pazuzu, all are historical variations on the primordial and anthropological archetype of Trickster, the demonic incarnation of liminality, ambivalence and paradox (Jung, 1972; Radin, 1972; Hyde, 1998). And as Weber warns social scientists and those who would let themselves in for politics (himself included), we necessarily and unavoidably make a pact with diabolical powers. Dealing with Trickster means acknowledging from the outset the uncertainty of outcomes and the unintended consequences of courses of action pursued with good intentions, for 'it is not true that good can follow only from good and evil only from evil, but that often the opposite is true'. And one grave risk is also known from the beginning, that would-be exorcists run the risk of becoming possessed themselves, for Weber knew very well what Nietzsche (1989: 89) had already said: that 'those who stare into the abyss should beware because the abyss begins to stare back; and those who fight with monsters should beware lest they become monsters themselves'.

Aesthetic ideas

We start on the same page as Weber on 'Politics as a Vocation' for it is only when we have brought ideals to light that we can do the hard political work of 'boring down steadily through thick planks with passion and judgment combined' (Weber, 1978: 225). This present book is concerned with imagining our way towards ideals that might guide our courses of political action. But where can we locate such ideals? Kant indicates where such resources may be found in terms of 'the pedagogical role of the aesthetic'. Aesthetic ideas, Kant says, can enable us to transcend the limits of both pure reason and practical reason and help 'to bring reason into harmony with itself' (Kant, 1914: 49).

> By an aesthetical Idea I understand that representation of the Imagination which occasions much thought, without, however, any definite thought, *i.e.* any *concept*, being capable of being adequate to it; it consequently cannot be completely compassed and made intelligible by language. ... Such representations of the Imagination we may call *Ideas*, partly because they at least strive after something which lies beyond the bounds of experience. (Kant, 1916: 49).

Aesthetic ideas – Kant includes metaphors, allegories and similes, poetic, mythic and religious language, however expressed – in visual arts, through music, film, dance, dramatic performance, literature, poetry – have transformative power because they help us to strain out beyond the confines of experience in the world towards what is beyond the world – they give us glimpses of an ideal realm of Beauty, Truth and the Good. Literature and poetry especially have this transformative, creative potential:

> The poet ventures to realise to sense, rational Ideas of invisible beings, the kingdom of the blessed, hell, eternity, creation, etc.; or even if he deals with things of which there are examples in experience – *e.g.* death, envy and all vices, also love, fame, and the like – he tries, by means of Imagination, which emulates the play of Reason in its quest after a maximum, to go beyond the limits of experience and to present them to Sense with a completeness of which there is no example in nature. (Kant, ibid.).

Ideals are beyond the world, but they are already present within the world, linguistically and symbolically encoded as 'collective representations that human groups have painstakingly forged over centuries, and in which they have amassed the best of their intellectual capital' (Durkheim, 1995: 15, 18ff). Ideals are collective representations generated in the lifeworld and institutionalized in language, though they have become lost, dissimulated and obscure. To imagine our way through the present crisis the ideas that we need are already present, for 'imagination is memory', James Joyce says, a principle that Joyce borrows from Vico, for whom imagination 'is nothing but the springing up again of reminiscences, and ingenuity or invention is nothing but the working over of what is remembered' (1999: 264); a formulation which Vico in turn inherits from the Greeks. Etymology, theology, mythology and folklore become important methodologies, and, as Vico found in his time, our poets (Yeats and Joyce especially, and others too) as much as our social scientists become our spirit guides into Ireland's domestic, political and moral economies.

Our present difficulties are characterized by stasis. We cannot imagine alternatives, so we are told that 'there is no alternative'. To think creatively social science needs to engage with aesthetic ideas, for this 'brings Reason into movement', Kant says. Literature and poetry 'enliven the mind by opening out to it the prospect into an illimitable field of kindred representations. ... Such a multiplicity of partial representations ... adds to a concept much ineffable thought, the feeling of which quickens the cognitive faculties' (Kant, 1914: 49). This book hopes to contribute to such a conversation between Irish social science and literature and poetry, and thereby to enable imaginative and creative thinking.

A guide to the book

An Introduction explores the issue of a collective representation of Ireland after the sudden death of the 'Celtic Tiger' and introduces the aesthetic idea that runs throughout; namely, the idea articulated by Yeats (1920a) in his famous poem 'The Second Coming'. In a period following crisis, in conditions of liminality and anomie, when 'Things fall apart; the centre cannot hold', Yeats asks: 'what rough beast, its hour come round at last, / slouches towards Bethlehem to be born?'

Three sections follow, on the Domestic, Moral and Political Economies of post-Celtic Tiger Ireland. Domestic, moral and political economies are not analytically separated in this book, for such analytical separation has been at the very source of the problem of the fragmentation of knowledge, the retreat into the present, and the losing sight of ideals. Instead, and quite deliberately, while the domestic, moral and political economies of contemporary Ireland are grouped thematically and in sequential order – Domestic, Moral and Political – all three are treated as an integrated whole within each chapter and throughout. In this way economics is reconciled and situated within its wider parental discourses of society as 'collective household' and the primary processes and principles of social integration, that is, morality. Not only is *oikos* house the root of 'economics', it is also the root of 'ecology', broadening the frame to integrate issues of environment and speaking to themes of sustainable development on one level, and at another level to the deep-ecological and ethnomethodological themes of mythology, lore and poetic unity that comprise the linguistic household of society. The philosophical, sociological and political-anthropological reframing of economics and the tripartite, holistic and normative structure reconnecting economics with historical and general anthropological deep human needs explore the grounds for a re-humanized political economics and suggest pathways to a sustainable future other than a second coming of recent patterns.

The first three chapters, on Domestic economy, are concerned with ideas of house and home. We explore the symbolic order and the imaginative structure, the meanings and values that we associate with house and home, both in the sense of the individual private dwelling house and more encompassing notions of our collective home as they circulate in general economy and in the economics of desire. Our discussion moves through the haunted houses of Ireland's 'ghost estates'; to the sophisticated financial instruments derived from mortgage-backed securities that were a lynchpin of global financialization and the epicentre of the crash; to the question of the fiscal and moral foundations of the collective household of Europe.

The next three chapters, on Moral economy, are concerned with ideas that are holy and sacred. We begin with a story about fundamental values and principles of fairness and justice as they are played out in a dispute over natural resources, a particular, contemporary conflict that reiterates the ancient Irish mythic story of the *Táin*. Now, as then, and as always, catastrophe follows when the moral principles of general economy are violated and inverted from reciprocal gift exchange to trickery and theft. The next chapter explores how neoliberal politics and economics have come to assume the status of theologies – metanarratives that purport to explain and to justify the genesis and the teleology of the prevailing social order so that they have become regimes of truth with normative imperatives to which 'there is no alternative'. The third chapter is concerned with the possibility of conversion, of an alternative, of turning around from the prevailing tyrannical neoliberal political–economic theology, which entails imagining and articulating a radiant ideal with normative and creative power.

The third three chapters, on Political economy, are concerned with ideas of laws and limits governing economics. The first chapter suggests correspondences between Plato's *Republic* and the Irish republic in the deformations and devolution of democracy into tyranny, tracing a red thread from the predicament of the ancient Athenians to contemporary Ireland in terms of the need to govern pleonexia, appetites without limits. The following chapter concerns the political and economic policies and practices of Irish development, in particular the designation – the naming – of Ireland's 'tax free zones', which has entailed deregulating limits, dissolving boundaries, instituting liminality as a development strategy; a development policy based on transgression, that while initially rewarding turns out to be debilitating; and we suggest practices that may ameliorate, redress and contain the dangerous forces that have been unleashed. The last, concluding, chapter imagines the subject, the ideal type of person who has been emerging under the auspices of the neoliberal revolution. This ominous subject, a self-interested individual who is increasingly isolated from interpellation within the normative frames of society, calls for imagining post-republican politics, in Ireland as elsewhere, in terms of a care of the self. Here, as throughout, the intention is not to be analytical, prescriptive and conclusive, but to suggest how we may change the aspects by which we view things and thereby create and imagine our way beyond the present.

Note

1 Immediately before the crash the Economic and Social Research Institute had been assuring the government and the public that we were living in 'the best of times' and that we were on course for further progress. But on the morning of the collapse of Lehman's, the ESRI's director was interviewed on RTE radio's 'Morning Ireland' and gave an account of events, based, she said, on what she had been hearing on the late night news channels from the US!

Introduction: 'What rough beast?' Monsters of post-Celtic Tiger Ireland

What rough beast is coming in the wake of the sudden death of the Celtic Tiger? Our hypothesis, formulated in the spirit of Yeats and Joyce, sees repetition and reiteration: that what will appear to us in the guise of the new is better understood in terms of recurrence.[1] For Joyce and for Yeats recurrence represents a philosophy of history, taken from the Greeks through Vico (1999) and Nietzsche (1995), attuned and oriented to the politics of the present. For Yeats (1920a) recurrence is represented in 'The Second Coming' by the figure of the spiral gyre: recurring cycles of history marked by moments of dissolution of order, liminality and the imposition of a new order. Modernity sees the acceleration, intensification and apotheosis of cycles of historical recurrence. What rough beast, Yeats asks, emerges from this civilization at the moment of its apotheosis and simultaneous decadence, when things fall apart? 'We are legion' is the demon's answer. The rough beast has many countenances: 'cold, egotistical calculation; the conduct of business without regard for persons; an iron cage of rationalized acquisitiveness' are faces that Weber (1958: 181) sees; 'naked, shameless, direct, brutal exploitation' is how Marx and Engels (1985: 16) describe it; a cult of egotistical individualism, amoral and self-destructive is how it appears to Durkheim(1966: 209); cultural dopes whose fears and desires are manipulated by the culture industry and mass society; the 'authoritarian personality' looking to the strong master are aspects of the beast according to Adorno and Horkheimer (1992: 120). The purportedly 'objective and self-regulating laws of the market' and the 'value-neutral' 'science' of economics; the 'fact' that 'there is no alternative' to a society organized on the neoliberal market principle that 'greed is good' is the beast's countenance in the current post-national, post-political, seemingly leaderless era.

Spiritus mundi of global neoliberalism

The rough beast is represented by one of the world's oldest and fully elaborated demonologies, the Assyrian demon of the desert storm, Pazuzu. Pazuzu – a canine, insect, serpent, raptor, humanoid – animal hybrid, is the dog-faced demon of the cold wind, destroyer of crops and cultivated lands, bearer of disease and plagues. Pazuzu is a demon of liminality; he forces choice. When Pazuzu comes around there is no room for equivocation; you must decide: succumb to barbarism and death, or defend civilization and life? Because of the absolute threat that he poses, Pazuzu can have the paradoxical and ambivalent effect of strengthening civilization, and for this reason Pazuzu is a threshold demon, a trickster figure used to drive off other demons: women in labour wore amulets of Pazuzu to protect themselves from Lamashtu, a lion-headed, donkey-eared, child-killing demon – a demon of ferocity and stupidity that steals the future.

An Assyrian relative of Sphinx, Manticore, Seth and similar monsters of chaos and ambiguity from Greece, Egypt and Mesopotomia, a 'vast image out of Spiritus Mundi' that troubles Yeats's sight in 'The Second Coming', Pazuzu is familiar to us as the demon from the iconic 1973 film *The Exorcist*. In *The Exorcist* Pazuzu is a metaphor for the era of 'tricky Dick' Nixon; demonic possession by Pazuzu representing the generation lost to the Vietnam war, political innocence lost through Watergate, and also in that same year the legalization of abortion and the subsequent fundamentalist polarization in American moral economy. Nozick's *Anarchy, State and Utopia*, the bible of neoliberalism not merely as economics but as a moral and political theology, was written in 1973. And especially from the point of view of our present interest, Pazuzu represents the CIA-engineered coup in Chile in 1973, the Chicago boys' laboratory of authoritarian neoliberalism and the 'shock doctrine' in Pinochet's dictatorship, the stolen child of Allende's democratic socialism and the dog-eat-dog morality of the enforced free market there (Klein, 2007: 91–121). Pazuzu is a Trickster, a devil that knows how to assume many guises, some of which are pleasing and beguiling. As a canine demon he is a two-faced friend who turns on those who thought they were his masters and savages them, just as global neoliberalism and our own local development strategy we thought would give us prosperity and security and we assured ourselves we were in control of, now turns on us and tears us apart.

Plutonomy and precariat

On the eve of the global financial crisis, researchers at the global banking giant Citigroup published an investment strategy report exploring opportunities associated with what they identified as the emerging 'plutonomy' (Kamper,

Macleod and Singh, 2005). Plutonomy refers to the sector of the economy that produces goods and services for the super-wealthy – off-shore banking and wealth management services, luxury yachts, jets, private islands and similar real estate, supercars, bespoke jewellery and the like, consumer goods for a new caste of global billionaires. As the world divides more and more into the super-wealthy and the very poor, Citigroup identifies stock in the businesses servicing the plutonomy as an investment opportunity which would be relatively safe even in the event of recession in the wider economy. The USA and Canada, Australia, the UK and Italy are already plutonomies, according to the Citigroup report, and the trend has been accelerating. Until recently some Irish were (or imagined themselves to be) amongst the number of the global plutonomy, and some still are even as the present crisis continues. National economies are thrown into deep recession, businesses go under, millions of people are unemployed, lose their homes, fall into poverty, but the plutonomy is still doing very well. The Forbes Rich List 2011 lists a 10 per cent rise in the number of billionaires since 2008, with their net worth rising quickly and steadily.

Pluto (Hades) is the original Dark Lord: God of the underworld and god of wealth (from jewels and precious metals buried in the earth, prior to that wealth stored underground, and prior to that again Pluto represents the chthonic power of dark soil). He is also the god of the interior of the body, the bowels and the viscera, and thereby of consumption, of devouring, digesting and defecation. Pluto's voracious economy of consumption frequently gives him gas – bubbles, gaseous emissions that issued from caves and crevases that the Greeks identified as the gates of Hell, and Pluto's breath has the sulphurous stench of flatus and corruption (Jones, 1974).

Pluto abducts Persephone (Prosperina, from *prosperene* – 'to emerge'), daughter of Demeter/Ceres. When she learns that Zeus was complicit in the rape of Persephone, Demeter (goddess of agriculture and bread, that is, of human food and life-sustaining resources – goddess of marriage, laws (stability) and the afterlife (continuity)) leaves Olympus and refuses to enable growth. The world falls into darkness and Zeus becomes fearful that the world will be destroyed. He intervenes with Demeter, but she refuses to cooperate until Persephone is restored. Zeus sends Hermes to intercede with Pluto, but Persephone has already tasted the fruit of Hades[2] and she will die without it. A compromise is reached: Persephone's time is divided between Pluto in the underworld and life with Demeter in the world, giving the corresponding seasons and cycles of autumn (scarcity and recession), winter (poverty and darkness), spring (recovery and growth) summer (prosperity and happiness). This is a mythic formula for a balanced and sustainable cosmopoiesis, but in a plutonomy Pluto takes possession of Persephone, holds her captive and the world becomes conflicted and falls towards darkness and death (Graves, 1960).

Plutonomy is a fusion of wealth and power and property wherein Pluto has an unfair share of Persephone. Plutonomies have existed many times in historical and anthropological societies from prehistory to the present day: in ancient Egypt, Greece and Rome; in European absolute monarchies, Tsarist Russia and Asiatic dynasties; in twentieth-century totalitarian regimes both Right and Left, in tribal, pre-imperial and in dictatorial post-colonial Africa; and again in the emerging configuration of concentrations of wealth and power in the constellation of neoliberal globalization in the form of the post-democratic 'corporate republic'. A corporate republic would be a re-privatized republic. While retaining some semblance of national democratic republican government, a corporate republic would be run primarily like a business, involving a board of directors and executives, as Greece, Italy and Ireland are presently managed and overseen by financial technocrats and former executives of Goldman-Sachs and similar banks. Utilities, including hospitals, schools, the army and the police force, would be privatized, and the social welfare functions carried out by the state are instead carried out by corporations in the form of benefits to employees and 'stakeholders'. These patterns are now well established in the Anglo-American plotonomy especially, and in other Western societies, including Ireland.

Recurrence of a dark age

The second coming of the rough beast means a recurrence of a social form resembling feudalism – the eclipse of the sovereign democratic republican nation state by transnational institutions – multinational corporations, banks and private hedge funds, the International Monetary Fund (IMF), and technocratic bureaucratic matrices of power/knowledge and regimes of governmentality – these are the new sovereign powers that command and dictate; panoptic disciplinary surveillance mechanisms, managerial and auditing practices permeating the capillaries of social relations; powers that are subjectivized, internalized, that in many ways we are complicit in, that 'we bring to bear on ourselves as we have become part of its mechanism' (Foucault, 1991: 217). We have come again to resemble, in many important respects, the serfs of the feudal dark ages, fully 'possessed' in the literal as well as figurative sense by the powers of the plutocracy. We are a new precariat, on our knees (precarious – from *pre care*, 'to pray'),[3] knuckling down, paying up, rendering ourselves to the Dark Lord of the Markets. Like the bondsmen of earlier epochs the precariat are praying in two senses: 'on our knees', begging, powerless and pleading; 'without a prayer'; but also in awe, dumbstruck, humble, worshipping in the cult of the Market and the celebrity entrepreneur.

Ireland's political unconscious

> The unconscious is that chapter of my history that is marked by a blank or occupied by a falsehood; it is the censored chapter. But the Truth can be found again; it is most often written down elsewhere. That is to say: in monuments: this is my body – that is to say the nucleus of the neurosis where the hysterical symptom reveals the structure of a Language and is deciphered like an inscription which, once recovered, can without serious loss be destroyed; in archival documents also: these are my childhood memories, just as impenetrable as are such documents when I do not know their source; in semantic evolution: this corresponds to my stock of words and acceptations of my own particular vocabulary, as it does to my style of life and my character; in traditions as well, and not just in them but also in the legends which, in a heroicized form transport my history; and lastly, in the traces which are inevitably preserved by the distortions necessitated by the linking of the adulterated chapter to the chapters surrounding it, and whose meaning will be re-established by my exegesis. (Lacan, 1994: 21)

The name Bram Stoker gave to his vampire, 'Dracula', is an Irish name: '*droch fholla*' which translates as 'bad' (*droch*) 'blood' (*fholla*) – as in the usage *tá drochfholla idir a chéile*, 'there is bad blood between them' – meaning a grudge, ill-feeling, a poisoned relationship.[4] *Drochfholla* – Dracula – is a condensed metaphor for Anglo-Irish relations in the nineteenth century; bad blood that courses through the veins and capillaries of a corrupt and corrupting Irish body politic. In this interminable stasis the collective Irish social body is preyed on by new generations of bloodsucking parasites in a never-ending repetition of the past, for 'he who fights with monsters should take care lest he become a monster' (Nietzsche, 1989, 89), and the history of Ireland is one of fighting with monsters and in the process becoming monsters ourselves.

The Count, the embodiment of this morbid condition, is the un-dead vestige of a remote past, descended from a once noble landed feudal lineage, but now decadent and corrupted. And not only do the un-dead aristocracy linger on, especially in the colonies, in places like nineteenth-century Ireland, but those who fight them, the modern bourgeoisie and bearers of Enlightenment, Reason and reform, become in turn bloodsucking monsters themselves. Count Dracula's estate is in Transylvania, at the edge of Enlightened Europe and the Traditional Orient, Christianity and Islam. This is an analogue of Ireland's place in the symbolic order and imaginative structure of the British imperium: backward, dark, Catholic, still ruled by a landed gentry that the peasants hold in awe and in dread. Castle Dracula is not an eastern outpost of European civilization in Transylvania, but on its western frontier, in the wilds of Ireland. During the land-wars of the latter half of the nineteenth century English landlords in Ireland moved from their Georgian country houses to neo-gothic medieval castles, built for security, complete with moat and bailey, defensive towers and battlements. Lord Ardilaun (of Guinness's and sprawling estates in Connaught) built Ashford Castle in this context. A visitor to the castle in 1880 – he might be Stoker's character Jonathan Harker visiting the Count – gives his impressions of his journey:

> After a week spent in the thin, mean poverty of the north-west, amid the sadness of ruined things this strangely beautiful castle renders me singularly happy. Here we are almost shut out of the storm and gloom of crime and poverty that enfolds the land, but even here the shadow of murder and outrage falls across our way. For as we sit at breakfast we hear the smothered detonation of dynamite exploding in the huge moat which our host is having cut through the solid rock, and sometimes small splinters of stone strike the windows. This new fortification, when finished, will separate the castle from the mainland. It is thirty feet deep by twenty feet wide. 'You see' says our host, 'I have a taste for the picturesque. The moat will be protected by battlements, and cannon will be placed at convenient distances. I shall be able to defend myself in case of invasion, and as the drawbridge will be raised at night it will be difficult for the dynamiters to get at me. (Pakenham, 1998: 124)

Similar Castle *drochfollas* were built throughout the countryside. Dromore Castle was built by Lord Limerick in 1878, an anachronistic Norman fortress on a precipice with most of the windows looking inwards on an enclosed courtyard. The result was cold, dark and damp, and the castle was never lived in save for a skeleton staff of loyal caretakers.[5] Count Dracula, and the Anglo-Irish Lords of the nineteenth century (and most recently non-residential cosmopolitan tax exiles, international bond-holders of Anglo-Irish debts to global banks and hedge funds), are absentee landlords, who live in London, Manhattan or the Cayman Islands, but to sustain themselves there they need the earth of the old estates, the bonded labour and the life-blood of their serfs. In the context of modern urban democratic society the hereditary landed gentry are a dark and ambiguous presence, provoking ambivalent feelings of respect and repugnance. The Anglo-Irish gentry in London are like the Count; ambiguously civil and bestial. A shapeshifter, Count Dracula morphs from a powerful nobleman to an effeminate dandy, from a cultured, cosmopolitan gentleman to a wolf, a rat, a lizard, a bat, a leech. Harker, the young English lawyer, perceives the Count with a mixture of awe and disgust:

> There he lay looking as if youth had been half-renewed, for the white hair and moustache were changed to dark iron grey; the cheeks were fuller, and the white skin seemed ruby red underneath; the mouth was redder than ever, for on the lips were gouts of fresh blood, which trickled from the corners of the mouth and ran over the chin and neck. Even the deep, burning eyes seemed set amongst

swollen flesh, for the lids and pouches underneath were bloated. It seemed as if the whole awful creature were simply gorged with blood; he lay like a filthy leech, exhausted with his repletion. (Stoker, 1993: 44)

Such decadent, blood-sucking, bloated monsters should belong to a bygone era. One hundred years before Stoker, Jonathan Swift (1996) had identified them as the Anglo-Irish aristocracy of the eighteenth century, a group that he ironically proposed may as well literally eat the children of their tenants as they are eating their parents figuratively as it is. The heroic lawyers of the Home Rule movement had fought with this monster, but just as it seemed exhausted and about to pass away, like Count Dracula the Anglo-Irish landlords kept rejuvenating and coming back to life. To kill this monster, just as with Dracula, Enlightened Reason would have to become alloyed with mysticism, passion and violence, and the vampire slayers would risk becoming monsters themselves.

Paddy the vampire slayer

The most fateful vampire slayer awakened during this period of cultural renaissance is Patrick Pearse, leader of the 1916 Rising and author of the Proclamation of the Irish Republic; the urbane schoolteacher who, like Mina, a victim of the vampire as well as a vampire slayer, becomes a bloodthirsty monster.[6] Pearse knows that to kill the monster he has to enlist the forces of the underworld, he has to raise the dead. In his necromantic oration at the graveside of O'Donovan-Rossa[7] he says that while it seems as though the Imperial monster has won, 'he has left us the graves of our Fenian dead, and while Ireland holds these graves Ireland unfree shall never be at peace'. 'Life springs from death,' Pearse says, 'and from the graves of patriot men and women spring living nations.' Thus Pearse calls back to life an Irish un-dead, bathed in blood, indestructible, an unholy, violent revolutionary power, ritually sanctified by Pearse's articulation of the Easter Rising with Christ's Resurrection. But though these men of death and resurrection have the power to kill the vampire, Pearse has repeated the curse. 'A terrible beauty is born,' Yeats (1920b:4) observes of Easter 1916, predicting that his own caste would be slain by this new generation. Pearse's un-dead men carry on, even when their work is done, and the Republic of Ireland has lived in the shadow of the gunman. 'They haven't gone away you know!'[8]

Metempsychosis of the gombeen man

But the gunman is not the only shadowy figure haunting modern Ireland. A much more insidious fiend is the 'gombeen man':

> A gombeen man is a man that linds you a few shillin's or a few pounds whin ye want it bad and then nivir laves ye till he has tuk all ye've got – yer land an' yer shanty an' yer holdin' an' yer money an' yer craps; an' he would take the blood out of yer body if he could sell it or use it anyhow. (Stoker, 2006: 28)

These bloodsuckers are the members of a new native Irish class of 'strong farmers', shopkeepers and publicans: land-grabbers and opportunists who fattened on evictions and emigration, paying tenants' rents over their heads and appropriating their holdings; profiteers who made their fortunes as middle men, hoarding food and grain during famine; publicans who set up shop adjacent to Public Works and Relief projects, as payment stations *cum* shebeens and taverns, to relieve the destitute of their relief. The gombeen man – from 'gambín' (Ir.) interest on a loan, from Middle English 'cambie' – exchange, barter, from Latin 'cambium'– is a village usurer, a native Irish petty bourgeois publican, merchant or estate agent, who, during the course of the nineteenth century, became the main supporter of the Home Rule movement. Irish Labour organizer James Connolly participated in Pearse's 1916 Rising, though he was aware that the vampire was no longer British but had already assumed new forms:

> those leeches who, as gombeen men, middlemen and dealers of one kind or another in the small country town, sucked the life-blood of the agricultural population around them. Anyone acquainted with rural Ireland knows that, next to the merciless grinding by the landlord the tenantry suffers most from the ruthless exploitation of the classes just mentioned, and that, indeed, the buying out of the landlords in many cases served only to gorge still further the ever rapacious maw of those parasites upon rural life. But whereas the landlords were ever regarded in Ireland as alien to Irish life, the gombeen men and their kind, from their position in the country towns, their ostentatious parade of religion and their loud-mouthed assertions of patriotism, were usually the dominant influences in the councils of the local Home Rule or other constitutional nation-alist organization. (Connolly, in Metscher, 2002: 256–257)

Stoker's character Renfield is representative of this incarnation of the rough beast. Renfield is diagnosed by Dr Seward as a 'zoophagous [life-eating] maniac' (Stoker, 1993: 70). He is in the service of the Count, his representa-tive, as the estate agent – the forerunner of the modern Irish gombeen politician – businessman/accountant is in the service of the landlord. Renfield collects flies, which he feeds to spiders, which in turn he feeds to birds, which he then devours. He would like to have a cat to eat. What he really aspires to, of course, is to become a vampire himself! Renfield represents the avarice of the new Irish indicted by Yeats who 'fumble in a greasy till / and add the ha'pence to the pence / and prayer to shivering prayer / 'til you have dried the marrow from the bone' (Yeats, 1916a: 32). The gombeen man is the obscene, insatiable greed of the post-colonial, post-Catholic, post-Nationalist, post-democratic-Republican Irish who have ruled for the twentieth century; a swarming horde of native, local vampires; they are un-dead and they continue to feed. Corruption of the body politic is their symptom. Exposed to sunlight after lengthy court Tribunals, and caught momentarily in the glare of grave crisis when the social body on which they have been gorging collapses into terminal debt, they slink away from public life, withdrawing to their crypts and vaults, only to re-emerge as 'independent candidates', 'special advisors', 'financial consultants' and 'board members' of new bodies politic. There they fasten their fangs again. Absentee proprietors, developers and speculators, they live an extra-corporeal existence; disembodied, de-territorialized, transnational, they avoid what is otherwise unavoidable for mortals – death and taxes. Like Renfield they serve mysterious foreign Masters – the share-holders of multinational corporations that use Ireland as a tax-minimizing profit siphon, sucking the fiscal life blood from the European social body; 'Senior Bondholders' of Ireland's private banking and sovereign debts; the IMF/ECB, and similar incarnations of the Dark Lord of the Markets.

Ireland's night of the living dead

Marx famously described capital as 'dead labour which, vampire-like, lives only by sucking living labour, and lives the more, the more labour it sucks' (1992: 342). As Shaviro says, 'The nineteenth century, with its classic régime of industrial capitalism, was the age of the vampire, but the network society of the late twentieth and twenty-first centuries is rather characterised by a plague of zombies' (2002: 281). But vampires and zombies are mutually interdepend-ent, for, as Shivaro notes, no predator or parasite can survive in the absence of prey, so vampire-capital can only extract its surplus by organizing its legions of zombie-labour. The zombie is the proletarian subject of the dawn of the dead as the age of global total capitalism. As Deleuze and Guattari put it, 'the only modern myth is the myth of zombies – mortified schizos, good for work' (Deleuze and Guattari, 1983: 335). McNally (2012) shows how the metaphors of vampires and zombies are especially useful for grasping and expressing the monster of the markets in contemporary global capitalism.

Post-Celtic Tiger Ireland is a haunted landscape of ghost estates and zombie banks cannibalizing the state (Kirby, 2010) but to see the full horror as Ireland's night of the living dead unfolds it is important to understand the cultural slippage around the figure of the zombie. In Anthropology and in Medicine the zombie is both 'real' and 'imaginary'.[9] The zombie is a liminal figure, suspended between life and death, between Western popular culture and non-Western lore and magic. The zombie is disturbing because of its 'categorical interstitiality' (Carroll, 1990: 27).

The zombie is a figure from the belief system of Haitian Vodoun, the blend of spiritualisms and rituals of the many different peoples who were uprooted from Africa and imported to Hispaniola during the slave trade. Under slavery, African culture and religion were suppressed, religious beliefs and practices were fragmented and recombined, and Roman Catholicism was mixed into the rituals to disguise the 'pagan' religion from the slaves' masters who had forbidden them to practise it. From this complex mixture of African tribal and Christian religious ideas and practices emerged the creoleized symbolic and imaginative structure that is Haitian Vodoun (Inglis, 2011: 354). Medical practitioners in Haiti regard zombification as the consequence of poisoning, Christian clergy see it as the product of sorcery, while Voudoun sorcerors (*boku*) tend not to share their esoteric knowledge with anthropologists, or indeed with anyone. According to the folklore, 'a person becomes ill, then appears to be dead and is placed in a tomb, and is then "stolen" by a *boku* and secretly returned to life and activity but not to full awareness and agency' (Littlewood and Douyon, 1997: 1094). In zombification the victim's agency is extracted by the *boku*, who retains this life force in a bottle or jar. The animated body remains without will or consciousness and becomes the slave of the *boku*, subdued by chaining, beating, poisoning and sorcery, and works secretly on his land or is sold to another *boku* (Littlewood and Douyon, 1997). Thus the figure of the dehumanized zombie whose will or agency has been stolen by a sorcerer is a Haitian collective representation of former slaves' fears of a return to the horrors of slavery. The Haitian fear is not of zombies, it is of *zombification*, of being turned into a zombie, a fearful nightmare the imaginative structure of which is rooted in the real experience of the brutal conditions of the lives of plantation slaves during the colonial period. The Haitian fear of zombies, then, is rather about 'the body-snatcher' – the zombie master – who 'takes the living person and destroys their soul, making a living but mentally and emotionally dead being who obeys his will' (Inglis, 2011: 354). Thus the figure of the zombie represents the fear of history repeating itself, of a return to enslavement by an imperial master.[10]

At the same time as the Young Irelanders were plotting their rebellion in 1798, and perhaps in part inspired by it, Haiti was already the first colony to become a republic, thanks to the revolution of former slaves who overthrew their French masters. Leaders of the Haitian revolts in 1791 were Boukman Dutty[11] and Cecile Fatiman, a mulatto *mambo*, a Vodoun priestess. Their

Vodoun ceremony to inaugurate the revolution combined animal sacrifice, a pact of blood brotherhood amongst the rebels and invocation of various divinities, all articulated with the Enlightenment principles of the American and French Revolutions.

Haiti was very much a social political anomaly and an object of wonder to nineteenth-century Europe (Inglis, 2011: 356). But as the early idealism of the Revolution degenerated into rivalry amongst the revolutionary leaders mirroring the Terror in France, combined with the machinations of the global powers of France, England and Spain as they vied for hegemony, Western observers began to look at Haiti not with admiration but with disgust and with deep ambivalence, for Haiti was a mirror for the failure of Western modernity to fulfil its own promises of Enlightenment: Reason and democracy; liberty, equality and fraternity. At the heart of the degeneration of Haiti, however, was not the 'pact with the Devil' as the French plantation owners liked to portray the origins of the Revolution in Vodoun and the mysterious 'blood ceremony' held in the *Bois Caiman*, but a 'pact with the devil' in the form of French banks. Under threat of political and economic isolation, backed up by the sanction of massive military intervention, Haiti was forced to pay reparations of 150 million francs (equivalent to 100 billion euro today) to absentee former plantation and slave owners in France. This burden of debt purportedly owed by Haitians to senior bond-holders in France bankrupted the nascent Republic and effectively mortgaged the future generations of Haiti in perpetuity. Anyone who wishes to imagine what state the former Republic of Ireland will be in one hundred years from now may have much to learn from the state of Haiti today.

Zombie precarity and vampire plutonomy

In 2010, the Irish government committed to the terms of an IMF–ECB–EU bailout, a programme of 'austerity budgets' which make huge cuts in social welfare rather than taxing the richest 1 per cent of the population who own 34 per cent of the national wealth, or the wealthiest 7 per cent of the Irish population whose combined wealth is more than 121 billion (Cronin, 2010). Subsequent budgets continue this pattern. The 2012 budget, for instance, disproportionately affects the worst off in Irish society: cuts to fuel allowance for the elderly; cuts to child benefits for large families; cuts in disability payments; cuts in community employment schemes (virtually wiped out); cuts in back-to-school clothing and footwear allowance; cuts in provision for job seekers; and cuts to rent supplements. At the same time there was a VAT increase, another regressive, indirect form of stealth taxation: the Household Charge, an increase in motor tax and planned reintroduction of third-level student fees. In total, €2.2 billion in cuts were announced as well as €1.6

billion in taxes. These cuts are occurring in a context where the gap between rich and poor is widening. According to the Central Statistics Office (2006) 'Survey on Income and Living Conditions', inequality in Ireland grew by more than 25 per cent in 2010. The average income of those in the top 20 per cent of the population was 5.5 times higher than the average of those in the poorest 20 per cent. A year earlier it had been just 4.3 times higher (Browne, 2011). The concentration of wealth in Ireland is one of the highest in the EU-15. According to Taft (2011), who has been trying to calculate who the 99 and 1 per cent in Ireland are, the top 1 per cent in Ireland own approximately €130.2 billion. Austerity budgets look to leave tax bands unchanged, with a rise in VAT, a flat rate property tax and the reduction of child benefit hitting those who can least afford it disproportionately while leaving the plutocracy relatively untouched – the rationale being that if plutocrats are taxed they will flee the country. In the words of Johnson (2011), 'We are all bondmaids now, the property of local chieftains themselves in thrall to feudal lords both domestic and overseas, and the state we are in is one that Cúchulainn would find not that unfamiliar at all.'

Monsters of the mythic age of globalization

'History ... is a nightmare from which I am trying to awake', Joyce says (1998:35). The recurrence of the nightmare in Irish history is a localized instantiation of the cycle of recurrence identified in Vico's *New Science* of the dark age of Gods, the mythic age of heroes and the historical age of men. Modernity is an intensification of this cycle as a spiralling vortex wherein features of all three recurring ages can be seen at once in the accelerated culture of globalization: the recurrence of the age of the Gods as the dark and obscure abstraction of forces and processes that are the Markets; the recurrence of the age of heroes in the celebration of the entrepreneur as Ideal-type subject; and the recurrence of the historical age of men as the public, mass society. During dark ages, Vico says, the gods mingle with men, giving birth to a progeny of monstrous doubles, ambivalently and paradoxically god-like heroes and mere mortals; patricians and plebeians, masters and bondsmen, Joyce's terrible twins Shem and Shaun. Seeming opposites, as antitheses they are in fact intimately bound together in a spiral dialectical dance. Patrician heroes are bestial monsters, for 'next to their heroic deeds, we must place the intolerable pride, the insatiable greed, the merciless cruelty with which the Patricians treated the unfortunate plebeians (Vico, 1999, 26: 104 /272) and plebeians who become heroic by overthrowing the patrician tyrants turn out themselves to be monsters, for in the Roman period of imaginary popular liberty, when the tyrants had been replaced by the Republic, the Republic became a new tyranny in which the majority of plebeians in fact continued to serve those plebeians who had become patricians (Vico, 1999: 68). And today, same as it ever was, *'precari uniti, contro i padroni'* is the political graffiti on the streets of Rome.

Monster – from *monstrere/monter* – means to show, to put on display, as the monstrance ritually displays the sacred host, for example. Monsters de-monster-ate boundaries, the mysteries that lie beyond the limit of what can be known (as in the usage 'here be monsters' on explorers' maps) and not only the obscurities beyond external limits but internal darknesses too, for the Other turns out to be the Other in the interior. Mary Shelly's (1987) monster created by Dr Frankenstein represents the paradox and ambivalence in the dialectics of Enlightenment and the democratic Revolution. The creature, the being created by the heroic modern Promethean enterprise of science, tech-nology and industry, remains nameless. The 'creature', that which we have created, the 'monster', is a metaphor for base humanity endowed with the power of reason and self-consciousness, a creature that demands recognition, demands rights, demands equality with its creator. As the creature's claims for equal recognition are not met it destroys those who brought it to life but who thought that they would circumscribe boundaries and limit its life, the Romantic aristocrats and modern progressive liberal democrats represented by Byron and Shelly and Wollstonecraft. Frankenstein's monster is the plebeian, the proletariat, the new monstrous public, the social body politic made up of many base parts, the popular mob, the masses that overthrew a nobility that, like Dracula, had become decadent. But the plebeian creature that becomes heroic by fighting patrician monsters for its rights to recognition becomes a monster himself; Terror follows every Revolution in one form or another. The eternal conflict between Heroes and men – patricians and plebeians, aristocratic masters and mass public bondsmen – is a motor driving history Vico tells us, one hundred years before Marx and Engels made it the central pivot of the *Communist Manifesto*. But whereas Marx was dazzled by a Hegelian Enlightenment vision of dialectical historical progress as linear, an upwards and always improving unfolding of *Geist*, Vico (and Joyce and Yeats) saw in the dialectic an eternal recurrence whereby periods of Enlightenment inevitably become decadent, declining again into dark ages.

A first glimpse of the second coming

In the period of decadence into a recurring dark age there are 'two great maladies', according to Vico (1999: 487) 'namely "the perfect tyranny of anarchy [the anarchy of the free market] and the unbridled liberty of free peoples"' (mass society, the herd of individual consumers). In response to these two pathologies of civilization three patterns recur historically, Vico says. The first is the restoration of internal monarchy by a charismatic leader, a demagogue who restores order by powerful violence. A second pattern is that the decadent society becomes subject to conquest by superior nations, the ceding of republican sovereignty to the IMF/ECB/EU 'Troika' being an initial form of the broader historical eclipse of a decadent Occident by an ascendant Orient, to ownership and rule by a global dynasty of despotic plutocrats. And the third pattern is that we become bestial again – solitary, competitive, un-cooperative, 'living like beasts, crowded together but divided amongst ourselves' (Vico, 1999: 487). Tendencies towards all three are the clear and unambiguous signs of our times.

We, individuated by the anarchy of the market and the unbridled liberty of mass consumerism, have become the 'rough beast'. Thoroughly possessed by our singular appetites, lost to the collective life of society, we fall as individuals into a void of chaos, which, as Vico explains, is the original monster, Orcus, that devours men whole. The Tea Party's assault on the fiscal institutions of republican and federal government, Eurosceptic neo-nationalism and balkanization, neoliberal individualism that would reduce the state to the function of authorizing Hobbsean free market anarchy, mean that we become the zombie mob of private individual consumers, crowded together but divided amongst ourselves; born-again Cyclopes, glowering from the mouths of our caves. In times of crisis – our present crisis – there is pandemonium: 'many demons' are unleashed and run through the herd as quickening furies. Only Hermes can call souls back from the dead. Hermes the communicator 'carries the law … calls souls back from Orcus, meaning he calls back to society those who were again dispersed in the lawless state of barbarism that devours men whole' (Vico, 1999: 168).

The Queen's 2011 visit to Ireland in this context gives us one of our first glimpses of the second coming. Simultaneously an anachronistic and a prophetic event –the Sovereign of the former Imperial power and amongst the world's wealthiest individuals, lays a wreath at the Garden of Remembrance for Republican national sovereignty in the former colony at precisely the moment at which national sovereignty is eclipsed and Ireland becomes a neo-feudal fiefdom, a neo-colony of bonded tax-serfs paying tribute to a global elite of senior bond-holders, a new absentee aristocracy of bankers.

Notes

1 The voyage of Ulysses in Homer is re-lived in the mundane everyday world of Joyce's modern hero Leopold Bloom, and in *Finnegans Wake* the history of the world is enfolded in the recurring themes of his protagonist's dreamwork. The Finnegans, Humphrey Chimpden Earwicker ('Here Comes Everybody'), Anna Livia Plurabelle, Shem and Shaun, metempsychotically assume the forms of figures from myth, religion and 'real' history, as well as anthropomorphically personifying rivers and landscape, time, space and number, and they reiterate and play out the great themes of human

history – conflict, the Fall, redemption – all the while retaining their mundane identities as ordinary people. In the portmanteau words of *Finnegans Wake* 'the signifier "stuffs" [garnishes, overdetermines] the signified' (Lacan, Seminar XX: 37): the spirit of one word enters another, as does the spirit of one situation, or of one being. The doubling, punning movement of lives, histories, thoughts, actions, overlapping, intersecting, crossing over into one another, reflects the recursive movement of history – history as recurrence, repetition, rather than linear progress. For Joyce 'All forms proceed by incessant doublings and undoublings in which they remain enantiomorphous – that is, resembling each other but not superposable. This gives the world a wholeness that is not characterized by unity, but by adhesiveness' (Ellman, 1977: 95).

2 Pomegranate, one of the oldest cultivated fruits, brought to Greece in Neolithic trade from Mesopotamia, is one of the earliest symbols of riches: the shape of the crown is derived from it, and garnet, one of the first precious gems to be used in jewellery and adornment, is derived etymologically from the seed of the pomegranate which it resembles. In Judaism the pomegranate is the forbidden fruit in the Garden of Eden. That Persephone becomes enthralled to Hades because of the pomegranate seeds suggests that once she has tasted riches she will not live without them again, even though they are associated with bondage and death. Mythologies of wealth are sustained by the dreams and desires of those who have been abducted and exploited.

3 This etymology is John O'Neill's; personal communication, June 2009.

4 Marxist, feminist and psychoanalytic interpretations concur that Bram Stoker's *Dracula* represents the return of the repressed political unconscious of Victorian modernity: variously and in combination Dracula represents anti-Semitism and fear of usury; liberal democracy's fear of a reactionary conservative restoration of tyrannical aristocracy; socialist fear of exploitative capitalism; Victorian patriarchy's fear of feminism, androgyny, homosexuality and sexuality in general; Christian, national and imperial fear of immigrants from the colonies, the Balkans, the Slavic hordes, the Ottoman Empire, 'Oriental despotism' and Islam. But, with the signal exception of Kiberd (2000), literary criticism of *Dracula* makes nothing of Bram Stoker's Irishness. It is as though the canon of English literary criticism consists of so many screen memories, various figurations of the return of the repressed that themselves are masks of what is 'really' repressed.

5 And the celebrity London architect William Goodwin, whom Lord Limerick had commissioned, was never paid for his work.

6 The ambiguity of Pearse's interest in cultivating boys as Classical heroes has been the subject of salacious controversy, while a curious detail that has received no attention is that he was always represented in profile, showing the right side of his face only. Pearse's Irish mother doted on him, but he had a cold and distant relation to his English father. An orator, poet and dramatist, Pearse struggled throughout his life to overcome a stammer, and he had a pronounced cast of his left eye. Pearse put his best (right) face forward, as though his self-consciousness of his 'two faces' were symptomatic of his unconscious awareness of the sinister dimension of his mission.

7 Patrick Pearse, '*Oration at the Grave of Jeremiah O'Donnovan Rossa*, Glasnevin Cemetery, Dublin, 1 August (2012), 1915.

8 Gerry Adams, Belfast, 13 August 1995, addressing a public demonstration, made this unscripted retort to a call from a member of the crowd to 'bring back the IRA'.

9 Zombie sightings across Haiti appear to be quite genuine. Ackermann and Gauthier's systematic review of clinical data documents the 'Properties of the Zombi' which

include: 'no will; no consciousness; no recognition of relatives and friends; eyes dull, glazed, vacant; air absent, stupid, dazed, sleepy; nasal voice; speaks little or not at all; emotionally and mentally dead; no memory' (1991: 480–481). Ackermann and Gauthier's is not a description of a flesh-eating monster, but of people suffering mental illness.

10 While Black Haitians understood the zombie as an analogue for the dehumanizing power of slavery, the zombie in the Western popular imaginary is very different. Haiti, Vodoun and the figure of the zombie are images of revulsion and hostility in the Western imagination, images of the unspeakable and mysterious, primitive, barbaric and bestial. Reporter William Seabrook represented Haitian Voudoun rites in his 1929 travelogue as 'blood-maddened, sex-maddened, god-maddened ... leaping, screaming writhing black bodies' (cited in Inglis, 2011: 357) which became popularized in the 1932 film *White Zombie* starring Bela Lugosi, reinforcing ideas about African primitivism and US superiority which formed the ideological justification of the US occupation of Haiti from 1915 to 1934. Haitians understand their zombi within a nexus of 'folk memory about the white slave masters and their power to destroy a slave both physically and spiritually' (Inglis, 2011: 357). The zombi is a passive, tragic figure, entirely under the rule of the zombi master. This bears little resemblance to the cannibalistic, aggressive and mobile figure of the zombie of Western popular culture. The Western construction of the zombie and Haitian voodoo is inextricably intertwined with colonial history, fear of slave rebellion, and of the fears (and desires) of dissolution into primitivism (Inglis, 2011: 353), illustrated, for instance, by a resurrection in the 1980s AIDS scare, where it was a common belief in the US that AIDS came from Haiti, and in particular from voodoo rituals of blood and sex and transgressing boundaries between human and animal, living and dead. The zombie of the global-American culture industry represents a dense cluster of intense fears and desires in the American libidinal economy. Variously and alternatively the zombie is the figure of White America's fear of racial miscegenation; fear of communism (*Invasion of the Body Snatchers*) and more recently of other ideologies (the Muslim terrorist as a 'zombie' under the spell of the 'evil Mullah'); dissolution of individuality in the masses (*Night of the Living Dead*) and, on the other hand, the desire for individual autonomy, freedom of will and self-elevation from the masses – whether mass consumerism or mass democracy – so that the central trope of the genre is a cathexis wherein a heroic lone survivor in the post-apocalypic frontier slaughters hordes of zombies (*I Am Legend*; *Twenty-eight Days Later*; *Zombieland*).

11 The patois name Boukman – 'Book-man', Dutty – 'dirty' indicates his background as a 'man of the book' that is, of the Quaran, a Muslim, a 'dirty' book in the eyes of the Masters.

Part I
DOMESTIC ECONOMY

1

Ireland's haunted houses

To be human is to dwell, Heidegger (1977: 325) says, and to dwell means to live with others as family and as neighbours. The house is a universal symbol of humanity. All societies have their own household gods, and Irish household gods figure prominently in David Creedon's *Ghosts of the Faithful Departed*,[1] an award-winning collection of photographs of abandoned houses in the Irish countryside. The Sacred Heart of Jesus, a picture of Christ with the names of the family written underneath, representing the security, well-being and continuity of the household and the promise of redemption; images and statuettes of the Madonna and Child representing the ontologically prior and more encompassing ideals of Motherhood – the Sacred Heart is the Mother's gift; origin and salvation come through her, as do all other gifts: sanctuary, care, and hospitality and charity to neighbours, friends and strangers. The ideal represented by the maternal goddess, the Madonna, is the gift relation, the fundamental social institution on which all civilization rests. The ruined house, the empty homes of the faithful departed, with their household gods broken and thrown down, represents cultural trauma and tragedy; the destruction of the collective household of Irish society.

Religious icons, furniture and décor, family memorabilia and household *bric a brac*, elements from real and imagined scenes, appear as images from dreams – the dreams which these houses' former residents had assembled around themselves, as well as the dream images and memories of home that we ourselves project into these scenes. They are 'phantasmagorias of the interior', shifting scenes of real and imagined elements that 'contain the residue of a collective dream world' (Benjamin, 1999a: 19). In this register of dream interpretation we could say that in the dust and detritus of ruined interiors we may find signposts on the royal road to the unconscious. Jung (1959) tells us that the house is a mirror of the psyche; that in the deep interior of the psyche-house dwell universal archetypes of the collective unconscious.

These archetypes, the Mother and the Trickster amongst them, are figurative collective representations of fundamental ideas, principles and powerful forces that perpetually animate human action and that underpin the institutions of collective life (Jung, 1972: 3–4), and if we are to understand our history, our experience and our current predicament we need to get to know the powerful forces that these mythic figures represent. We will use the residue in the interiors of Irish houses as 'material' with which to conduct a 'political dream interpretation' (Benjamin, in Miller, 1996) of Ireland's collective unconscious. By working through the dreams and archetypes of the Irish collective unconscious we hope to contribute towards our awakening and redemption, for as Benjamin says, 'each epoch not only dreams the next, but also, in dreaming, strives toward the moment of waking. ... In the convulsions of the commodity economy we begin to recognize the monuments of the bourgeoisie as ruins even before they have crumbled' (1999: 13).

Let us begin with *Heart of the Home*. A wan daylight illuminates a single empty fireside chair upholstered in a modern pattern; comfortable, cushioned, but worn and tattered, this is a poor person's easy-chair. It is pulled up close to the fire for warmth. The fireplace is painted a rich crimson. The paint is peeling and flaking away. The fire has been quenched a long time. The grate, with its pot-hooks hanging idle, is filled with twigs; a crow's nest in the chimney has fallen through. The floor is littered with dirt and debris. The mantelpiece is covered with a chintz cloth, once bright, now discoloured, on which lie a battery, a small picture of the Crucifixion and a vial of medication. Hanging over the fireplace is a Sacred Heart picture, Christ's serene face gazing on an empty scene where an elderly person sat for years, suffered and died, cold and alone.

What is one's reaction to such images? How do they make people feel? People say (we have listened to their reactions at exhibitions): 'These photographs are so beautiful! I know this house! I've been in this kitchen! I know these things! I used to sit on a chair, or play with an ornament just like that! This is my grandmother's house!' After that moment of recognition, when we find ourselves in the picture, as it were, we awaken to its beauty: 'What colour! Look at the light!' A whole world, maybe a scene from our early childhood, is revealed and illuminated for us. These photographs transport us, as though we travel back in time to a harmonious and familiar place, the ancestral maternal home, and they awaken in us feelings of nostalgia. This sentimental sense of familiarity and harmony evoked for us by these images are awakened by what is Beautiful in a work of art.

But this recognition of harmony and beauty isn't one's only reaction. As you are drawn into the image, just as you discover the familiar, at the very same moment you find yourself feeling shocked and disturbed. For these beautiful scenes are scenes of ruin and decay, of loss, of dereliction and destruction – layers of dust and ashes, rusted, broken things, cobwebs, empty chairs by quenched fires in cold rooms, mouldering beds and mildewed clothes. They are images of death, of dead houses, the homes of the dead, haunted by the ghosts of the faithful departed. As we might expect when we are confronted by death, when we see a ghost, we are shocked, frightened; we feel vertigo; we draw back, we want to hold on to something. When an abyss confronts us, the abyss of the ocean viewed from a cliff top, or the abyss of death, we try to shut down disturbing thoughts, fears and anxieties, feelings that these images begin to move in us. These troubling feelings, creeping anxieties that send shivers down our spine, are being awakened by what is Sublime in a work of art. In *Critique of Judgment* Kant distinguishes between the Beautiful and the Sublime, noting that whereas beauty 'is connected with the form of the object', having 'boundaries', the sublime 'is to be found in a formless object', represented by a 'boundlessness' (2007: 23). Schopenhauer elaborates, noting how the pleasure offered by the beautiful is associated with a benign object, whereas the pleasure of the sublime, by contrast, is associated with an overpowering or vast malignant object of great magnitude, one that could destroy the observer (1966: 39).

Just as we stand back, to steady ourselves, to catch our breath as it were, at the same time we lean forward, to take a closer look. Here, with these images, we are drawn in by the texture, the layers, the dense fabric composed of light and shadow, of colours and darkness, of bright and shining things juxtaposed with grime and filth. Our perception oscillates between the boundaries formed by the cosy home and family life, and, simultaneously, the boundlessness of time and death. We feel a compelling fascination; we cannot turn away from these images. They are powerful. Powerful art combines the principles of the Beautiful and the Sublime. The tension between the Beautiful and the Sublime in a work of art causes ambivalence, mixed feelings. Art doesn't solve the problem of the ambivalence of the Beautiful and the Sublime. It doesn't reconcile them with one another, for the Beautiful and the Sublime, like Life and Death, are entirely different things; the very antithesis and negation of one another, they cannot be resolved simply into a 'pretty picture', a mere decoration. Rather, they stand in opposition to one another: One, and its Other, in dynamic tension. An artist tries to capture this essential moment, to give us an epiphany. 'Epiphany' is a theological term imported into the discourse of aesthetics, most famously by Joyce's *A Portrait of the Artist as a Young Man* (2003). It refers to the moment when the power of God (who cannot be seen or represented) is revealed, displays itself, and becomes visible in the mundane world. In secular terms epiphanies are those fleeting moments when the organizing principles of our existence are revealed to us, so we may gaze in wonder and amazement. Creedon gives us an Irish epiphany in *Ghosts of the Faithful Departed*.

The fireplace, the hearth, the kitchen. These are the essential spaces of the home; and the home, Bachelard (1994) says, is always a maternal space. Hestia (Gr.) Vesta (Rm) was the Classical mythological goddess of the home (Graves, 1960). She has an equivalent in every one of the world's treasure trove of religions, mythologies and anthropologies. Her Irish form is St. Bridget, a Christianized incarnation of an earlier pagan oracle, *Brigid*, the bright one, goddess of spring, of fire and builder of households. She is an idealized representation of the archetype in the collective unconscious of the Mother. The etymologies of the goddesses of the home come from the roots '*sta*' and '*est*' in the most ancient languages – Sanskrit, Hebrew, Greek – as in the word '*stationary*', the fixed, permanent point of light and heat around which civilization is anchored; and from *est*, to be – Hestia has no ancestral genealogy in Greek mythology: she simply 'is'. When this fixed point becomes undone, in Yeats's words, 'things fall apart/ the centre cannot hold/ mere anarchy is loosed upon the world' (1920a: 10). The hearth is the heart of the home. The fireside, source and centre of light, warmth and hospitality, is universal anthropologically and in the history of civilizations. It is something that we share with all of humanity. The goddess Hestia/Vesta also appears in the words 'feast', '*fiesta*' and perhaps in Irish (though it is probably a false etymology it has good resonance) in the words '*feis*' and '*feasa*', words meaning the celebration of life and of wisdom respectively. Hestia/Vesta/Brigid is also the site of sanctuary, safety and of hospitality, of welcoming the stranger. What does it mean when the fire goes out in the hearth? It represents nothing less than the end of civilization: life extinguished. It is conventional to think of Hell as burning everlasting fire, but it is much more likely that Hell is cold, dark and damp, a ruined, desolate, empty place, as it is in Scandinavian mythology – *Hel*. These images of ruined homes and quenched hearths show us the antithesis of life; the cold, heartless spaces that Yeats foresees in 'The Second Coming'.

Creedon's photographs taken in 2005, three years before the economic collapse, are in a sense images taken at *Samhainn*, the period in the pagan Celtic calendar when, following the dog days of hot summer and after the autumn harvest, the season transforms into the long, cold, dark winter – corresponding in this case to the seasonal change from the harvest of affluence after a summer of globalization to the harsh winter of depression. This is a period of liminality; we are standing on the *limen*, the sacred stone of the doorway marking the threshold; we are in a portal between one dimension and another. Standing in this liminal portal between worlds we are in the very zone of metempsychosis, the space of the transmigration of souls. This portal is a primordial and recurring space represented in various ways on the Irish landscape, perhaps most iconically by the passage grave dolmen at *Poll na mBrón*, a sculptural monument representing the passage of the dead back into the Earth to emerge again in an afterlife. The ruined houses of the faithful departed are similar portals of liminality. When we step into these liminal spaces and attune to their energies we may glimpse spirits in the process of metempsychosis. Here, we seem to be looking into our collective past life; some of what we see is grim and depressing, a failed social model ending in poverty and emigration; the promise of care betrayed by a history of neglect, cruelty and abuse; a nightmarish convolute of Ireland's collective dream-state, masked by the dream image of happy families in cosy homesteads. At this moment, when we seem to be awakening from a dream, we perceive aspects of Hestia that we have often willfully chosen to ignore – the goddess as conservative guardian of morality and religion; the matriarch as stern matron; mother Ireland, mother church, mother as smothering. As the dream dispels, we glimpse the shade of the ancestral maternal archetype, Hestia, goddess of the hearth and home, radiant, but also tarnished, as she fades into the ether. The ancestral spirits we glimpse in these photographs are melancholy spirits of a waning power; they are, for the most part, benign shades of traditional community. But in any liminal space, as well as the spirits of departed ancestors transmigrating to the past, there are unclean spirits too: malevolent demons have passed through these rooms, wreaking havoc and destruction.

Creedon's photographs capture a schism, a moment of historical and cultural rupture and transformation. They capture the eclipse of a form of life that was centred around the communal hearth, the sacred space of the home, the household economy of familial communism ruled by the goddess Hestia as the maternal archetype, constituted and reproduced through the gift relation. Her power has waned. Her fire has been quenched, her pot has gone, and now instead of the fireplace we have an empty place, the free space of the marketplace, ruled by Hermes (Gr.) Mercury (Rm). Hermes is a Trickster archetype, the youthful, homeless, wheeling-dealing deity of the market, sophistry and thievery. Celtic Tiger Ireland emerged under the auspices of the spirit of Hermes' free market. In the 1960s, following a long period of moribund economic stagnation and mass emigration, the Irish state decisively abandoned the development model of autarchic economic self-sufficiency based on family farms and small business, and embraced the free market. Joining the European Economic Community on one side, and attracting foreign direct investment by American transnational corporations by offering low taxes and access to European markets on the other, Ireland became a crossroads of economic globalization, ruled by Hermes, cosmopolitan deity of the crossroads. Youthful Hermes ran through the Irish household, throwing open the windows and doors, exposing the scandals and hypocrisy whereby Hestia neglected her children, or, worse, cruelly mistreated a great number of them in the name of 'care'; disrupting beliefs and traditions that had become sedimented and petrified. He has been a welcome breath of fresh air, as Hermes frequently appears in mythology. But, as all Tricksters, the new God has a dark side, and recently, just as Hestia's mask slipped, Hermes' mask has slipped too, and we glimpse his other countenance.

Hermes/Mercury stands for the marketization of all social relations. By the Mercurial power of the market everything is dissolved and liquidated into cash value in a process of reverse transubstantiation. Whereas Hestia represents the transubstantiation of material necessities into ideal forms that have normative power – the family, the community and the society constituted and reproduced by the gift relation mediated through the maternal household – Hermes stands for de-sublimation, from Ideal to material; the liquefaction of ideals into commodities. The market is 'the frightful leveller'; it annihilates and liquefies every social institution with which it comes into contact, so that all values 'float with the same specific gravity in the constantly moving stream of money' (Simmel, 1964: 414). The free market of Hermes the Trickster is the source of the nihilism that has been at the heart / hearth of Celtic Tiger Ireland. The Trickster, whether ancient or neoliberal, is born out of chaos, he dwells in chaos, and his actions, while exciting, and – sometimes, for some people – beneficial in the short term, always and invariably end in more chaos. We are now living through catastrophic market failure caused by financial wizardry and bankers' tricky deals and pyramid housing schemes, and some of our local tricksters, Charlie, Bertie and their developer friends, have, as Trickster typically does, slipped away quietly from the scene of disaster.

If we are to exorcise the haunted houses of Ireland's landscape it is more than a matter of helping spirits to pass over, mourning the past, laying certain things to rest, making atonement with those who suffered under the old order and coming to terms with our collective memories, both beautiful and shameful, in the wake of the death of the collective motherland. Waking the dead is also a vigil. It means being awake and watchful to the new dangers that present themselves in liminal periods of historical metempsychosis: it means protecting the present and taking responsibility for the future: it means preventing evil spirits from breaking through and taking possession of our souls, and insofar as these Mercurial spirits are already amongst us, it means grappling with them and governing them. In Yeats's poetic geometry of the historical process, the inverted cones of the spiralling gyre are drawing apart from one another; they have reached the very point of separation, and at that moment of rupture things are in danger of falling apart, unleashing 'the blood dimmed tide' (1920a: 10). Let us try to look in the eye of the rough beast that is coming – he has in fact been amongst us for some time already – and see what holy charms we might use to repel or at least to contain him – for as Benjamin (1992: 254) tells us in his theses on the philosophy of history, '*even the dead* will not be safe' from the historical forces of darkness, and we are dealing now with 'an enemy who has not ceased to be victorious'.

The most sinister and uncanny thing about how the antichrist works is that rather than coming from the outside, as an alien malevolent Other, the rough beast is already within. It is commonplace for the Irish to blame our problems on externals: historically, the English oppressor; more recently, a perceived materialism, consumerism and loss of community has been blamed on 'Americanization'; and now, impending hardships are exteriorized to the abstract forces of global economics. But the devil usually works through a 'familiar'; his hobgoblin sits by the hearth of the home. When Hermes came to the house of the Gods, Hestia freely gave up her seat to him. Padraic Colum (1989: 26), perhaps unintentionally, puts his finger on one of the well-springs of evil in modern Irish culture: 'Oh, to have a little house / to own the hearth and stool and all'. The historical desire for the security of possession, Lee (1989: 517) tells us, becomes the 'possessor principle', the prioritization of possession, the aggressive defence of the principle of private ownership as the very keystone of modern Irish morality, a principle laid down as a foundation in the Constitution, and enshrined, like a circular, fortified *Dún*, enclosing the Irish *conscience collective*. The possessor principle, the desire expressed by Colum's 'Old Woman of the Roads' for sovereign security through possession of the house, through private ownership of the little white magical things that might brighten her heart – 'A dresser filled with shining delft / speckled with white and blue and brown' (Colum, 1989: 26) – turns, by Satanic black magic into demonic possession by those very same objects. From small, covetous beginnings – Yeats's (1916a: 233) indictment of the gombeen man 'fumbling in a greasy till, add[ing] the ha'pence to the pence' – desire grows and becomes insatiable – 'to own the hearth and stool and all'. The shining ornaments in the dresser will never be enough. We must own it *all*. By the possessor principle the possessor becomes possessed by the fetish object of his/her own desire. As Kavanagh (1964: 36) puts it, the modern Irish peasant, whether in Monaghan in the 1940s or reincarnated as the builder/developer in Dublin in the 2000s, is caught by 'the grip of irregular fields'. Our 'Great Hunger' (Kavanagh, 1964) our desire – for security, for sovereignty in the form of private ownership of land, a house, real estate – devours the soul from the inside out. This is the specific and peculiar idiom and accent of modern Irish consumerism, a form more generally represented in civilization-devolved-to-mindless-consumerism by the zombie.

A Thoroughly Modern Haunting

What is this Irish landscape of the present and the not-too-distant-future? It seems familiar, but it is different. It looks perhaps like Goldsmith's (1770) 'Deserted Village'. Goldsmith's houses had been abandoned by peasants who had left for the city, to work in the dark satanic mills of Manchester. But they were fleeing what Marx and Engels (1985: 225) called 'the idiocy of rural life' and they were people who were going to places where they might 'make history, with will and consciousness'. These people were not yet zombies, though that became the fate of millions of their grandchildren as we glimpse them again on T. S. Eliot's (1996) *The Waste Land*; London, epicentre of early twentieth-century metropolitan civilization, appearing as a fractured and incoherent cultural and spiritual wasteland. And for those few Irish who had not emigrated to London or its equivalents, but who had remained in Ireland hoping to be nourished by the modern Irish Republic, Kavanagh (1964: 57) says that they had nothing but 'the hungry fiend screaming an apocalypse of clay in every corner of the land'. We glimpse another version of the landscape of the recurring future-present in the barren stages of Samuel Beckett (2006): the lunar/nuclear *mis en scene* of *Waiting for Godot*, *Endgame* and *Krapp's Last Tape*, wherein, all the content of fantasy and illusion stripped away, the individual is confronted by what Lacan (1981) has called 'the Lack', the unnamable void of meaninglessness and groundlessness that yawns open under the feet of modern civilization. The interiors of the houses of Celtic Tiger Ireland seem to be brighter, richer, fuller places than the nightmares depicted by Kavanagh and Beckett. But are they? Have we awoken from the nightmare of our history? Or is this another convolute in the interior structure of the dream – dreaming we have awakened in order that we may carry on sleeping?

The interior of the contemporary Irish 'dream home', the 'ideal home' as a wilderness of mirrors, is a shrine to the 'cult of the individual' (Durkheim, 1974). The central cult object over the mantlepiece is no longer the traditional picture of the Sacred Heart or the Madonna with the serene gaze, but, typically, a large, gilt-framed mirror over the cold hearth, reflecting the empty room and the grinning visage of the occupant – if there is an occupant; for, if the house is not entirely standing empty on a ghost estate, as often as not the place of the occupant is filled by a placeholder, a sales agent in the so-called 'showhouse'. Potential homeowners wander through, pilgrims in the grotto of commodity fetishism; the shrunken family of one-dimensional man, shades of our former selves, or more tragically, simulacra of the fully human selves that we might have become. In the showhouse we encounter a thoroughly modern form of haunting, the ghost in the machine. The iron cage of rationalized acquisitiveness, Weber (1958: 178) says, thoroughly disenchanted and systematically cleansed of all higher spiritual values, is 'haunted by the ghosts of dead religious beliefs'. Lacking, and thereby desiring re-enchantment, we are seeking something in the showhouse as commodity fetish. In the real estate brochures and property supplements we were promised a 'home with character', a house with 'personality', a 'starter family home' in a 'new neighbourhood community'; an 'executive residence' in an 'exclusive gated enclave'; all simulacra of the wholeness and continuity of neighbourhood, community, society and of collective life. 'There is no such thing as society',

Margaret Thatcher famously declared at the beginning of the neoliberal revolution. 'There are individual men and women, and there are families.' It is the soul-less individuals of this market dogma and its empty, solipsistic theology who occupy Ireland's new, haunted houses.

Ghosts of the Faithful Departed is a *memento mori*, a reminder of mortality: remember man thou art but dust, and into dust thou shalt return. These aren't nostalgic souvenirs, images of a vanished past, haunted by ghosts of the faithful departed, but rather, and as well, they are portents and premonitions of a holocaust to come, a catastrophe already upon us. Just as these photographs represent epiphanies, they are also images of apocalypse. These are images of the quiet, cold spaces that are in the eye of the hurricane, the storm of history that is now breaking upon us – the recurrence of poverty, desolation and emigration – whereby our new houses, the new houses that we have built during the Celtic Tiger, become emptied once again – abandoned by the builders and developers, repossessed by the banks and mortgage lenders; bereft of parents and emptied of children, big, cold houses, where the fires have gone out, or where there was never a fire lit; houses where there are no ancestral spirits as they have never been – and probably never will be – lived in at all; these vacant, soul-less houses are 'haunted by a lack of ghosts' (Frye, 1977: 22). A society that has sold its soul to materialism has left us short of places to shelter. The devil has now come knocking on our doors.

How will we know this devil when he comes calling? The Celtic Tiger is dead. We need a picture of the rough beast in his next metempsychosis. While his specifically Irish form hasn't yet fully materialized we do have to hand a powerful image of high-modern lycanthropy that might serve as a placeholder for the time being. This figure of man-devolved-into-wolf – '*wer-wolf*' – is the well-known cartoon figure of Wile E Coyote. Wile E Coyote and the Road Runner are cartoon anti-heroes of the decline of American civilization into market-driven nihilistic mass consumerism wherein *homo homini lupis est* – 'man is a wolf to man'. In the North American Native mythology analysed in Radin's (1972) famous study, Coyote is a Trickster archetype. Native American Coyote myths are tales 'told to account for the history of the universe' embracing cosmogony, religion and tradition, history, law and economics, and tragedy and comedy (Bright, 1993: xii). Wile E Coyote stands for humanity as individual animal appetite. His intelligence and cunning are singularly devoted to his ungoverned desire. He represents the political and libidinal economies of an unregulated market. Coyote stands for possessive individualism chasing obscure and fetishized goals of progress and abundance (represented by Roadrunner) through a barren desert landscape (representing modern civilization). In trying to catch Roadrunner, Coyote employs cunning but also science and technology represented by the various gadgets and devices supplied by the 'Acme Co.' – rockets, telescopes, invisible paint, superfoods, technical models and mathematical formulae – the paraphernalia of espionage and the cold war arms race (which of course was actually happening in America's deserts at the time the cartoon was penned, just as Coyote's mad pursuit whips up a storm now in other deserts). Furthermore, the formulae and models used by Coyote represent the market dogma of Friedman's Chicago School economics and rational choice theory that have been the hallmarks of global American hegemony. 'Acme', meaning 'American Corporations Make Everything' and *acme* meaning the pinnacle of development envisaged by modernization theory's *Stages of Economic Growth* (Rostow, 1960) as the stage of global mass consumption, is an overdetermined signifier for the dominant mindset of American civilization as hyper-individuated technocratic free market utopia.

But Wile E Coyote's reliance on technologies employed only in the narrow instrumental goal of satisfying his immediate appetite invariably rebound on him. The result is always the same – catastrophe! He runs out over the edge of the canyon. He is suspended momentarily in the air, carried on by his momentum, or clinging by his fingertips to the remnants of his fantasy, until he looks down at the lack of ground beneath his feet. And then, when the disjuncture between the imaginary and the symbolic orders reveals the Real, he falls. The only question that remains is 'how far?' He falls to the bottom of the canyon floor and crashes painfully in a cloud of dust and, typically, the wreckage of his tricks and schemes – a flying contraption, a ticking bomb (Acme's market failures, like banks and private enterprise's debts and liabilities passed on to the public and the taxpayer and the subsequent cuts and austerity measures) come plummeting after him, and just as he is picking himself up they land on his head and clobber him again. But Coyote always survives. An archetype, he is indestructible, like a vampire cursed to be forever un-dead; driven only by a thirst that is impossible to slake, he gets up, charred and smoking from the explosion, crushed and broken under the debris, and he repeats the cycle all over again. This is the horror of living in the modern wilderness where community and society have been eclipsed by the market. Like Coyote, we seem to learn nothing, and under the spell of progress through technology – cathected in fantasies of the divine powers of market logics and rational action to deliver affluence, reduced to the impoverished form of frantic circulation of digitized financial products, leveraged on our dream houses and a superabundance of commodity fetishes – we remain trapped in a nightmare of history as perpetual recurrence of the present. We bail out the banks, transfer the debt burden to the public, suffer the cuts, frontload the pain, reboot the markets, return again to the Acme catalogue, and begin the mad cycle all over. Like Wile E Coyote, the post-Celtic Tiger Irish are suspended in thin air over the abyss, clinging to the remnants of the illusion of affluence, afraid to look down, about to fall. Now falling; falling; falling. ... It's a long way down!

How deep is the canyon? Our race to the bottom

In the 1930s in the aftermath of the Wall Street Crash, anthropologist Gregory Bateson (1958, 1972) developed the concept of schismogenesis as an aetiology of social conflict. While Bateson developed the concept to explain the escalation of ritualized rivalry to the point of violent rupture amongst tribal peoples of New Guinea, he intended it as a formulation of a general process of political anthropology that could also account for Europe's downward spiral to modern barbarism. 'The nations of Europe are far advanced in symmetrical schismogenesis and are ready to fly at one another's throats; while within each nation are to be observed growing hostilities between the various social strata' (Bateson, 1972: 70). European schismogenesis ultimately took the forms of fascism and communism, culminating in catastrophe – World War II and the Holocaust, purges, gulags and the bureaucratic–authoritarian state.

Bateson identifies two forms of schismogenesis. The first he calls symmetrical, a competitive relationship between equals: for example, the international rivalry amongst European economic and political powers and the arms race. In the contemporary context, symmetrical schismogenesis appears as competition between nations to win international investment; a rivalry that involves their competing in a downward spiral to reduce corporate taxation, deregulate markets, cut public services, cut wages and become 'more competitive'. Ireland led this 'race to the bottom' in Europe, leading other EU countries, and especially the accession states of Eastern Europe, away from the Nordic and the Rhinish social models, towards an ultra-liberal unregulated free market. The second form Bateson identifies is complementary schismogenesis, that is, rivalry and antagonism amongst unequal social groups, for example gender, racial and class conflicts. In Bateson's time, as in ours, symmetrical and complementary schismogenic processes occurred simultaneously, and they have become amplified. The Celtic Tiger deepened and sharpened social divisions, and Ireland is now one of the most unequal societies in the OEDC. Underinvestment in social infrastructure (health care, education, public transport) combined with regressive fiscal policy and loss of control of the national revenue base in a context of economic globalization means that the Irish state has neither the economic nor the political resources with which to intervene. Instead, with Coyote's tunnel vision, it 'sticks with the plan', barrelling ahead towards further catastrophe.

Schismogenesis can be restrained by identifying external or internal enemies (Bateson, 1972: 71–72), historical examples being the consolidation of collective identity by fascist movements in Germany, Spain, Austria, and in the corresponding totalitarianisms in Russia and Eastern countries by mobilizing sentiments of nationalism, racism and anti-Semitism, and by the identification of scapegoats, 'thieves of enjoyment' (Zižek, 1990) – 'jews', 'immigrants' and other 'vermin'. As recession bites we may see an upsurge of these phenomena in post-Celtic Tiger Ireland, as there is in Greece and throughout Europe in the form of fascism and extreme nationalism. The schismogenic process can also be restrained, or at least moderated, by temporary or occasional inversions of relations of inequality. Tokenistic representation of minorities – a Nigerian or a Latvian elected to an Irish town council; carnivalesque festivals celebrating multiculturalism – for a day; lotteries, gambling and celebrity systems that occasionally catapult someone into affluence by 'a stroke of luck', reinforcing the notion that social structure is an arbitrary matter of personal fortune: these phenomena have become staples of contemporary popular culture. But the most important process by which schismogenesis can be counteracted, and even turned around, is by the gift relation.

Reversing Ireland's downward spiral: the return of Hestia and the gift of home

What might we do to reverse the downward spiral, to restore equilibrium to the turning gyre? The ancient, deep anthropological magic against demonic chaos and barbarism has always been the gift. The gift relation is the most fundamental and anthropologically universal social institution. The gift is a cardinal virtue in all of the world's religions. It is formative and constitutive of all social relations, and is the foundation of civilization. Its reciprocal, obligatory and incremental principles placate aggrieved members of the community, and inveigle the potentially hostile outsider into the mutually sustaining civilizing process. The gift relation reverses violence, theft and hostility, and redeems conflict arising from division and inequality into the miracle of society.

The gift relation was analysed and formulated by French social science with the purpose of identifying principles that would underpin and fortify France's Third Republic and prevent recurring cycles of revolutionary violence on the one hand and totalitarianism on the other. Mauss (2002) argued that the anthropologically universal principle of the gift relation could be adapted to become the core integrating principle not only of modern France, but also of other European states, and indeed of modern civilization. The grammar of the gift relation, in Mauss's analysis, consists of three principles: Reciprocity – the gift is given; the gift is received; and the gift is returned; Obligation – the recipient of the gift is obliged to return the gift; and the recipient of the reciprocated gift becomes obliged to give again; and Increment – the gift must be reciprocated by a gift of (at least) equal (and preferably greater) value, thereby amplifying the reciprocal and obligatory dimensions of social relations. The logic of the gift relation has been adapted and developed to achieve social integration and harmony in modern contexts that were riven by endemic social conflict and revolutionary violence, and in fact became the basis of the modern Western democratic republican welfare state. At the same time as these principles of modern republicanism were being developed in France, in Germany, Bismarck introduced universal health care, pensions and unemployment insurance to unite conflicting regional and class factions, and there were similar developments in the UK, where, for example, Titmuss, the architect of the British National Health Service, premised this core institution of modern British society on the principle of the gift relation.

Modern society cannot be reduced to Adam Smith's and Milton Friedman's network market relations mediated by Hermes, because the great accumulation of wisdom in humanity's mythic and moral patrimony knows that Hermes is a Trickster, one of whose core characteristics is his tendency to run amok. The deep meaning of 'Economics' has always been from the management of the household, the *Oikos*, and the free market must ultimately be accountable to Hestia's domestic science, the arts and graces of balanced and fair distribution that achieve equilibrium, harmonious life and sustainability for the whole household. Modern society, the power of the market made accountable to Hestia, is a collective household structured by the grammar of the gift, in a total system of gift relations wherein 'gifts' in the form of fair wages, housing, health care, education and social security are exchanged for labour, political legitimization, loyalty, duty, civil responsibility and social harmony. The paragons of this stabilized, equitable and harmonious social model have, for many decades now, been the Nordic countries, some of the core member states of the EU, namely France, Germany and – once upon a time – the UK. We need to learn from the continued success of the Nordic and Rhinish social models, restore our commitments to the foundations of social integration and counteract the sinister forces of the theft relation with the white magic of the gracious gift. But is post-Celtic Tiger Ireland willing to learn?

Ireland has some 100,000 unsold houses, 'toxic assets' owned by developers, owed to Irish and international banks, under the stewardship of the National Assets Management Agency. There are also some 160,000 unoccupied rental spaces. Dublin has 10,000 homeless people, there are approximately 28,000 households on the housing lists for social housing and many more people are trapped in substandard and decrepit dwellings in neighbourhoods blighted by poverty and violence. A likely possibility is that the Irish state will purchase the surplus housing stock from Ireland's builders and developers and use these state-acquired housing units for social housing provision. By such a strategy government could simultaneously bail out its friends in the banking and construction industries (who, as the main beneficiaries of the Celtic Tiger, were sponsors and supporters of government during the boom) and appear to be generously addressing the needs of the poor, thereby using the gift of the house to reverse the vicious circle and restore equilibrium to the spiralling gyre.

But this will probably turn out to be a poisoned gift, as gifts from Hermes and other tricksters very often are. There is a long and ignoble tradition of such dubious 'gifts' – the Trojan horse; the shiny red apple proffered by the Witch; the counterfeit coin given to the beggar in Edgar Alan Poe's macabre story – Trickster's gifts that, far from helping, actually cause harm to the recipient. This may well turn out to be the nature of the gift of Ireland's toxic houses to the poor and the homeless. Ireland's surplus houses were never built to be homes, to be dwelt in by people and families living amongst neighbours and communities. Typically, they were built as tax shelters: tax-incentivized buy-to-let investment properties, or holiday houses in beautiful but remote locations, or minor suburban estates built by local developers like tumorous growths on rural villages that were already in terminal decline. These houses are surplus to requirements because they were built in isolation, without services, infrastructure or connections; without schools, or shops or jobs. Into these houses throughout the Irish countryside will be poured a distilled, residual, urban population of the multiply disadvantaged and the socially excluded. These new Irish 'neighbourhoods' will quickly become nightmares; exurban ghettos and *banlieues*, ticking social bombs that will explode in our faces and leave us once again, like Coyote, standing burnt and blinking in the midst of ruins and ashes.

Note

1   *Ghosts of the Faithful Departed* can be viewed at: http://www.davidcreedon.com (Accessed 10 June 2012).

2

The value of house and home

The house, the residence, is the only rampart against the dread of nothingness, darkness and the obscurity of the past. Its walls contain all that mankind has patiently amassed over hundreds of centuries. It opposes escape, loss and absence by erecting an internal order, a civility, a passion of its own. Its liberty flourishes where there is stability and finitude, not openness and infinity. ... Man's identity is thus residential. (Kant, in Perrot, 1990: 342)

Heidegger tells us that *bauen*, to build, means also to dwell, and dwelling is the particular way in which human beings inhabit the earth: to be human is to build, to dwell, which 'also means at the same time to cherish and protect, to preserve and to care for, specifically to till the soil, to cultivate the vine' (1977: 325). The very foundations of our idea of the house are inextricably bound up with what it is to be human, which entails cherishing, protecting and caring for; all of which, Heidegger says, for all of its extraordinariness, 'remains for our everyday experience that which is from the outset "habitual"' (Heidegger, ibid.). The grounds of the metaphysics of what it is 'to be' are to be found in the phenomenology of dwelling and the taken-for-granted *habitus* of home-making and inhabiting. From a phenomenology of dwelling, Heidegger suggests, we might recover normative principles that have become concealed from us, ironically because they have become habitual.

Living is round

In Ireland all of the ancient forms of settlement – *dún, rath/lios, cranóg, clogheen/clachán* (stone ringfort, earthen ringfort, island enclosure, cluster of houses) – are round, and they are the prefixes of geographical placenames which are also the names of ancestral households. *Dún*, a stone ringfort, derives from the verb *dún*, 'to close'. The noun 'wall' is '*balla*', and the verb '*ballaigh*' means 'to gather'. Both these roots underpin '*baile*', 'home', and 'at home' – *abhaile*. *Teach*, 'house', is derived from *'teacht'* – to come, as in to come together, to combine; and *cónaí* from *cónaigh* – to dwell, to reside – is *có naí*, 'with baby'. *Naodh* is a suckling baby, which in turn is closely related to *naomh*, meaning 'sacred' or 'holy'. *Teach conaithe*, a dwelling house, means the coming together to give birth, instigating the sacred institution of society.[1]

A related etymological cluster is found in *'comharsa'*, which may be translated as 'neighbour'. To dwell means to dwell with others, a meaning Heidegger says 'has been preserved in the German word *nachbar*, neighbour. The *nachbar* is ... 'he who [builds] dwells nearby' (Heidegger, 1977: 325). To dwell is to dwell with others nearby, so that to dwell is not a monadic caring for oneself but entails cultivating reciprocal care for and amongst others who also dwell. *Comharsan* derives from *comhair*, meaning 'combined work', 'mutual assistance'; and also *os comhair*, meaning 'facing', 'in front of'; and also *'cumhair'*, meaning help, strength and power. So *comharsan* is one who faces (as in a circular gathering), one who dwells (who remains before me) and one who is part of a combined strength of mutual assistance.

The circular hearth, home and dwelling, discourse and knowledge are inextricably linked.[2] Fire was first used to clear the forests. The burnt-out circular clearing formed a defensive perimeter, the fire providing heat, light and protection from animals, especially at night. The circular gathering of the primitive family around the fire became the locus of a civilizing process (Goudsblom, 1992). The domestication of fire develops social solidarity in the division of labour that tending the fire necessitated, and communicative action – the language that coordinated collective action – presupposes. Vico (1999: 244) says that the clearing became an 'eye' to the heavens, from whence we gazed upwards to eternity and the realm of the Gods, and complementing the heavens, Bachelard suggests, the hearths and huts of human dwelling became an earthly constellation. The immemorial, legendary house is the circle of light shed by the fire, the round, primitive hut of prehistoric man (Bachelard, 1994: 31).[3] Communication, mutual recognition, self-reflection and theosophical speculation begin in the primitive scene of gazing into the fire and into the heavens.[4]

That the form of dwelling and human well-being is round is evidenced by the multiplicity and diversity of anthropological forms of housing and primitive settlement that are circular: the beehive houses of Hama, Syria, continuously inhabited since 6000 BC; the Mongolian yurt, the igloo, the adobe huts of the Masai, the Zulu and Kalahari Bushmen; the houses of the Kogi and Arhuaco of the Sierra Nevada and Central South America, peoples that are separated by continents and by oceans. In the circular settlements of the !Kung the hearth of each family hut is situated two arms' length from the next, the exact bodily distance of the gift relation – one outstretched arm giving, the other receiving, the central area encircled by these hearths is the social space for dividing food and for dancing (Hanson, 1998: 4). By extending hospitality across the threshold, from inhabitant-to-inhabitant to inhabitant-to-outsider/stranger, the household marks and reiterates its threshold, while simultaneously the household's gift to those formerly outside, perhaps hostile, enabling them to establish their own household, with its own threshold, ensuring the safety of the household by the outsiders' now being under obligation and becoming subject to the influence of the idea of the civilized household. The circular gift relation demonstrates the superiority of the household as a form of life both economically and morally over the needful state of homelessness and disorder. The gift relation that constitutes the household initiates what has become social security, in that in the event of the household becoming needy it can call in the debt morally and materially. Amongst the pre-Celtic Neolithic civilizations in Britain and in Ireland the spiral expanding outwards from a centre point of origin is the graphic decorative motif of a fundamental understanding of the virtuous circle, that sustainable living is round.[5]

Vesta's temple in Rome was round, like the huts of the aboriginal inhabitants of the Tiber valley and surrounding hills. The geometric principle of Vesta's temple's circular structure, that every point on the circumference is equidistant from the centre, represents the formal abstract principle of equality: all members contained within the circle, gathered around the fire of the collective household, the family, the tribe, the community, the city, are recognized by others as being due their fair share of common resources for their contributing to the collective well-being. This is the principle of Weber's primitive communism. The house and home are originally round – communal, collective, whole, a continuous and eternal cycle of birth, life and death, and rebirth – and in this form lay integrity and sustainability.[6] Modern civilization broadens the circle of society, though at the cost of dissolving community, to such an extent that, as Yeats says, 'the centre cannot hold / mere anarchy is loosed upon the world' (1920a: 10). We are presently living through such a moment of dissolution. What caused the de-centring?

The value of modern houses

A central feature of the experience of modernity, an experience greatly amplified during the recent period of neoliberal globalization, has been the expansion of limits and the dissolution of boundaries as financial markets and their informational infrastructure have extended beyond the fiscal regulatory frameworks of nation states. The indefiniteness and boundlessness of the spatial frame of global markets, the opacity and complexity of their media and processes, become a source of collective stimuli. Indistinctness of boundaries has a stimulating and seductive effect, Simmel (1997: 145–146) says, like a

meeting convened in darkness: the outer boundaries fade and the focus intensifies on the immediate as 'fantasy expands darkness into exaggerated
possibilities; one feels surrounded by fantastically indefinite and unlimited
space'. The intensified focus on the immediate due to spatial limitlessness is
further amplified by temporal de-containment: global trade in financial
markets takes place around the clock, Wall Street opening, London and
Frankfurt trading, Tokyo closing; and an inner temporal expansion whereby
currency and interest rate fluctuations are traded instantaneously by
automated systems. De-framing takes place too on the linguistic and cognitive
level: the Classical modern narrative framing of political economy, from Adam
Smith and Marx through Keynes and Friedman, has been superseded since the
1970s so that economics in general and financial derivatives trade in particular take place on the basis of mathematical models and algorithms that even
financial services professionals themselves scarcely understand. The global
financial market is 'the most computationally intensive activity in the modern
world' (MacKenzie, 2008: 25), a 'streaming epistemic system' (Knorr Cetina
and Preda, 2007: 117), 'clearly defined in terms of prices, news, relevant
economic indicators at any given moment' but 'ill defined with respect to the
direction they will take at the next moment'; a processual reality, an infinite
succession of non-identical matter projecting itself forward as changing
screen, a reality that changes all the time 'stable only long enough to enable
transactions to occur'.

In the context of this techno-financial sublime wherein liminality and
liquessence are greatly intensified there is a corresponding increasing significance to spatial fixity as 'every immobile asset around which economic
transactions of any kind occur is [a] pivot point for unstable conditions and
interactions' (Simmel, 1997a: 146). 'The reason why mortgages tend to be
connected almost exclusively to immovable assets,' Simmel says, 'is a combination of the stationary character and the indestructibility of these assets ...
the mortgaged object can remain in the hands of the debtor and yet be
completely secure for the creditor' (1997a: 146). Insurance was a relatively
insignificant dimension of the money economy in Simmel's time, but it came
to play a central role in subsequent and especially in the most recent economic
crisis. Insurance, developed by Lloyds of London in the early modern finance
industry, so that a ship and its cargo, valued according to the risk of its safe
arrival or its loss, could become a security, is the prototype of contemporary
financial investment vehicles. 'The principle of insurance has made those
objects that are totally lacking in any fixed position in space eligible for
mortgage lending' (Simmel, 1997a: 147). Insurance exponentially increases
money's character of abstraction, as each derivative insurance policy, a
financial product whose value is derived from the risk of earlier insurances,
abstracts financial markets from the original fixed, literal, 'concrete' asset on

which it is leveraged. Credit Default Swaps (CDSs) and Collateralized Debt Obligations (CDOs) as insurance policies derived from Mortgage Backed Securities (MBSs) are the lynchpin of the 84–trillion dollar financial derivatives market, and the sub-prime section of that market was the epicentre of the crash (MacKenzie, 2008).

Why did the value of houses, and thereby mortgages, increase so much during the recent period of neoliberal globalization? The value of the house can be understood in terms of what Simmel (1997b) formulates as *The Conflict in Modern Culture* between the hypertrophy of objective culture and the relative underdevelopment of subjective culture. As the structures and institutions of modern society become more vast, impersonal and opaque – the workings of global political economy and financial markets as they seem to the average citizen, for instance – people search for security and certainty at a smaller scale; for points of unconditional mooring in a world of flux and contingency. The house, as Kant says, becomes a rampart against the vast obscurities of the outer world; it erects a civil and stable internal order. As the modern world becomes more complex, more extensive, more 'objective', the house, perceived as a safe haven of subjective culture, tends to become more valued. As well as the effects of this general dialectic between objective and subjective culture, the nature of money itself plays a special role. As Simmel explains (1964a: 414–415), 'money as absolute means, the universal solvent, dissolves and reduces all values to the question of "how much?" Everything floats with the same specific value in the constantly moving stream of money, and as all things have equal value, differentiated only by quantity, nothing is of any value' (1964a: 414–415). Following the money to its source, the stream appears through the lens of historical materialism in terms of naked, brutal exploitation. Conrad's *Heart of Darkness*, Weber's *Protestant Ethic and the Spirit of Capitalism* and Simmel's *Philosophy of Money* (originally published in 1899, 1904 and 1905, respectively) go deeper, and show that the river of ivory, rubber and oil, slicked with the blood of labour, or today's sophisticated financial derivative instruments flow from madness and horror: the modern economy is a feverish vortex of desires emanating from nihilism. For Simmel, money is an annihilating power -'the frightful leveller. ... It hollows out the core of things, their individuality, their specific value and their incomparability in a way that is beyond repair' (1964a: 414–415). We shall return to the problem of nihilism and the heart of darkness in the modern household below, but for the time being let us consider the value of the rampart that stands against it. Against the tendency of money economy towards cultural nihilism, Kant and Simmel suggest, the house retains a value that cannot be so easily reduced to cash value because its use value is entwined with its concrete, material endurance as residence, as dwelling place.

As late as the nineteenth century, Simmel reminds us, even in cities, individual houses typically had proper names, as though houses were persons! 'The house that is called by its own name [gives] its inhabitants a feeling of spatial individuality, of belonging to a qualitatively fixed point in space. Through the name associated with it, the house forms a much more autonomous, individually nuanced existence' (Simmel, 1997b: 149). As Kant (2002: 36) points out, not everything has a monetary value: 'Everything has either a *price* or a *dignity*. Whatever has a price can be replaced by something else as equivalent. Whatever by contrast is exalted above all price and so admits no equivalent has a dignity.' But it is not so 'either/or', as Kant asserts, for some things (and the house, Kant himself suggests, may be a rather special type of thing) have *both* price *and* dignity. Through dwelling, whereby subjective culture is developed and institutionalized, the substantive value of house and home becomes intertwined in the collective personality, biography, character and name of the household. Whereas the housing market splits them, in ordinary language usage 'house and home' are synonyms for a unified whole, the household, an entity constituted by a web of libidinal attachments, with 'personality', 'character' and dignity that resists financial liquefaction and commodification. According to Simmel, 'it is the money form of profit which distorts the notion of value. Whenever profit appears only in terms of "use value" and where only its immediate concrete quantity is taken into account, then the idea of its growth is confined to sober limits' (1990: 250). From the perspective of the householder this is primarily how the house appears – substantive value as concrete actuality, as residence, dwelling place, as identity, as the end in an otherwise endless sequence of purposes that money can serve. The house and home is an enduring final object of enjoyment providing spatial and temporal boundaries to life, a mooring for meaningful life-projects of autonomous individual and familial self-realization.

The ideal value of real estate

Whereas modernity and globalization open limitless horizons, the house establishes stability and finitude as it constitutes an end in the otherwise endless sequence of purposes. Moreover, and in addition to the way in which its exchange value is inseparable from its use value as dwelling in the realm of subjective culture, the house as 'real estate' retains a moment of 'ideal value'. According to Simmel, what is 'real' about the value of real estate is that it contains a portion of an absolute, ideal value that is relatively indestructible, and thus 'it grants a certain dignity which distinguishes it from all other types of possession'. This special value of real estate continues throughout history, because 'whereas movable objects might be exchanged against one another, immobile property was – *cum grano salis* – something incomparable: it was value as such, the immovable ground above and beyond which real economic activity was carried on' (Simmel, 1990: 241). What is 'real' about real estate is that house and home stands in the place of what Lacan (1978) terms the Real: the abyss of nothingness and meaninglessness over which human existence is suspended. Herein lies the affinity between private property and nihilism – the little piece of the Real that adheres to real estate. In our rational, though patho-logical-fetishistic attachment to our house as private property we express our existential anxiety arising from the meaningless thrownness of existence.

In Weber's (1978b) formulation the *oikos*, the household, is that deep nexus of economy and society, the locus of wealth in its *ur-form*: 'The size and inclusiveness of the house varies. But it is the most widespread economic group and involves continuous and intensive social action. It is the funda-mental basis of loyalty and authority, which in turn is the basis of many other groups. ... The principle of household communism, according to which everybody contributes what he can and takes what he needs (as far as the supply of goods suffices), constitutes even today the essential feature of our family household, but is limited in the main to household consump-tion' (Weber, 1978b: 359). The *oikos* for Weber is an ideal-type socio-economic institution, a primordial and transcendent form preserved and expressed by the etymology of 'economics' as meaning 'the care of the household'. Weber's *oikos* corresponds in Simmel's paradigm to an endur-ing social form, an institution with innumerable substantive anthropological and historical variations at the level of life's contents while retaining all the while a coherence and cohesion of social form. Just as 'the stranger' is the social type in which 'the tension between closeness and remoteness, involve-ment and detachment finds equilibrium' (Simmel, 1964b: 402) and just as 'it is the function of "the metropolis" to provide an arena for the struggle between the individual and the super-individual contents of life and their reconciliation' (Simmel, 1964a: 423) the modern household can be formu-lated as the institution in which tensions between external objective culture and subjective internal culture are brought to terms with one another. In the genealogy of the spirit of capitalism, as the Calvinist throws himself into working in his vocation in order to avoid doubt of being amongst the elect while at the same time avoiding expenditure of accumulated wealth on pleas-ure, the household becomes the theatre in which this inner and outer conflict is played out. In Weber's formulation, 'the puritan outlook that stood at the cradle of modern economic man' 'set the clean and solid comfort of the middle-class home as an ideal' (Weber, 1958: 171).

The provision and the maintenance of the household become for the husband and housewife an exterior manifestation of goodness, that, even though it cannot of itself assure one's being amongst the elect, represents nonetheless 'the methodical development of one's own state of grace to a higher and higher degree of certainty and perfection' (Weber, 1958: 133).

Careful domestic economy restricts consumption and the irrational use of wealth, and, from the point of view of the inner world and the libidinal economy of the subject, ascetic domesticity opened up a world of work that is never finished, demanding 'hard, continuous bodily or mental labour' (Weber, 1958: 158). Thus homemaking and housekeeping serve within the genealogy of the Protestant ethic and the spirit of capitalism as a worthy vocation and a means of avoiding doubt: 'the home was the anvil on which adult manhood was forged' (Vickery, 2009: 52). In this formulation the well-ordered household is an ideal and an end in itself within the symbolic order of the emerging spirit of capitalism that holds the place of the Real and saves the puritan ascetic proto-modern householder from the psychosis-inducing terror of not being amongst the elect. The modern household began as a part of the puritan's vocation and like other dimensions of the Protestant ethic it gradually became secularized and massified in the broader objective culture of the iron cage of rationalized acquisitiveness, where compulsive economic activity 'no longer related to the highest spiritual and cultural values ... stripped of its religious and ethical meaning, tends to become associated with purely mundane passions ... this nullity imagines that it has attained a level of civilization never before achieved' (Weber, 1958: 182). Herein lies the source of the deep ambivalance of the modern relationship of home ownership; its association with petty bourgeois conservatism and aggressive defensiveness on the one hand, and, on the other, terrible entrapment in banal routine.[7]

The emotional wealth of the household

The history of family life shows a progressive improvement of the status of women in respect to recognition of subjectivity and equality, and, especially, the centrality of the emotions, specifically love, as the core of family life (Simmel, 1964: 128–130; Frisby, 1998). A libidinal economy of reciprocal relations of erotic passion, care and affection, mutual loyalty and responsibility, love relations that are 'more than life' stands at the centre of the household. The idea of modern marriage, and 'marriage-like free love' – which is Simmel's inclusive term for the multiplicity and variety of stabilized institutionalized contemporary post-conventional intimate relations – 'is the commonness of *all* life contents insofar as they determine the value and fate of the personality, immediately or through their effects' (Simmel, 1964d: 328). In a thriving union, Simmel says, individuals who 'give themselves wholly to one another' do not in fact 'wholly' give themselves away, 'because their wealth consists in a continuous development in which every abandon is at once followed by new treasures ... from an inexhaustible reservoir of latent psychological treasures and hence can no more reveal and give them away at a stroke than a tree can give away next year's fruits with those of the season' (Simmel,

1964d: 328). It is this inexhaustible wealth of a libidinal economy upon which the contemporary household is built. This is a constantly increasing emotional capital that in healthy modern intimate relations is perpetually replenished, constituting a miraculous 'surplus' that sustains the integrity of the form of the household and generates its added value.

But of course this ideal modern form of marriage or marriage-like household-constituting emotional commerce is by no means always realized, and neither is it easily sustained, and where it is, it is often at a high price of repression and resentment. The conditions of contemporary life, the complex web of political-economic and cultural relations within which modern intimate relations are negotiated, the always unstable equilibrium of individuals' inner life played out against a constantly expanding outer horizon of alternative possibilities and the progressive loosening of the constraints of conventional morality threaten modern love, marriage and household, however configured, from both within and without, as Simmel (and indeed the Webers) knew very well.[8]

While the *oikos* diminishes in size and significance in terms of the material economy and becomes associated primarily with subjective culture, because of the richness of its libidinal economy the modern household assumes an increased value amid the flux, indeterminacy and nihilism of the broader objective culture. Zelizer, developing a theme of Simmel's, argues that children have become 'economically worthless but emotionally priceless' (1981: 1036). The same inversion takes place with respect to the household: the trace of Ideal value that accrues to the household is its core nexus of priceless emotional relations – and in Simmel's formulation this priceless nexus is increasing in value as it becomes more difficult to achieve and to maintain. The ideal value of the household increases in proportion as it recedes in reality from our grasp. In societies where the housing market boomed, a high rate of divorce and household decomposition on the one hand is matched by remarriage and the re-composition of second and third new households on the other. Hence the enduring and amplified value of the idealized household as an end in an otherwise endless sequence of purposes, as a repository of value as such, and thus as mother lode, *agalma:*[9] a source of primary collateral from which all other collateral is derived. It is the anthropologically deep-seated and, under conditions of modernity, progressively elaborated treasure trove, the elusive, idealized object of the household constituted through the reciprocal complex of libidinal and material economies as an irreducible core of value that has anchored the wider economic trade in financial derivatives.

Liquescence, liminality and the solidity of household value

The value of real estate resonates with deep-seated needs of the household's domestic economy of emotional and material asymmetrical reciprocal relations of interdependency. In times of insecurity and liminality the house assumes added and amplified value. The amplification of the value of the house as a bulwark against insecurity is ancient. For the Greeks to sell a family home or landed property was 'an offence not only against the children, but also against the ancestors, because it disrupted the continuity of the family' (Simmel, 1990: 240). As Simmel notes, the Greek prohibition on the sale of real estate was instituted at the apex of Classical civilization, at the cusp of decline.[10]

The recent history of the real estate market reiterates this lesson: while currency and stock market bubbles burst and crash, comparatively, until very recently, real estate prices, even when inflated, deflate gradually, fall back slightly and recover steadily. Owner-occupiers who dwell in their house as home, for whom their primary relation is their property's ongoing and enduring use value rather than its exchange value, batten down the hatches and weather the economic storm. Within five years of the UK property crash of the early 1990s homeowners in south-east England who had experienced the highest levels of negative equity had fully recovered their lost value and within the following ten years saw their real estate increase in value by over 100 per cent (Boleat, 1995). In the US, while stock values crashed in the aftermath of the dot.com bubble, ENRON and other corporate scandals, the housing market saw extraordinary growth, in parts of the State of California by over 100 per cent within one year.

The boom in housing prices, in the US, the UK and beyond, can be understood primarily in terms of how modernity is increasingly characterized by liquescence (Bauman, 2000) and permanent liminality (Szakolczai, 2000), and neoliberal globalization is an intensification and acceleration of these collective historical experiences of hypertrophy. The heightened value of the house emerges against the insecurities of the risk society (Beck, 1992), the destabilization of the fiscal and legal bases of national citizenship and the identity insecurities of the post-national constellation (Habermas, 2001), the ephemerality of postmodern culture and accelerated social transformation (Baudrilliard, 1987; Jameson, 1991; Virilio, 1995). The new poor, having no longer a role in production, attempt to become consumers (Bauman, 2005) and so they focus on that commodity *par excellence*, the house, as primary asset, saving, investment, and as theatre for the performance of the ethic of consumerism. The sub-prime mortgage borrower is Bauman's 'flawed consumer'. Labour no longer defines value, according to the theories of the new finance capitalism. Workers are no longer needed, only consumers, and as surplus and redundant populations tend towards precarity they are recast in terms of being flawed consumers. In this emerging form we can see not only a defensive retreat to the interior but also the persistence of a deep need to articulate and to realize an idea of the good life. The care and attention given to interior décor, the work of continuous 'home improvement' so characteristic of contemporary life, even amongst such flawed consumers, as a mask and as a compensation for their precarity, practices easily disparaged as commodity fetishism can be more sympathetically understood as attempted elaborations of subjective culture and the search for meaningful life projects in the face of the hypertrophic growth of the objective culture of globalization.

'Sub-prime' borrowers' desire for a dream home

The sub-prime mortgage crisis arose because economic restructuring and flexibilization under conditions of globalization have amplified the desire for security amongst the economically least secure borrowers whose jobs are being outsourced and flexibilized. 'Sub-prime' precarious borrowers are precisely Simmel's subjects of modern culture whose life chances are unstable and incoherent, for whom self-realization through meaningful autonomous life projects is foreclosed. 'The question as to what value really is, like the question as to what being really is, is unanswerable', Simmel says (1990: 62), except insofar as their ideal unity is made comprehensible to the unitary soul, that is to say, their external objectivity is apprehended as being subjectively meaningful. 'In whatever empirical or transcendental sense the difference between objects and subjects is conceived, value is never a "quality" of the objects, but a judgement upon them that remains inherent in the subject' (Simmel, 1990: 63).

The value – *werth* (worth) – of an object, Simmel says, is determined by the dialectics of desire:

> The content of our desire becomes an object as soon as it is opposed to us, not only in the sense of being impervious to us, but also in terms of its distance as something not-yet-enjoyed, the subjective aspect of this condition being desire. ... Objects are not difficult to acquire because they are valuable, but we call those objects valuable that resist our desire to possess them. (1990: 66–67)

Desire and value are amplified by the desire that others have for the same object.[11] It is not the use value or exchange value of the object, but moreover and primarily the 'psychological, even metaphysical presuppositions' that come into play in economic relations between suppliers and consumers – and other consumers: that is, by the presence of a third term: a competing desire that thwarts the dyadic economic relation, and by creating opposition and distance raises the value of the object. This amplifying effect of a third term opens a spiral of competitive relations, constituting a libidinal economy underpinning and at the heart of the money economy.

Simmel's theory of the triangulation of desire in the libidinal economy that underpins political economy anticipates Girard's explicit formulation of desire as a feverish mimesis and Lacan's desire as desire for recognition to mask a constitutive lack in the subject. In Girard's formulation 'the mediated nature of desire can be illustrated as a triangle, i.e. as a relation between subject–model/mediator–object' (1976: 15). In this relationship the object of desire – in this case the house – is not the goal. The subject actually desires to be the model – the other subject, a hypothesized, idealized subject – and only desires the object so as to imitate the model. As the subject and the model desire the same object, competition and rivalry ensue, and when the same object is desired by many its original value becomes inflated. This is exactly what happens in a 'bubble', such as land and property markets.

Economic insecurity and socially unsecured financial derivatives

The domestic economy is integrated with the wider 'real' economy and the de-materialized, financial derivatives markets of MBSs through a libidinal and moral economy of the *oikos*, wherein there is a presumed contract between people with aspirations of becoming owners of a private home, with secured means of income, accumulated savings, and all of the sublimated libidinal energies and self-discipline, conscientious planning and mutual commitment to the personally shaped future vested in the family home and its dependants, an island of intimate sociality and solidarity within the broader sea of the so-called 'market society'. It is not the house but the *oikos* – the household – and the homemaking project holistically combined as a meaningful and self-suffi-cient sustainable totality that together constitute the 'asset backed security' (ABS), the nexus of wealth wherein economy and society are ineluctably bound up with one another.

The sub-prime mortgage market is a further refinement of the uncoupling of the relationship between the money economy of the market and the libidinal–moral–domestic economy of the *oikos* (Weber, 1978b: 375) and becomes increasingly based on relatively fictive 'households'. Some 40 per cent of all US house purchases in 2006 were not 'primary residences' but specula-tive 'investment properties' and 'holiday houses'. As well as this froth, which is a common historical feature of real estate booms, the problematic bubble was in the new territory of the sub-prime market which was opened up through the development of a plethora of new 'sophisticated' financial products: adjustable rate mortgages (ARMs), with 'teaser' low entry rates that would later increase; 100 per cent mortgages with zero down payment; loans based on stated (rather than proven) resources, such as 'stated income, verified assets' (SIVAs), 'no income, verified assets' (NIVAs) and eventually 'no income, no job, no assets' (NINJAs). Online mortgage companies, often branch enterprises of real estate and construction companies, developed 'automated underwriting' of loan applications for houses that they were selling or building, ensuring loan approval without any review of applicants' assets, prospects or ability to make repayments. Over 40 per cent of all sub-prime lending in the US was concentrated in the 'dream states' of Nevada, Florida and California, where immigrants pursue the American dream and Americans dream of retiring. At the height of the boom there were 45,000 mortgage sales agents working the California market (McDonald, 2009). The rate of functional illiteracy in the State of California is over 30 per cent. A substantial proportion of 'sophisticated' mortgage products were sold to clients who had difficulty reading the loan agreements. In this market not only is there an accelerated and intensified uncoupling of the economy from the *oikos*, but the *oikos* itself is increasingly fictive; it shrinks from the historical extended household to the nuclear, atomized and particulate household units of the contemporary post-family – striving to reconstitute itself; and it fades from the radiant ideal of the anthropological universal and transcendent form of the house and home to the mere simulacrum: the residual and vestigial image of the beautiful home flickering on the wall of the cave, which has a mesmerizing effect none the less for that as it now shines ever more brightly.

Sub-prime lenders then 'bundled' mortgages, that is – in an idiom of the narcotics trade that found a new usage in financial markets – they 'cut' (combined sub-prime, insecure loans with traditional secure mortgages, as cocaine is cut with milk powder) into packages of MBSs containing several thousand mortgages, and sold MBSs on to larger banks, which bundled them again with other sub-prime mortgages and sold them to other financial institutions and investment banks as mortgage derivatives. ABSs, MBSs and CDOs, based as they were on the traditionally secure value of real estate and the low default rate of households, enjoyed artificially high credit ratings, and risks were further displaced through CDSs, insurance policies held by still other financial institutions extending throughout a globalized banking system. Taken together this constituted an outward spiralling system of risk displacement and amplification, a housing pyramid scheme with foundations in acute insecurities at the level of subjective culture and the individual household.

The moral grammar of financial sophistry[12]

The value of house and home ('real estate') has, from deep historical times up to the present, been a substantive 'real' value anchored in libidinal attachments, meaningful symbolic networks, norms and cultural ideals. The derivative value, abstracted away from the substantive, as it becomes distant from all contexts of meaningful morality, as the real economy becomes decoupled from the speculative financial economy, becomes a-moral; based on 'nothing'. The collapse of the sub-prime mortgage derivatives market illustrates Plato's indictment of the Sophists as that fantastic class of the image-making craft who build on the *nulla*/nihil/nothing so that the false assumes the appearance of the real (Horvath, 2009a). Plato traces the various declensions and permutations of sophistry as the art of the trader as a money-making species. Simmel's formulation of the stranger closely corresponds with Plato's characterization of the sophist, as 'throughout the history of economics the stranger everywhere appears as the trader, or the trader as stranger'. The stranger's role in 'intermediary trade, and often (as though sublimated from it) in pure finance, gives him the specific character of *mobility*' (Simmel, 1964b: 403). Plato's sophist is a protean and slippery creature who assumes a variety of guises and appearances. He is 'the paid hunter after wealth and youth, who baits his hooks with pleasure and flattery' (Plato, 1892: 223) (sophisticated sales techniques); 'the trader in the goods of the soul' (1892: 224) (ideals of the beautiful household founded on a wealth of love); 'retailer and manufacturer of the same wares' (1892: 224) (the developer/realtor/ mortgage broker combined in the same company at the level of the housing market, and, at the level of banking and finance, the designer and trader in the dream-image of the household and sophisticated loans and financial investment products); 'the eristic disputator, combative and acquisitive' (1892: 226) (the trader/broker/dealer on the trading floor fighting in the bonus culture of the finance industry); the 'purger, who separates and differentiates' (1892: 231) (the market analyst who rates and apportions risk). Plato systematically deconstructs the grammar of sophistry so that the quintessential hallmark of the species comes into view: the sophist, Plato says, is 'a magician and imitator of true being ... a mimic ... a juggler [who] imitates creation by copying images, mixing being & nonbeing... haphazardly, thus proliferating falsity' (1892: 235) by 'the phantastic art of making appearances ... appearances, since they appear only and are not really like' (1892: 236). Making money, or more accurately, creating the appearance of money, is the work of what Plato calls 'the image making and phantastic art' (1892: 261) ... the 'juggling part of productive activity' (Szakolczai, 2009b: 12).

The semblance of true being created out of non-being is the 'derivative': the seeming value derived from the nullity of the 'mortgage backed security' where there is in reality no *oikos*, only a fictive household whose reality is undermined, flawed, non-existent. The sophisticated nullity then metastasizes. Metastasis is the quality of being able to change and to travel and to change the constitution of where it travels to. Cancer, for example, begins as a primary tumour, becomes mobile and invasive and metastasizes to distant locations in the body, destroying those organs too. Similarly, sophistic forms of contemporary economics not only separate and travel away from the *oikos*, but return and invade it so that the household begins to function as though it were a corporation. In the mortgage market of the 'noughties' households that had some substance, that had endured and prospered, were inveigled to 'release some of the value locked up in the home' by re-mortgaging to fund current expenditure. Householders thereby became the pillagers of their own commonwealth, undermining the security of their own foundations and tearing otherwise sustainable households asunder.

In the wider economy as the MBS is bundled the nullity multiplies exponentially, proliferates, inflates – a bubble, containing nothing. The 'bundled' compound nothingness is masked by ratings agencies, which are paid by the banks to rate their investment products, 'bundles' of securities in which secure investments are 'cut' with worthless 'junk' mortgages. Whether they are blinded by past historical performances of 'real' households' historical record as reliable investments, or whether the ratings agencies were aware of the nullity and engaged in masking, giving 'triple A' ratings to investments that bear only the vestigial after-image of household security that they knew were in truth worth 'nothing' (*nihils*, NINJAs) – the effect is the same: the creation of the seeming 'something' – money – out of nothing, by the 'unreal class of the image-making craft'.

As the nullity inflates it unleashes a spiral of mimetic desire: because others are seen to be making money everyone wants to 'get into the game': the 'property game' at the subjective cultural level of 'househunting'; the 'hot mortgage market' for the local and regional lending agencies; the 'securities game' at the objective cultural level of the economy, and so on. The consumer housing market and the banking and financial system become a vast, spiralling mimetic game – 'casino capitalism' (Strange, 1986), expanding and feeding on nothing. Money is 'made' in the sense that the mimetic spiral of desire for images in which real and unreal elements are mixed is set in motion, as set out above, when investors compete to buy into derivatives so that their 'investment value' escalates far beyond their current market value and is based instead on investors' expectations of the price that other future investors may be prepared to pay for them. The financial crisis caused by sub-prime derivatives trading resonates with a historical case of Simmel's era: 'In the period 1830–80 German agriculture produced steadily increasing annual returns, which gave rise to the idea that this was an infinite process; therefore estates were not bought for a price that corresponded to their current value but to their expected future profit – this is the reason for the current distressed condition of agriculture' (1990: 250). Simmel is writing some twenty-five years after the German land bubble, indicating the duration of recessionary aftershock of a major real estate crash.

Beginning in 2006 sub-prime mortgage defaults began to rise steeply and

for the first time in the history of modern economics lending agencies saw
borrowers default on their very first mortgage repayment. The fictive households wherein coherent and enduring meaningful life projects were supposed
to be being built were being at the same time undermined by broader social
and cultural currents: would-be homemakers cannot constitute an *oikos* as
they are beset by conditions of objective culture that mitigate against the very
possibility of the *oikos* – flexibilized short-term employment (Sennett, 1998),
precarious economic relations that have their correlate in the intimate sphere
in the form of temporary short-term-commitment social relationships
wherein libidinal energies become de-sublimated and discharge themselves
formlessly through the instant gratification of individual consumption and in
the insecure, unstable and vulnerable configurations of postmodern family
life. As these fictive households fail to materialize, dissolve and otherwise
cannot meet their mortgage obligations, the rate of default and repossession
increases sharply and the value of derivative investments leveraged on
mortgage backed securities collapses along with the fictive households themselves.

The value of modern love

Against this depressing vista Simmel invests some hope in the power of
modern love, which Simmel says is a specifically contemporary social form of
intimate relationship; a relationship of progressively egalitarian reciprocity
wherein individuals 'give unreservedly to one another all of their being and
having' ... gifts of 'hopes, idealizations, hidden beauties, attractions of which
not even [the partners to the love relation] are conscious' (Simmel, 1964d:
329). These gifts are drawn from what Simmel calls 'the inexhaustibility of
their inner life and growth' ... 'the fertile depth of relations [that] suspects and
honours something even more ultimate behind every ultimateness revealed'
(1964d: 329). This is an incremental and mutually enriching economy of
gifting in which 'there lies a beauty, a spontaneous devotion to the other, an
opening up and flowering from the "virgin soil" of the soul' (1964c: 393) that
'overflows to the other being exclusively and entirely in colour, form and
temperament' (1964d: 329). Furthermore, the dyadic relationship is enriched
by the introduction of a 'third term' which saves the parties to the dyad from
losing their individuality and descending into a trivial identity, and draws
them, individually and collectively, into a broader society in ways that simultaneously decompose ossifying social forms and reinvigorate creativity and
subjective culture. Modern intimate relations are, for Simmel, an ideal form of
sociation wherein a miraculous surplus value, 'something super-personal that
is valuable and sacred in itself' (1964d: 129) is generated. Even in hyper-indi-
vidualized conditions of contemporary life, and moreover accentuated by the

very experience of individuation, a higher, third element, springs from modern love. This higher, third element is society intruding into the household and the household, reinvigorated, reciprocally extruding into society. The reciprocal dynamic between private household and social life is the delicate triadic flower that, however vulnerable and endangered it is by the crushing weight of objective culture and the annihilating power of the market, continues to thrive on the waste-land of late capitalism's money economy.

Notes

1 These etymologies can be traced through standard Irish dictionaries. Here we have used Dineen (1996).

2 See also Freud's hypothesis on the origins of civilization and how women become guardians of the fire (Freud, 1961: 22, n.2).

3 The most ancient African peoples, the Masai of the Horn of Africa and the Kalahari Bushmen, whose archaeological anthropology can be traced continuously for 20,000 years, still live in circular huts and have central communal fires.

4 Goudsblom's (1992) discussion of fire and the civilizing process, based on Elias (1994), argues that the domestication of fire reaches into deepest antiquity, 400,000 years, or 10,000 generations. The guardian of the fire, the woman who tends the hearth and home, is a figure of extreme antiquity, an archetype that is anthropologically deep-seated in the collective unconscious. Oracles and Sybils are amongst the most ancient social institutions.

5 For a meditation on this theme see Trinh T. Minh-ha (1985).

6 To be outside of the household was to both pose a threat to the household and/or to stand in need of the household's hospitality, protection and charity. And moreover, to be isolated or to isolate oneself from the collective wisdom of the household is to be foolish and irrational, as evidenced by the etymology of the 'idiot' as 'singular', 'individual' as 'standing out', as in 'idiosyncratic'.

7 As a consequence the house is the *locus classicus* of modern horror, from E. A. Poe to *The Amityville Horror*. Hence the other great theme of modern subjectivity given special importance by Simmel: the freedom of the nomad and the stranger, who comes today and stays tomorrow, and never quite gets over the freedom of coming and going (Simmel, 1964a: 402). The undertone to the harmony of the modern bourgeois home has been the *fugue* and the affair: the man who dissociates from his household responsibilities into an alternate identity; Conrad's Kurtz who loses himself to the heart of darkness while his 'intended' waits in the empty London apartment; the housewife who entertains a 'gentleman caller'; a social form diversely represented by Dr Jekyll and Mr Hyde, the *double entendres* of Vermeer's interiors, Ibsen's *A Doll's House* and the shenanigans of Wisteria Lane; an ambivalence that Simmel was familiar with in his professional career and in his private life.

8 The standard account of Simmel's private life is that 'Simmel and his wife Gertrud, whom he had married in 1890, lived a comfortable and fairly sheltered bourgeois life. His wife was a philosopher in her own right who published, under the pseudonym Marie-Luise Enckendorf, on such diverse topics as the philosophy of religion and of sexuality; she made his home a stage for cultivated gatherings where the sociability

about which Simmel wrote so perceptively found a perfect setting' (Coser, 1977: 195). Against this view, we also know that Simmel came from a household destabilized by his father's early death and difficult relations with his mother, and that Simmel's own home life was unconventional. Simmel had a lover of many years, Gertrud Kantorowitcz. Gertrud Kantorowitcz and Simmel's wife were close friends, and Gertrud Kantorowitcz was always amongst the select company of the Simmels' salon. Both Gertruds were together by Simmel's deathbed and he entrusted his last works to them. It was several years later that Gertrud Simmel discovered that Georg and Gertrud Kantorowitcz were much more than friends, and that they had a lovechild together. Gertrud Simmel turned furiously against her deceased husband and asked that Hans, their son, similarly radically reappraise his memory of his father (Weber, 1988: xlii).

9 *Agalma* is an ancient Greek term for a gift to the gods, and thereby endowed with magical powers beyond its apparent superficial value. Over time, the term *agalma* has come to mean something beautiful – an object to be treasured. Lacan introduced the term in his *Seminar VIII* (1961), writing on Socrates' Symposium. The *agalma* is defined by love; it is the inestimable object of desire that ignites our desire: the *agalma* is the treasure which we seek in analysis, the unconscious truth we wish to know – which may of course be entirely 'lacking'!

10 Similarly in Rome, where the architectural geometry of the Roman house was symptomatic of a fundamental insecurity as the Empire at its full expanse coincided with its decadence: 'Body, house, forum, city, empire: all are based on linear imagery. ... This visual language expressed the need of an uneasy, unequal and unwieldy people seeking the reassurance of place; the forms sought to convey that a durable, essential Rome stood somehow outside the ruptures of history. And though Hadrian spoke this language masterfully, he may have known it was all a fiction' (Sennett, 1996: 121).

11 All desire, Girard (1976) says, is desire 'to be': desire for the fullness of being that we impute to the model. If the model/mediator is external, transcendent – if it belongs to a different order entirely (a saint or a hero are Girard's examples) – then we engage in a kind of folly that nonetheless remains optimistic. Hero worship and celebrity fandom are commonplace examples. But if the model/mediator is 'internal', that is, if s/he is someone just like us, an equal, as we are (at least formally) in modern consumer society, then the model transforms into a rival and an obstacle to the acquisition of the object, whose value increases as the rivalry grows.

12 For the following discussion I am indebted to Agnese Horvath, who led a discussion on Plato's sophist, the *nulla* and metastasis at the Fourth Socrates Symposium, 7–9 November 2009, Firenze, Palazzo Guidi.

3

Foundations of Europe's collective household

There is no document of civilization which is not at the same time a document of barbarism'. (Benjamin, 1992: 248)

Of the many dream-houses of the world's civilizations the Pantheon in Rome is possibly the most beautiful: a perfectly proportioned hemisphere within a cylinder, an apotheosis of architecture expressing the harmonization of religious and civic ideals. Hadrian had this beautiful house erected, though he had it accredited to an earlier consul, Agrippa, because Hadrian's accession to power after the popular and respected Trajan was marred by skullduggery and the murder of his rivals. Covering his tracks and attempting to regain respectability, Hadrian demolished the remains of Nero's 'golden house' which occupied the future site of the Pantheon, an embarrassing monument to the megalomaniac vanity and decadence which had almost ruined Rome, and he replaced it with a temple of good order and geometrical perfection, as though to make a definitive statement with this 'ideal home' that the great project of Roman civilization was safely back on track. The interior of the Pantheon is an abstract geometrical and sculptural representation of idealized Roman and cosmic order: the Gods in their shrines overlooking the grid pattern on the floor representing the plan of a Roman city; at the centre of the floor is an umbilicus, leading down to the interior mother lode, the *mundus*, representing the foodstore upon which the collective life of the city depends; and overhead, at the centre of the dome, the *oculus*, an eye open to the heavens (Sennett, 1996).

The collective dream-house of United Europe is similarly a materialized constellation of gods and goods – peace and harmony amongst historical enemies governed by Reason and legitimated by democracy; progress through science and technology; limitless horizons of economic growth; security, prosperity and abundance. Its 'dark side', its barbaric aspects, include democratic

deficit, technocratic instrumental rationality and the uber-bureaucracy of the
supra-state. All subsequent EU treaties and referenda are elaborations of the
Treaty of Rome, clarifying and consolidating its constitutional and legal basis,
streamlining and rationalizing its complex decision making and executive
functions, a process that many people feel will do nothing to redress, and in
fact will exacerbate, the problems of the EU's technocracy. To get a bead on
the ambivalence of the Treaty of Rome, the tensions of civilization and
barbarism that animate the EU, we will revisit what Benjamin might have
called the *ur-phenomenon*, the original 'Treaty of Rome'.

The mythic Treaty of Rome

In *Rome: The Book of Foundations* Serres (1991) uses the vast and rich diversity
of archaeological, historical and mythological trackings and tracings of the
origins of Rome to demonstrate an important point of epistemology, namely
that there are no definite foundations, no single story of origins, for there are
many beginnings. Myth collects multiple and various origins, synthesizes and
distils them into an archetypical history. In the central salon of the Capitoline
museum, where the ceremony of the signing of the Treaty of Rome, establishing what was to become today's EU, was held in 1957, a series of Renaissance
frescoes depict an earlier, primordial, fundamental 'treaty of Rome', namely
the mythic cycle of the foundation of Rome. The first fresco shows the
discovery of Romulus and Remus being nursed by the she-wolf. The second
depicts Romulus marking the boundary of Rome with a plough. The third
depicts the duel of the Orazi and the Curiazi, champions of the rival tribes of
the Romans and the Albans. The fourth depicts the rape of the Sabine women.
And the fifth in the cycle depicts the institutionalization of the cult of Vesta.
The ceremonial signing of the Treaty of Rome inaugurating what has become
the EU was staged and ritually enacted against the backdrop of this earlier,
primordial *ur*-treaty that underpinned Roman civilization. What resonances
and continuities exist between an ancient, mythic and ideal treaty and its
modern descendant? Why did the original treaty come undone; why did Rome
fall from civilization back into barbarism, and what lessons can modern
European civilization learn from the original treaty of Rome that might
prevent the EU, which emerged in the wake of the mechanized barbarism of
the world wars and the Holocaust, sliding back into a new dark age?

The Capitoline – capital – the hill, mound, the accumulated and protected
foodstore is, with the Palatine, one of the original Roman settlements. The
original circular shrine to the she-wolf has recently been identified on the
Palatine, a site corresponding also, probably, to the *mundus*, the underground
foodstore of the aboriginal Romans, perhaps even more remotely a cave that
was the wolves' den, taken over by the earliest settlers. The totemic animal of

the early Romans is the she-wolf. The she-wolf represents the first dimension of the primordial 'Treaty of Rome' – a 'treaty' that seeks to reconcile and harmonize relations between opposites: Animal–Human; Nature–Culture; Barbarism–Civilization. The myth of Romulus and Remus nursed by the she-wolf is a collective representation of this treaty. The reconciliation of opposites is achieved by the mediation of the gift relation. This is the essential basis of social order. This order is not based on simple equality between the parties to the exchange. Rather it is an order of asymmetry and dynamic equilibrium emerging from irreducible particularities and essential differences between the parties to the reciprocal gift relation. The wolf is a wolf, fierce and implacable Nature; Romulus and Remus are babies, vulnerable Humans. In the quintessential representation of this primordial gift exchange between the she-wolf and the human children, that is the famous bronze sculpture of the Capitoline she-wolf from 500BC (the figures of Romulus and Remus were added in the Renaissance) all of this is expressed. The she-wolf is unmistakably savage. Her ears are pricked, her eyes wide, her nostrils flaring; her fangs bared. She stands alert, poised, in a pure state of Nature. Her paps are swollen with milk, representing a superabundant natural fecundity. Why does she nurse the babies, care for them rather than eat them? This is an unfathomable mystery, as inexplicable as the gift of life. But the wolf's mysterious gift of care costs her. The she-wolf's ribs are showing through her skin.

In the Roman mythic cycle the first primordial 'Treaty of Rome' is represented by the myth of the she-wolf's mysterious gift of care to Romulus and Remus. This is followed by the foundation of the city, represented by the story of Romulus' circumscribing the city boundary with a plough. As Vico (1999: 235–236) explains, this myth is a collective representation of the development of agriculture, tillage and the generation of surplus, enabling permanent settlement, but also the need for defence against the wandering barbarians who would trespass on the tilled fields and raid the storehouses of the civilized. The underground *mundus* now becomes the *torre*, from the fortified round grain silo, but the *mundus* is preserved as a symbolic, sacred site. The first fruits of the harvest are ritualistically thrown into the *mundus* to appease the gods of the underworld, representations of the threat of starvation and death from a time before the household had learned how to harvest and store. The *mundus* now becomes the symbolic centre of every Roman settlement. It represents the treasury, the accumulated commonwealth upon which the survival of the collective household depends. But as this accumulation of valuable resources becomes institutionalized, the rival tribes are still embroiled in a state of perpetual war over territory and resources, intensified by the presence of accumulated goods. The myth of Romulus ploughing the boundary of Rome is a collective representation of the development of a social order based on strong demarcations and differentiations between insiders and outsiders, between civilized Romans who produce and accumulate wealth, and barbarian Others, rival clans who might wish to raid and steal Roman resources, and vice versa – the Romans would raid them too – distinctions that are ritualistically iterated and reiterated, and that become the frontiers of social conflict. This vicious circle is represented by the duel to the death between the Orazi and the Curiazi, brothers belonging to the rival clans of Romans and Albans. (Grant (1973: 163–164) shows the parallels between the Classical 'duel of the champions' and the Celtic myths of the Ulster cycle.) According to the myth the duelling brothers share the same birthday and they are related to one another through tribal intermarriage. They symbolize all enemies, ancient and modern, who share a great deal with one another despite – or perhaps because of – their historical rivalry. The mortal combat of the brothers represents the nihilistic vicious circle of schismogenesis, a symmetrical conflict between rivals ceasing only in death. In this case the Romans eventually emerge as Pyrrhic victors, teetering on the brink of mutual annihilation –as of course was the story of Europe before the EU.

The third phase of the Roman mythic cycle represented by the duel of the Orazi and Curiazi leads to what we might identify as a second primordial 'Treaty of Rome'. This is represented by the fourth moment in the Roman mythic cycle, the rape of the Sabine women. The Romans and the Sabines, like the Albans, were rival tribes warring since time immemorial over resources. The Romans raided and abducted the Sabine women. The Sabines counterattacked. No doubt this had happened countless times before – raiding one another for food, slaves, women and cattle – the Celtic mythic saga of the *Táin bó Cuailnge* is one of countless examples in the anthropological record. The Sabine women, now captives of the Romans but many by now also having become the wives and daughters and grandchildren of their enemies and vice versa, pleaded with Romulus and with the Sabine leader to stop the carnage of the tit-for-tat vicious circle of violence, spiralling downwards and destroying one another's societies, a constant threat to life itself, both Roman and Sabine. As a result of the pleas of the Sabine women a truce ensued, beginning a 'virtuous circle', spiralling outwards and upwards in the opposite direction, building civilization. This is the second primordial Treaty of Rome, between the Romans and the Sabines. These two phases in the mythic cycle of the founding of Rome – the duel of the Orazi and the Curiazi and the rape of the Sabine women – have at their heart the issue of recognition. In both cases the central drama is what Hegel (1977: 104–111) and more recently Honneth (1996) have formulated respectively in terms of the 'master/slave dialectic of self-consciousness' and the struggle for recognition as 'the moral grammar of social conflict'. In this struggle the enemy protagonists come to recognize one another: as husbands and fathers, as brothers and as sons in the case of the Duel, and as wives and mothers, sisters and daughters in the case of the Rape.

In both myths the protagonists come to be seen by one another no longer as mere objects, enemies and chattel, but as subjects, persons, mutually recognizing one another as deserving of respect.

The fifth element of the Roman mythic cycle, the founding of the cult of Vesta, by Romulus's successor, Numa, a Sabine king, represents the institutionalization of this mutual recognition and respect between the diverse and previously hostile parties. The cult of Vesta represents the house and hearth of Roman civilization. Insofar as Vico says 'the civil institutions of all peoples begin in religion' (1999: 6), the cult of Vesta is the moral bedrock of Roman domestic political economy, the foundation upon which the whole of Roman civilization is built.[1] The cult of Vesta has two essential elements: first, the strict taboo governing the violation of women; and second, the principle of reciprocal distribution of resources. The cult of Vesta institutionalizes the gift relation as sacred principles: that the gift, especially the mystical and primordially natural gifts of life – giving birth to children, and care, nourishment – must be freely given, not forcibly taken; and that the sharing of resources through reciprocal gift relations builds civilization, whereas theft leads to schismogenesis, nihilism and death. These are the basic integrating principles of the collective household of Roman civilization. Vesta is the goddess of social integration. In the mythic cycle of the foundation of Rome the institutionalization of the cult of Vesta is a collective representation of how the gift relation, the reciprocal and equalizing exchange of goods, builds mutual recognition, respect and trust around the collective treasury represented by Vesta's sanctuary.

Whereas Vesta's temple in the Roman forum is a modest, beautiful and graceful circular structure, the adjacent house of the Vestals is large and elaborate. The inner sanctum of Vesta's temple represented a storeroom, originally a granary. Ritual duties of the temple included baking and distributing a sacred cake made of salt, water and spelt flour, the bread of life, primitive and elemental, representing a remote ancestral cookery.[2] As the Roman state was understood as a community of families Vesta was at the centre of both private and public life, underpinning and transcending both. Together, the Vestals' buildings stand at the centre of the earliest forum, when the warring tribes of the seven hills had made sufficient peace with one another to abandon their defensive heights and construct a city on the common ground between them, originally marshy and insalubrious, gradually reclaimed and built over. The Vestals' buildings were adjacent to the king's dwelling. The Vestals' house was a large, cloistered villa, with enclosed gardens and fountains, surrounded by a kitchen, bakery and mill, and upstairs the Vestals' bedrooms and a commodious *Tabulerum* (a conference room, or parlour). In many respects the Vestals' house resembled a convent: an orderly house, a sacred house, an ideal collective dream-home founded on the virtues of chastity and charity. The Vestals' virginity represents the principle of incorruptibility – the incorruptibility of public office, especially the offices of the Treasury, which persists today in the impartiality of the Civil Service, paradigmatically the offices of the Revenue Commissioners.

Rome's Vesta was originally the Greeks' Hestia, and, prior to her, personifications of the original deity Gaia, the Earth Mother and her various manifestations, Cybele, Berecynthia, goddess of cultivated lands. Cybele's crown represents the principle of enclosure; it encloses the *orbis terrarium*, the circle of lands, locally the settlement, but extending to the world around (Vico, 1999: 690). Vesta (Gaia/Cybele/Berecynthia/Hestia) is crowned with towers, or strongly situated, well-defended lands, *torres/terrae*. From her crown there began to take shape the so-called *orbus-terranu*, or world of nations (Vico, 1999: 722). From such towers came the Latin *extorris*, exiled, as if *exterris*, driven from the land. The first lands ploughed, *arate*, were the world's first altars, *area*. On these lands Vesta sacrificed to Jupiter (Hestia / Zeus equivalents) the impious people who had violated the first altars, meaning they had trespassed and stolen from the fields of grain. These first sacrificial victims, *hostiae*, were called victims from Latin *victus*, vanquished, because they were isolated and weak; ... they were called *hostiae* because such impious folk were justly deemed the enemies *hostes* (hostile) of the entire human race (they threatened the food supply of the settlement). 'Theseus founded the city of Athens on the Altar of the Unfortunates. He justly regarded as unfortunate the lawless and godless men who had fled the conflicts caused by their abominable promiscuity and had taken refuge in the strongholds. These refugees arrived alone, weak and in need of all the benefits which the pious derived from civilization. ... The first victims were consecrated to Hestia and then killed on the altars of civilization. The sacrificial victims were the violent and impious people who trespassed on the heroes' tilled fields' (Vico, 1999: 770–776 *passim*). Vico goes on to explain how Roman city walls were originally and traditionally laid out and circumscribed by a plough, and the traditional Roman hedge was elder (bloodwort). The blood-red juice of the elderberry represented human blood. '*Sang*', blood, was originally the area marked by the blood of those who were killed for trespassing on the cultivated areas, the blood of the burglar rather than, as might be assumed, the common bloodline of those within the household. This idea is preserved in the root of 'sanction', the bloody punishment for transgression, which originally meant the transgression on Vesta's cultivated lands and theft from the household. The heroic origin of the word *terra* is preserved in the Latin noun *territorium*, territory, meaning a district over which dominion is exercised. The true origin of the verb *terrere*, to frighten, derives from the bloody rites by which Vesta guarded the boundaries of the cultivated fields. The first house was a foodstore. This original meaning is preserved today in the etymology of *casa*–house (Sp.), which is also a box, a store – *caja* and a bank, a treasury – *caixa*. In Rome, and down to Victorian England, a key was a symbol of women's power, the key by which the matriarch of the household locked treasure chests and cellars, and the key is the symbol of the state, the American Department of the Treasury for instance. The Treasury which was the foundation and the heart of the household was both the material store (of food, money) guarded by the mother – the mother lode – and the symbolic surplus, the *agalma*, the sacred treasure of the mother's original supernatural gift of fertility upon which the constitution and survival of the whole depend.

In contrast to the massive and monumental structures characteristic of Roman civilization, Vesta's temple is always a modest, graceful building. Slender, delicate columns support a light roof, sheltering a small altar on which a fire continuously burnt. The Vestal fire was attended to constantly; if it went out it was an ominous portent. Once a year it was ritualistically quenched, and then re-lit in the primordial manner of rubbing sticks together. The Vestal priestesses distributed the new fire, as well as bread baked with spelt, water and salt, to each Roman household. Vesta's rituals of caring for the fire and distributing fire and bread, and the circular structure of the temple (which was also a sanctuary) represent a formal principle of religious equality amongst Romans. All Roman people – patricians and plebians, new Roman subjects from the colonies, men, women, children and even slaves – are all equal in Vesta's eyes. Echoes and antecedents of this fundamental principle of civilization are the principles underpinning modern legal-rational authority and the state bureaucracy, namely the principle that all people are equal in the eyes of the Law. The principles of recognition and distribution institutional-ized by the cult of Vesta are not that everyone gets the same or gives the same. Ancient Rome, with its strict apartheid divisions between patricians and plebeians and its rigid patriarchy, was an enormously unequal and stratified society in every respect – except in this formal religious principle: there are heroic patrician citizens and lowly plebeian subjects, but everyone receives recognition and redistribution from Vesta according to their due as Romans. This principle institutionalized in the cult of Vesta solves centuries of warfare ensuing from symmetrical schismogenesis between the rival tribes in the prehistory of Rome, as it has done in the prehistory of the EU. But while the principles institutionalized by the cult of Vesta provided Rome with the basis of a 'global domestic policy' reconciling several rival tribes into the collective Roman fold, the problem of conflict now became internal. The sharply drawn distinctions between patrician and plebeian classes, distinctions that were ritu-alistically reiterated in gross and subtle ways, down to the fine grain of everyday life in Rome, became the frontier of what Bateson (1958) calls 'complementary schismogenesis' – the conflict not between symmetrically evenly matched rival clans, but between ruling elites and subalterns within the same community. The subsequent history of the rise and fall of Rome is that of the incessant struggle and antagonism between the Patricians and Plebeians as the Plebeians sought to pursue the realization of equality of recognition and distribution intimated in the cult of Vesta.

Complementary schismogenic conflict was endemic in Rome, as Vico describes: 'Alongside the heroic deeds we must place the intolerable pride, the insatiable greed, and the merciless cruelty with which the Roman Patricians treated the unfortunate Plebeians' (1999: 26). Agrarian strife between rival tribes became subsumed and internalized in Rome as perpetual conflict between heroic patricians and subjected Plebeians who toiled as bondsmen in fields owned by the patricians, who paid them thides and taxes, and who were conscripted into their legions. Schismogenic tensions, in Rome as elsewhere, were counteracted to some extent, Bateson says, by 'factors which unify the two groups in loyalty and opposition to an outside element [such as] ... a symbolic individual, an enemy people' (1958: 70). Thus conflict internal to Rome was diluted by Rome's conflict with Barbarians, Gauls, Huns and other external threats, and by internal dissidents such as Christians. The Coliseum and other theatres of power were spaces where the vast gulf between Patricians and Plebeians was momentarily bridged by their mutual involvement in the spectacle of cruelty and the collective effervescence of mass entertainment. But the bridging between Patricians and Plebeians occasionally achieved by the circus, like carnival, was always only temporary relief from the schismogenesis endemic to a vastly unequal civilization: a civilization founded upon inequality, and yet a civilization in which the integrating religious principle of the cult of Vesta was that of reciprocal recognition and distribution amongst people formally equal as Romans.

Roman history, Vico says, will baffle anyone 'who attempts to find any Roman virtue in such great arrogance, any moderation in such avarice, any mercy in such cruelty, or any justice in such inequality' (1999: 302). When the history of plutocratic global neoliberalism is examined the very same may well be said. But if politics can be thought of as 'the activity of amending the traditions and arrangements existing between people by exploring and pursuing what is intimated in them' (Oakeshott, cited in Mouffe, 1988: 39) we can formulate the internal political and juridical history of ancient Rome (just as the modern EU) in terms of the fundamental tension, the latent and overt conflict, and the continuous antagonism between monarchy and democracy; and emerging from that conflict in which revolutionary violence, democratic politics, bureaucratic regulation and technocratic management, statecraft, diplomacy and rhetorical eloquence all play a role, is the development of Roman jurisprudence and the gradual extension of rights and privileges of full citizenship to Plebeians.

The fall of Rome and the sapping of the foundations of Europe's collective household

There is a memorable scene in Monty Python's *The Life of Brian* (1979) in which a cell of the revolutionary People's Front of Judea is justifying its subversive campaign against Rome. The Chair, Reg (John Cleese) is flanked by PFJ members Stan (Eric Idle) and Francis (Michael Palin).

[Reg] They've taken everything we have, and not just from us, but from our fathers, and from our fathers' fathers'

[Stan] And from our fathers' fathers' fathers ...

[Reg] And what have they ever given us in return?

[From the floor] The aqueduct.

[Reg] Huh? Yeah, OK, yeah. They did give us the aqueduct. ...

[From the floor] And the sanitation.

[Stan] Oh, yeah, the sanitation Reg! Remember what the city used to be like?

[Reg] Yeah. All right. I'll grant you the aqueduct and the sanitation are two things the Romans have done.

[From the floor] And the roads.

[Reg] Well yeah, obviously the roads. ... But apart from the aqueduct, sanitation and the roads, what have the Romans ever done for us?

[From the floor] Irrigation. ...

[From the floor] Medicine. ...

[From the floor] Education ...

[Reg] Yeah, all right. Fair enough ...

[From the floor] And the wine ...

[Francis] Yeah, yeah. That's something we'd really miss, if the Romans left, huh?

[From the floor] And the public baths.

[Stan] And it's safe to walk the streets at night now ...

[Francis] Yeah, they certainly know how to keep order. Let's face it. They're the only ones who could in a place like this!

[Reg] All right. But apart from the sanitation, the medicine, education, wine, public order, irrigation, roads, a fresh water system, and public health, what have the Romans ever done for us?

[From the floor] Brought peace.

[Reg] Peace? Oh shut up!

This farce is played out in a thousand scenes in Irish politics, civil society and everyday life in Ireland, amplified since the arrival of austere Roman discipline in the shape of the EU–IMF–ECB Troika. We complain about authoritarian bureaucracy and centralized power, about the loss of political autonomy and the loss of private homes and livelihoods, about the impossible burden of debts purportedly owed to French and German bond-holders. But at the same time we gratefully accept not just the most recent bailout that pays for current wages and public services, but for decades previously the EU-funded infrastructure and development grant-aid, and the 93 per cent of Irish farmers' income that comes from the EU in the form of direct payments, price interventions and subsidies. Eurosceptics also readily concede that Ireland has benefited enormously from European development grant aid and other financial supports, but at the same time they argue that Europe will cost us 'more taxes' and especially that the prospect of the harmonization of corporate taxation across the EU will undermine Ireland's development strategy of attracting foreign direct investment by a corporate tax rate of less than half of the EU average. Furthermore, we even grant that Ireland's problems may not reside so much in the central bureaucracies and economic technocracies of Brussels and Frankfurt, or that European ideas – or even the abstract ideal of a United Europe – are not wrong in themselves. Rather, many respondents to the question of 'what has Europe done for us?' say that the problems with being ruled by the Treaty of Rome arise from sources closer to home – incompetent and shambolic Irish bureaucracies; localist political cultures of clientelism and brokerage; nest-feathering and petty corruption. Like the People's Front of Judea, many Irish are inclined to say that it's a good job that the EU/IMF/ECB Troika is in fact running things now, for, 'Let's face it. They're the only ones who could keep order in a place like this!' We pay lip-service to the idea of Europe as long as the cheques keep coming, and with bitter reluctance we 'render to Caesar', as it were. As was the case in Rome, the local rulers of the provinces on the fringes, like Pontius Pilate in Judea, take the laws from the Senate and the Forum, but they interpret them in accordance with local customary practices, in the hopes that the central authorities, preoccupied with their own power struggles and political intrigues and with their energies concentrated on other battlefields, will overlook seemingly minor problems happening on the margins. But in the long history of the rise and fall of Roman civilization – from kings and tyrants to the Republic; from the Republic to Empire, to decadence, dissolution and eventual collapse, this problem of corruption in the provinces recurs repeatedly. Roman civilization was ever only as strong as its least-committed provinces.

Roman civilization at its full expanse was much larger than the present EU, stretching in Africa as far south to what is now Sudan, north to the Rhine; from Syria and Persia in the east to the Scottish borders in the north-west, incorporating hundreds of linguistic and ethnic minorities and their local and regional cultures. The task of administrating this vast civilization from its centre in Rome, or from one of Rome's second cities or regional capitals – Constantinople, Tarragon, Cartage, Tournai or Colchester – was unimaginably more difficult than administrating EU affairs from Brussels as there were no means of communication other than messages relayed to and from the centre, and to travel from one end to the other or from any point on the frontier to the centre would have taken months; even the most urgent dispatches took several weeks (Heather, 2005: 104).

Maintaining the army consumed up to three quarters of total revenues, so that the military, the key of Rome's strength, eventually became its weakness. At first, the revenue stream supporting Rome came in the form of loot from Rome's sacking of enemy cities, or as tribute paid to Rome by subordinated regional powers. Tax farming was first introduced in Pergamum, a Greek city controlling most of what is now Turkey, which became a Roman settlement in 133BC. Through tax farming Rome's revenue became effectively outsourced to private sector independent subcontractors. A contract to provide Rome with a set sum was sold to the highest bidder, typically a local Roman nobleman, often a consortium of wealthy investors, Romans and Romanized local nobles and their extended retinues. Tax farmers returned the agreed sum to Rome, and retained whatever surplus from their tax-raising activities as private profit. Through this mechanism the extortion of revenues from Roman settlements became much more systematic (Holland, 2003: 40). But even in the matter of taxation the state bureaucracy's role was limited to allocating overall sums to the cities of the Empire, their colonies' tax farmers, and monitoring the transfer of monies back to the central coffers. The difficult work, the allocation of individual tax bills and the actual collection of money, was handled at a local level. Even there, so long as the agreed tax-take flowed out of the cities and into the Roman Treasury, local communities were left to be 'largely self-governing communities. Keep Roman central government happy, and life could often be lived as the locals wanted' (Heather, 2005: 105–106). Under these circumstances it is hardly surprising that, according to the historians, the Roman provinces from the north-west to the near east 'ran themselves', and by the same measure the fall of Rome came about by the Empire unravelling at the edges.

This unravelling at the edges in the provinces may be illustrated by any number of examples – Pontius Pilate's trouble with Jesus Christ in Judea, for instance. According to the Gospel of Luke, amongst other historical sources, resistance to Roman rule, especially Roman taxes, was widespread in Judea, and Jesus was brought before Pontius Pilate accused of treason and sedition, and more specifically of encouraging people not to pay taxes:

> Then the whole assembly rose and led him off to Pilate. And they began to accuse him, saying, 'We have found this man subverting our nation. He opposes payment of taxes to Caesar and claims to be Christ, Messiah, a king.' (Luke 23: 1–4)

Pilate, as both Roman Praetor and private tax farmer, was personally responsible for collecting taxes in Judea and returning them to Rome, so the charge against Jesus was as serious a charge as could be made against a Roman subject. Local administrators and their retinue, like Pilate, ruthlessly extorted their subject communities. There is ample historical evidence that such tax protest as Jesus was charged with was widespread in the Roman provinces, as the burden of heavy taxes was exactly the point at which the common people felt the imperial weight of Rome. And there is biblical evidence that Jesus had in fact preached against tax collecting, and that he made a special mission of converting tax collectors, persuading them to abandon their official duties and to follow him instead. The ambivalence of Jesus's position is however expressed in answer to the question asked him as to whether or not it was sinful that the Jews should pay taxes to Rome. Jesus famously responded, 'Render unto Caesar the things which are Caesars, and unto God the things that are God's' (Matthew 22: 21). It would seem that to some extent Jesus was scapegoated for tax protest and sedition that was widespread in Judea. Pilate's finding Jesus 'not guilty' seems to recognize that Jesus represented a common problem facing Roman administrators, hardly worth making a big deal over, other than to have him flogged and released as an example to other rabble rousers, as Pilate proposed, and then to wash his hands of the matter. When Pilate eventually found himself in the position of having to slake Jesus's local enemies' thirst for blood, the only charge that would stick that would have merited crucifixion was the seditious claim imputed to Jesus to be king of the Jews, a claim he did not deny when Pilate asked him directly. No one, including Pilate, could have predicted just how much trouble the new cult from Judea would eventually cause the Roman Empire. Gibbon (2005) famously argues that Christianity's new ethics of charity and humility gradually sapped Rome's vital spirit and led to the decline and fall of the Empire, but irrespective of Gibbon's thesis it is perfectly clear that at the time, to most of those involved – Pilate, his retinue and his chain of command back to Rome – this was a minor and insignificant event in the grand imperial scheme of things. Threats to the revenue foundations of the Roman Empire were more forceful than those of Christ and his followers: tax riots in cities such as Antioch, and Pontus, whose king, Mithridates, harried by Roman extortion, routed a legion, slaughtered thousands of Roman merchants, seized the chief tax farmer and had him executed by pouring molten gold down his throat (Holland, 2003: 46–47); or external threats by rival imperial military powers, the Persians in Syria for example, that eventually wrested much of the eastern provinces from Rome, or the attrition of Carthage by the Nubians and with the decline of the north African settlements a loss of fully seven-eighths of the tax revenues from that part of the Empire, Rome's most prosperous colony that subvented so many other Imperial projects. The gradual fall of Rome was ultimately caused by the paradox that as the Empire grew to its full expanse so its revenue base became increasingly unstable and unable to support it (Rawson, 1988; Heather, 2005). As Roman civilization was expanding revenues poured back to Rome in the form of labour (slaves) and capital (the product of newly conquered lands), and as new territories became settled Roman provinces, regular and predictable revenue streams in the form of taxes from new cities and villas flowed back to Rome. While the Empire was engaging enemies, defeating them, enslaving them and conquering their territories, this economic growth was booming, but it was not sustainable. The Roman Empire had a northern frontier extending 4000 miles east to west and it required an enormous military commitment to defend it against Scots and Irish barbarians at one edge and Huns at another, to Sythians at another frontier, and to sundry pirates and raiding corsairs – not to mention the People's Front of Judea! And the cost of funding a standing professional army – garrisoned at every corner of an enormous Empire, from Hadrian's wall to Antioch, from Gibraltar to the Rhine, a professional army in defensive posture, not conquering new territories and winning fresh spoils but simply maintaining security, protecting the villas and ranches of Roman planter nobility and fortifying the citadels of newly Romanized local nobility – became steadily more economically unsustainable.

Weber (1978b: 1055, 1104) attributes the decline and fall of the Roman Empire to exactly this: to the parasitic role of parvenu Romans in the provinces. In developing from a littoral (coastal) Empire to an inland Empire a manorial economy developed. This had the effect of choking the money supply as these estates were largely autarkic. Landowners became more politically dominant, and their imperative was to defend their estates. 'The decline in the offensive capacity of the Roman army, so clearly apparent in the dispersal of the entire body of troops along the full length of the northern frontier was certainly the result of an increase in the standing of the class of resident provincial landowners.' This new class comprised Roman planters, and more significantly native local – formerly barbarian, recently Romanized – nobility, who had recently acquired Roman citizenship and rights, and who now aspired to the affluent lifestyles of the great imperial cities; an avaricious class of *nouveau* Romans in Gaul, Britain, Iberia and central Europe that now demanded of the Roman army that it defend its property and secure its prosperous lifestyle. In many instances prominent individuals gravitated from the provinces towards the central Imperial court, attaining high office in the Senate, in the army and at the Treasury, while retaining their provincial loyalties and their non-Roman partisanships, as Ireland's MEPs and European Commissioners do today.

Thus emerged an internal contradiction – less revenue, but more demands for spending on the needs of the elite – that systematically undermined the Treasury foundation, the *mundus* upon which the whole of Roman civilization depended. Just as today the dominance of transnational corporations and their post-national global corporate elite that structure their commercial operations so that they are at the fringes of the EU in order to minimize their tax liabilities, in Liechtenstein, Monaco, Luxembourg, Ireland, or on tax-free virtual islands within Ireland such as Dublin's International Financial Services Centre. Like the manorial elite of the Roman era, post-national global capitalism systematically deprives the EU of essential revenues, while at the same time demanding centrally funded services and expenditures – the underwriting of their losses by taxpayers; provision of infrastructure, public services, defence and security to shore up and protect their private interests.

Ireland and the new barbarism

Throughout the years of the Celtic Tiger, Ireland, like Judea, was one of the EU's non-committal provinces. St. Patrick came to Ireland as booty, abducted like the Sabine women in a slave raid to Hadrian's England by Irish barbarians. The Romans had come to Ireland several times, but thought it not worth the trouble of conquest. Patricus escaped, returned and through Christianity he eventually Romanized us. The organized, disciplined violence of the Roman armies maintained only a precarious hold over law and order in the outer provinces. While civilization was Roman at the centre, all around old customary practices continued. Local chieftains paid lip-service to Rome; they performed being Roman, 'acted Roman' when circumstances required it, but otherwise continued as usual. Rome understood this, and usually tolerated it. Patricus' Irish Christianity exemplifies this elasticity, and Irish Christianity from antiquity to modern Catholicism remained in many ways as much pagan as Roman, as Irish political culture today remains closer neither to Boston nor to Berlin, but to Ballymagash! The decline and fall of Rome came about through a combination of fraying at the edges and corruption at the centre, and when Rome fell, and then Constantinople, Christianity survived on its outer fringes in Clonmacnoise and Kells as illuminated islands of civilization while Europe sank in a sea of darkness. Ireland's gift to European civilization was the preservation of the Word in illuminated manuscripts of the sacred scriptures and reintroduction of Christianity by missionary St. Columbanus and others bearing the good news of the gift from God to barbarous France and Germany. But those days are long gone, and recently we have played the barbarian role again.

'The history of the modern state is the history of taxation, the bureaucracy of the treasury the true core of administration' (Habermas, 1991: 17). By globalization the revenue base of the nation state is fundamentally altered, so much so that the conditions of globalization and the post-national constellation, Habermas (2001) says, call for a new 'global domestic policy'. Similarly, Bourdieu says that the global neoliberal erosion of the revenue base of the republican state is nothing less than an assault on modern civilization by the tyranny of the market, 'a civilization associated with the existence of public service, the civilization of republican equality of rights, rights to education, to health, culture, work' (1999: 24). The utopian civilizing project of the modern national republican welfare state as collective household has depended on revenue redistribution. However, though a great deal of noise is made about the emerging superpowers – China and India especially – Bourdieu says that 'the emphasis placed on [globalization] conceals the fact that the main danger comes from the internal competition of other European countries' ... 'social dumping' ... countries with less social welfare ... [lower taxes] derive competitive advantage ... but in so doing they pull down the others which are forced to abandon their welfare systems ... To break out of this downward spiral [which Ireland has been leading] we need to combine 'to protect social gains and generalize them to all Europeans' (Bourdieu, 1999: 24–36, *passim*).

The post-revolutionary democratic republic culminating in the national state of the late twentieth century is the modern 'Ideal home', the foundation of which was the generalized gift relation institutionalized in the form of progressive redistributive taxation funding public services, social security, education and health. The EU takes this collective domestic economy project to a supranational level. The amount each country pays to the EU depends on its GDP, and how much revenue it raises from VAT, customs duties and agricultural levies on imports from outside the EU. From the beginning Portugal, Ireland, Greece and Spain all received more than twice as much as they paid in. Germany is by far the biggest net contributor, along with some of the smaller, rich countries like the Netherlands, Sweden and Austria. France and Italy's budget contributions have been cushioned by subsidies for their large agricultural sectors, while the UK's net contributions have been lessened by its special budget rebate. The Rhinish social model in Germany, France, Benelux and the Netherlands; the Nordic social model in Scandinavia; the UK's NHS, housing, social security, education, all together the collective home of European Union is founded on the total social fact that is the gift relation. In this and subsequent European treaties Ireland benefits from fore-giveness; it is given gifts in advance. Its non-involvement in the war against fascist and communist totalitarianism is fore-given; its cultural backwardness is fore-given with opt-out clauses in progressive legislation; its economic poverty is fore-given by massive development grant aid. In all of this, Ireland is morally, politically and materially obliged to reciprocate. But, between 1990 and 2000 25 per cent of all investment by US multinationals in Europe came to Ireland, and profits from US companies based in Ireland doubled from 13.4 billion USD to 26.8 billion USD in 2002, and in the post-crisis this pattern remains (Gravelle, 2010). If taxes on these profits were paid at the EU average rate of corporate tax, 25 per cent, 7 billion euros would have been contributed to central EU funds for general redistribution. In Ireland, which doesn't contribute to central funds, certain provisions of the Irish tax code mean that the nominal rate is different from the effective rate, for instance Microsoft in 2007 netted 1.7 billion euros in profits from its EU operations, based in Ireland for tax purposes, but paid just 460,000 euros in tax, a rate of 3.8 per cent.

The antithesis to the Roman Pantheon, the dream-house of regeneration after the decadence of Nero, is Dermot Desmond's and Charlie Haughey's dream-house, Dublin's International Financial Services Centre (IFSC). The Pantheon's *oculus*, *umbilicus* and *mundus*, the eye of the heavens beaming down on the holistic ideal home of Roman civilization, nourished by an umbilical cord, founded on the *mundus*, the common store, into which were placed the first fruits of the harvest as ritual gift to assuage the powers of the underworld, is absolutely inverted in the architectural principles of the IFSC, which is an ideal house dedicated to obscurity, darkness – turning a blind eye to the theft of the commonwealth through a siphon and sinkhole. The IFSC, the onshore offshore bank where global corporations syphon off profits made in EU markets, tax free, has been the sinkhole of Europe, whereby vital revenues are sapped from the democratic institutions of the collective polity and transferred to the private coffers of the global plutocracy, undermining the foundations of the collective household.

Notes

1 One of Vesta's intact temples in Rome, near the Circus Massimo, is on the Via Sabina, 'on the warpath', the route of the warring tribes' raids, possibly built as a memorial to their new concord.
2 Vestals could forgive condemned criminals, for example, and as their dwelling was adjacent to the palace and other central offices they could be politically influential.

Part II
MORAL ECONOMY

4

Fair trade and free market

This place here, this isn't Ireland at all. This is another world! The law of the land doesn't apply here. This is Shell country. It's like the army zone in Baghdad. They're a law unto themselves and the [local] law is on their side – the guards, the government, the army, the courts, the media. ... It's like something straight out of the 'X Files.' It's beyond belief! (Note from a fireside conversation, Shell to Sea solidarity camp, Rossport, Co. Mayo, June 2009[1])

The space and time of this story are the mythic world of authoritarian neoliberal globalization, a world of giant corporations and epic conflicts, of local heroes and (eco)warriors pitted against dark powers; a twilight zone of the divided and conflicted, the gigantic and the bizarre. In this phantasmagoric mythic world we hear a story that uses myth against myth ... a dialectical fairytale to wake us from our dream-sleep (Benjamin, 1999a).

Elements drawn from many registers are combined in surprising ways that make the seemingly disparate and strange into a coherent story that is deployed to counter mythic powers. In the remarkable fragment above, the traditional opening, declaring the space/time in which the story takes place to be 'another world', where things happen that are 'beyond belief', is articulated with elements from the phantasmagorias of global American popular culture: the Wild West – 'this is Shell country'; CNN and Fox News war coverage from inside Baghdad's Green Zone; and the paranormal/science-fictional/conspiratorial military-industrial entertainment complex represented by the 'X Files'.

And later in the same conversation, a conversation that ranged fluently across the chemical composition of unrefined natural gas, the blast radius of pipeline rupture at pressures over 300 bar, price per barrel projections on global markets post-peak oil and the legalities of compulsory purchase orders, what had been initially formulated as 'beyond belief' is, by another speaker, rearticulated as familiar, mundane and all too real – at least in terms of the experiences of this community, for whom generations of migration between rural periphery to global metropolis and back again have made people keenly intelligent and wise to the world:

> They thought they were dealing with peasants I suppose. But they're not you know. Did they think we hadn't seen all this before – big business, corrupt politicians, crooked cops? Sure that's all over the world – Chicago, London, Boston ... it's the same thing. We're well used to that here!

And from another storyteller:

> The issue here isn't whether we're closer to Boston or Berlin, it's whether we're closer to Nigeria than to Norway![2] (Ethnographic fieldnotes by authors, June 2009)

In the same articulations sober and even jaded accounts of extraordinary events and experiences that belong none the less to mundane reality are fused with magical tropes. In this next instance the agency of global power appears in the guise of the wish-granting genie:

> Lookat! Have you seen Belmullet? It's pre-Celtic Tiger Ireland! Sure there's nothin' there, you'd think. But there's lads flying around in new Imprezas [a powerful car favoured by 'boy racers']. This place never saw a boom before, and even now there's no recession either. Every house is rented. You couldn't get a place! There's about six hundred there in town with Shell one way or another, and more offshore, and on the site. Shell come into a place like Belmullet and they say 'What's wanted here? Well, there you are!' (Ethnographic fieldnotes by authors, June 2009)

This discursive frame composed of elements drawn from the realm of reality and the register of fantasy – a frame that is similar to the magic-realist literary genre developed by García-Márquez (1998) to depict the exotic and grotesque baroque political culture of post-colonial Latin America in the shadow of American puppet dictatorships – enables people to construct narratives that link local events with the most globally far-flung; the banal and seemingly innocuous with the most complex, obscure and sinister:

> Eastern European muscle, former army conscripts, bully-boys – sure that's how Shell do the dirty work all over the world – Nigeria, South America ... Oh they know all about that – Foreign Affairs, the Army – that was completely set up. And the cover-up afterwards – deny everything, spin it: 'he was only a gobshite', 'a fantasist'. Not at all! We knew what he was, and the Bolivians knew too. (Ethnographic fieldnotes by authors, June 2009)

The ability of this narrative form to grasp and articulate the purported machinations of transnational corporations in global political-economy is combined also with a self-reflexive understanding of the politics of envy and resentment that operate in the intimate world of a local community, and how these two realms – the abstract global and the intimate local – are articulated with one another (using the magic formula of the number three) so as to ferment trouble and set in motion a self-destructive mimetic spiral of conflict:

> They get people fighting amongst themselves and then they stand back and let it happen. It's exactly what they want to happen – sure they're dab hands at it, aren't they doing it all over the world for years! Here's how it's done: Three stage payments; a down payment of ten [thousand], another payment when the pipe is laid down, and a final payment when the gas is flowing. How that works is to put people against one another. Some people are waiting on money; some have spent it already before they've got it even, on cars and things, and now of course, as they see it, it's their neighbours – protesters – who are holding up the payments. ... It's very easy! Pay one person a few thousand, nothing to the next person, the neighbours get to hear of it and before you know it there's the recipe for begrudgery. (Ethnographic fieldnotes by authors, June 2009)

This fluent narrative linking abstract-remote and specific–intimate is nourished by a collective lifelong experience of living with liminality, having one foot planted in the local-historical and another in the contemporary geopolitical:

> People have gone from here to all over [alluding to headstones in the local cemetery bearing inscriptions 'of Nottingham and Rossport'; 'of Poolatomas and New York]. ... People here have a long memory. People here are connected to the past and they know what's going on in the world too.
> Michael Davitt and the Land League – that was all started here. The boycott – it was us who came up with that! This, now, Shell: Sure they're the Landlords now!'[3] ... And isn't that what's wanted now too, a rent strike – a national mortgage strike – to boycott the bondholders? (Ethnographic fieldnotes by authors, June 2009)

'That's the story now for you!'

We pick up the story at an occasion of storytelling common to so many stories. We are in the west of Ireland, in Rossport, Co. Mayo, at the Shell-to-Sea solidarity camp. People are telling stories of their experiences with Shell. It's a well-known story, at least it is in some circles, and we will trace the arc of it here again, because (according to some people) even though it's a new story, a story that has been threshed out and rehashed by the media and in the Courts and in the Dáil, investigated by the planners and thoroughly laid out in inquiries and reports, first-person narratives – *Our Story: The Rossport Five* (Garavan *et al.* 2006) and in the form of a comprehensive saga related by *Irish Times* journalist Lorna Siggins (2010) – *Once Upon A Time in The West* – it's a story that has been hushed up and distorted or even erased entirely. On the other hand, maybe we've heard it all before – or something very like it at any rate – for in many ways it's 'the same old story'! So here's the story again, the bare bones of it anyway.

The Corrib natural gas field, currently valued at 50 billion euro (one of several oil and gas deposits off Ireland's coast with an estimated current value of between 500 billion and 2 trillion euro)[4] is being developed by a consortium controlled by Shell Oil. Providence Resources, controlled by Tony O'Reilly (who also controls Independent News and Media) is a private Irish-based member of the consortium. Norway's Statoil is another. The gas is to be brought ashore by a high-pressure pipeline to a refinery, both under construction. The development carries risks of explosion as well as environmental pollution and health hazards to people living in the vicinity, a small community in a sparsely populated rural area of subsistence farming and fishing that for many generations has experienced economic underdevelopment and emigration. The development and its associated works and services spin-offs mean employment opportunities, though these are mostly specialized jobs and therefore for outside the immediate area. These jobs and their local services spin-offs comprise most of the benefit to the local, and indeed the wider, economy. This is because the terms under which the Shell consortium is operating, terms set by the Irish government, are extraordinarily generous. Fiscal and licensing terms negotiated between 1987 and 1992 by Fianna Fail Resources and Finance Ministers, Ray Burke and Bertie Ahern respectively (the former subsequently jailed for corruption and the latter forced to resign from office under pressure of ongoing tribunal investigations into political corruption) mean that Irish Revenue receives minimal royalties from the oil and gas fields, and 100 per cent of development and operating costs can be written off against tax for twenty-five years. The oil industry itself acknowledges that these are the most favourable terms anywhere in the world.

Earlier, in the 1970s, the Irish government turned down an offer of assistance from the Norwegian government to establish a state company similar to Norway's Statoil to develop Ireland's oil and gas resources. Whereas Ireland's current legislation explicitly prohibits any state involvement, Norway's 70 per cent stake in Statoil means that its oil has since become the fiscal foundation of that country's prosperity, funding the health, education and pensions needs of Norway's future generations.

Locally, at the development sites, residents and landowners have been protesting the project. In 2002, a comprehensive report by the Planning Authority endorsed and upheld the arguments of the local community, concluding that the development was fundamentally flawed. Shortly afterwards oil company representatives met with then *Taoiseach* Bertie Ahern and senior government officials, and within a week with the Chairman of the Planning Authority. The earlier findings of the Planning Authority's report were overturned. In 2005, five local residents were jailed indefinitely for contempt of court for refusing Shell access to lands that had been compulsorily purchased by Ministerial order. The 'Rossport Five', as they became known, generated attention and support locally, nationally and internationally and, embarrassed by the affair, the state duly released them. Development at the site has been progressing since then through a strategy of 'project splitting', which means that the overall development has been divided into several discrete projects, each one brought forward for planning permission individually, to be integrated and operationalized at a later stage, but in the meantime circumventing protests at the risks posed by the development overall. The whole development, as well as each of its 'split project' component elements, have been vigorously contested by local residents, supported by environmental campaigners who have established a solidarity camp nearby. Meanwhile the local community has also been 'splitting' – some accepting the now modified development, some opposing it on all grounds.

Work on the Shell on-and offshore sites is carried out under the protection of a 500-strong private security firm employed by Shell, backed up by a large force of *Gardai* with Army and Navy support. Protesters have been harassed, intimidated and severely beaten by private and state security forces, arrested on spurious charges, tried, prosecuted and jailed indefinitely (Garavan et al., 2006; McCaughan, 2008: 58–60). Local community interests have received financial support from Shell, and some say that people, including public servants, have been 'bought' (Leonard, 2007: 185, McCaughan, 2008: 23, 113). Coverage in the Irish media, much of which is owned by Independent News and Media, has been sparse, trivializing and/or criminalizing protesters; or, more typically, celebrating the development and reiterating the government's position: that the protests are impeding a development of strategic national importance and jeopardizing the state's development policy of economic growth through attracting foreign direct investment by low corporation tax and fast-tracked infrastructure (Connolly and Lynch 2005; Leonard 2007). The conflict continues, fought daily along several lines: acts of protest, ranging from peaceful civil disobedience to actively obstructing machinery and similar skirmishes, are met with baton-wielding *Gardai* and Shell private security, resulting in hospitalizations, arrests and hunger strikes. Simultaneously, people are doggedly contesting each stage of the development on technical and legal-procedural grounds (Siggins, 2010). Campaign-hardened local residents and their supporters are acknowledged by Shell's legal and technical consultants and by state agencies as having become formidable adversaries. The 'Shell to Sea' campaign, now some ten years running, has won some victories: the development has been slowed, the route of the pipeline has been changed, curtailed by numerous safety, environmental and design improvements. But the fiscal and licensing terms within which the exploitation of Irish natural resources is being developed have, however, not yet been revisited, and the even bigger question of hydro-carbon-based economic growth in the context of global climate change and planetary ecological self-destruction is hardly heard at all.[4]

What does this story mean?

We formulate the Corrib gas story in terms of its reiteration of themes in an ancient Irish mythic cycle, the *Táin Bó Cuailnge*, a story about the fundamental importance of gift relations and of principles of fair trade and reciprocity, and of what happens when these relations become corrupted by trickery. When gift relations become corrupted, scrambled and inverted, a process of schismogenesis – breaking, splitting, conflict – begins: conflict characterized by mimetic desire, intensified rivalry and reciprocal violence; a process that spirals out of control so that social institutions become undone and civilization descends into a dark age.[5]

Tracks, traces and foundations

While this story is told in Mayo in 2009 we could indeed be anywhere at any time in the world's histories, for all communities, Nancy (1991) tells us, are formed in a timeless and anthropologically universal familiar place of sharing experiences through storytelling; the people gathered together, over a shared meal, sitting around a fireside. The story is laid out, unfolded, related and presented as a gift to those people present: 'That's the story now for you!' What does it mean to pass the story around as a gift? Benjamin (1999c) tells us that ancient stories contain powers that, though they may have been locked up for countless generations, can impact upon the present and change the future as powerfully as when they were first recounted. Civilization begins when people gather to hear a story. The timeless foundation of the conversation of the world, making sense together (O'Neill, 1975), is the seat of the storyteller: the Sybill's Rock at Delphi, seat of the Neolithic matriarch, has its direct Irish archeological equivalents in the An *Suíochán* – the housekeeper's chair at Lough Gur (Dames, 1992) – and the Hag's Rock, the rock of ages, the petrified face of An *Cailleach* (O'Crualaoich, 2003). The *Cailleach* is a Celtic idiomatic representation of an archetype of deep antiquity, the primal Earth Mother. The *Cailleach*'s name is ambiguous: it may be from *caille*, a veil, suggesting a link with the veiled Greco-Roman goddess Hestia/Vesta, goddess of the domestic hearth, settlement, inviolable sovereignty; it may be from 'loss' (*caill*), representing the seasonal aspect of the Earth Mother in her winter form as harsh nature, the loss of fertility, to be followed by her other face, Brigid, the bright maiden of spring and returning fertility. *Cailleach* – 'lost'/'discarded' – may also refer to her diminished status from the Bronze Age onward, a female principle now disparaged and come to mean crone or even witch, though as a formerly powerful deity she is still feared and revered. Her name may also be derived from *ciall/ciallmhar*, meaning wisdom, intelligence and good sense.

Another track leading forward a few thousand years finds us gathered around the Tholstol, the *taler sthol*, the tale-teller's stool, the Vikings' deliberative assembly and seat of authority in Dublin and Limerick. A millennium later takes us to the *seanchaí* and the *bean feasa*, seated by the hearth, the diminished shades of the bardic poet and the *cailleach*, respectively, and their more formalized roles, first of hedge-school teacher, later the local school teacher,[6] picking up the threads of a scrambled language and a shredded history; and to the present mythic age of globalization where in comparison to immense, techno-sublime global powers our stories have become small, multiple, fragmented; dissimulated and drowned out in a white noise of news bulletins, soundbites, emails and twitters; an ecstasy of communication in which all too often mere raw information is misrecognized for knowledge digested and institutionalized in forms of wisdom and lore. But stories continue to be told and while they may sometimes be fragmented and partial they are always being pieced together to make good sense and to restore wholeness to the world, for as Rilke (in Bauman, 1995: ii) says, 'the story of shattered life can be told only in bits and pieces'.

The story of Shell and Corrib gas, 'The Great Gas Giveaway' as it has come to be known, is a Vichean recurrence in that the story resonates with and reiterates an ancient Irish story, the '*Táin Bó Cuailnge*', the Cattle Raid of Cooley. Both stories concern the pursuit of wealth and moral-practical relations of gift and theft, and they hinge on the fulcrum of justice and fairness. As a reiteration of the themes of the *Táin* the Great Gas Giveaway re-presents the accumulated wisdom of many generations distilled and preserved, translated and transmitted for the edification of the present and the protection of the future. Like all stories in the world's treasury of lore it has mythic qualities and epic proportions; it is an historical saga; some details are maybe lost and confused or misremembered; there are moments of fable and embellishment, borrowings and cross-fertilizations. Nor is the *Táin* a uniquely Irish story, for similar stories of herding, of exchange and of theft leading to cycles of reciprocal and mimetic violence are common across ancient civilization – Hermes' theft of Apollo's cattle, for instance; the reciprocal raids between the Romans and the Sabines; violent duels between brothers who become enemies, and so on, stories attesting to highly generalized, deep anthropological patterns of experience and cultural traffic. Above all, though, it is a normatively oriented sacred story with a teleology and eschatology: it tells us where we are going and what will become of us in the end, including the conditions of possibility for redemption. Along the way the story conveys deep truths about social relations and human character, of virtues and vices represented by heroes and villains. Like all true stories it is oriented to illuminating normative principles for the guidance and preservation of the 'Good Life'. The stories of the Great Gas Giveaway and the *Táin Bó Cuailnge* tell of what happens when relations of gift exchange on which society is founded are distorted by hubris and pleonexia: by vanity, foolishness, betrayal, greed, power and trickery. When gift relations based on reciprocity and fair exchange are distorted by power and trickery to become theft relations, society splits, schisms emerge and deepen, and a spiral of mimetic violence is unleashed. The basis of collective life is undermined for future generations. Civilization becomes unsustainable and descends into a dark age, a recurrence of barbarism. The stories disclose grievous moral error and warn of their dire consequences, and they intimate what needs to be done in order that things may be set right.

Where should we begin to tell this story? Authoritarian neoliberal globalization's political-economic consensus post-9/11; or post-1989? The Reagan/Thatcher revolution; or the eclipse of Keynes by Hayek and Friedman? The successful gas drilling in 1999; or exploration and knowledge of reserves in the 1980s, or 1970s? Changing natural resources development legislation in the 1990s and 1980s; or the legislation of the 1970s? Ireland declining to emulate Norway in the 1970s, or the political culture from the foundation of the Irish state, enshrined in the Constitution as the preference for private over public ownership; or the long historical experiences of colonial dispossession and the Nativist and Catholic social relations of status and class from which that ideology emerged? Or further back still? Or sideways, into the baroque micro-world of Fianna Fail in Mayo with its rogues gallery of colonial mimics, 'cute hoors' and the endemic culture of petty corruption grown up to become the Celtic Tiger's crony capitalism (O'Carroll, 1987; Keohane, 2005)?

Following tracks and traces backwards and forwards through time and across cultures in search of historical foundations, Serres (1991) has shown,[7] leads us not through infinite regress to a pointless nowhere but rather to a multiplicity of beginnings. Such a genealogy reveals that there is no one epistemological point of origin, no singular solid empirical ground. Contrary to historians who caricature a purportedly Irish propensity for 'telling tales and making it up' (Foster, 2001), and against whose 'mere stories' historians imagine they hold the authority of historical 'truth', there is in fact no History: there are only stories and their re-tellings. All stories, fragments, traces, opinions and words – *logi* and *doxai* – Arendt (1990) reminds us, contain a grain of truth, insofar as they express the world that is common to all, the general condition, as it appears and discloses itself from a particular point of view. In the end all we have to work with are these *doxai*, representations of reality as it appears from particular points of view. This does not mean that we become mired in relativism. We will always be able to sort out stories, showing that some are more coherent and convincing than others. Some will be revealed to be no more than fragments, gossip and hearsay, and some can be shown with good reason to be lies, 'spin' and systematically distorted communications. But this sorting out is done always within the interpretive horizon of a particular tradition and the hermeneutic circle of community of interlocutors trying to understand our past, make sense of our present and take care of our future.

Recurrence of the *Táin*, foretold: corruption of the gift relation

One of the preambles to the epic saga of the *Táin Bó Cuailnge* is related in an illuminated eleventh-century manuscript from Clonmacnoise, the *Leabhar na hÚidhre*, (Carey, 2009), a book which contains myth and legend, history, geography and folklore as well as sacred scripture, their fluent combination in the one manuscript showing not carelessness or pre-Enlightenment confusion of fact and fantasy, but, on the contrary, a testament to the wisdom of the Saints and Scholars in their practice of not analytically disassembling knowledge into discrete pieces and separate stories, but of treating it holistically as an integrated body of wisdom and ideals to be respected as such by inscribing and enshrining it in a holy book: an illuminated manuscript, a powerful book of radiant ideas to light our road ahead. The story as it was written at Clonmacnoise, transcribed by several scribes working in succession, was already very ancient at the time of its being written down; translated from oral Gaelic dialects and transcribed in old, middle and early modern Irish and Latin, refracted and influenced in recursive transductions and transaccidentations, but the core of the story rings across the ages as clear as a bell.

Crunnuc MacAgnomain – his name from *crunne*, meaning gathering, settlement, dwelling – lives with his children in their lonesome household in the mountains of Connaught, his wife, the children's mother, having passed away. One day, out of the blue, a woman walks up to Crunnuc's door, crosses the threshold and makes herself at home in the house. She feeds the children; she shares Crunnuc's bed. The household prospers and flourishes under her care. She becomes pregnant. One day Crunnuc goes to the Fair in Ulster. 'Say nothing about me to the people you meet there', the woman warns Crunnuc. 'Don't worry', says he, 'I will hold my tongue.' At the Fair, as well as trade and commerce there is gaming and competition. A race is to be run against King Conchobor of Ulster's chariot. Conchobor, a usurper who attained power by bribery and trickery, personifies what the Greeks called *pleonexia*, an insatiable lust for political and economic power, grasping and over-reaching beyond any sense of limit and just measure, the fundamental problem addressed by Plato's *Republic* and Aristotle's *Ethics*. Crunnuc, standing amongst the spectators, remarks that the King's chariot is fast but that his wife is faster! Conchobor's men overhear and report it. 'Bring her here and prove your boast', the King commands, 'or be put to death.' She is summoned. 'You can see that I am heavily pregnant', she says. 'Wait at least until I have given birth before you make me run.' The King refuses. The spectators laugh and show no sympathy. 'You should know that I am Macha of the *Sidhe*', she says.

Her name, Macha, is richly overdetermined with significances: it means 'fertile plain' or 'herd of cattle'; derived from '*mac*' – son, or more generally offspring; *maclóg* – womb, and *macnas* – playfulness, liveliness. She is fecundity, Life. She has come from nowhere, she simply 'is'. As a spirit she bears family resemblances to her Greek sisters Demeter, Aphrodite and Hestia. Cleaned up by Christianity she becomes Brigid the firegiver and homebuilder. She represents the original Gift, the resources of Nature. An aspect of the Neolithic *Cailleach* and her sacred herds, Macha is a pre-Bronze Age personification of principles of autonomous femininity and territorial sovereignty.

Though now facing off against a supernatural being Conchobor does not back down. Pride of losing face before his subjects and his own hubris lead him to insist that the race be run, and so it is. Macha crosses the finish line beating Conchobor's chariot, and immediately she gives birth to twins, a boy and a girl. She then curses the people of Ulster: 'For the next nine generations, at the hour of greatest need you will be as vulnerable as a woman in labour.'[8]

This is one of several *réamhscéala* – fore-tales, ominous predictions – of the *Táin Bó Cuailnge*. Most share a central theme, namely the disruption of the life-sustaining gift relation of reciprocal fair exchange by injustice and trickery, foolishness and greed; and the catastrophic consequences that follow from that, leading to collective weakness, death, poverty and mutual destruction.

Crunnuc is the incompetent husband who, whether through foolishness, carelessness or vanity, overawed or caught up in the exuberance of the Fair, fails to take good care of the home. Echoing the advice mothers give to their children to this day to be prudent and temperate, Macha asks Crunnuc not to 'give away the farm'. But Crunnuc betrays Macha; he gives away the gift that has given herself to his household. Crunnuc is the minister who mismanages the *oikos*. He makes a bad job of husbanding his household's god-given resources. He feels compelled by Conchobor, an arrogant, dark power under whose guidance people have become affluent but frivolous and morally decadent. He might have refused, backed down, talked his way out of the challenge, but just as the people of Ulster have lost sight of virtues of fairness and justice, Crunnuc for his part lacks the virtues of prudence, courage and foresight. Macha is brought forth. The crowd will not wait. They want her to perform now. The Fair is the central economic and political institution of the community. Here, people meet to trade their goods and services. Fair trade exchanges are asymmetrical and reciprocal. The things exchanged are not equivalent; they are not the same thing, goods with the same value exactly; so one party may get a somewhat better deal than the other party to the exchange, but the trade is experienced to be mutually beneficial to the parties so that they settle for the time being. This asymmetrical reciprocity encourages them to trade again, to settle things up next time, and so on. Exchange unites: people partake freely in an asymmetrical though mutually satisfactory exchange. They go away happy for the time being, and they will return and trade with one another again, establishing, developing and deepening a relationship that is economic, political, moral and juridical all at once: the gift relation is 'a total social fact', as Mauss (2002) says, an anthropologically universal foundation of general economy and human culture. This dynamically balanced fair exchange derived from the gift relation is the anthropological and historically general unifying principle of society and political economy (Mauss 2002). It is a general principle expressed in the particular, locally, in the contemporary English vernacular equivalence of 'fair' and 'just', and in Irish wherein the etymology of 'aonaigh' (fair, market) is derived from 'aon' (one). 'Aonaigh' has another meaning too –'fury', 'rage', intimating what transpires if deals go wrong, if they are experienced as iniquitous and unfair. And this is not fair play! This cannot be right! Demanding that a pregnant woman race against the King's chariot for the price of her husband's life is completely and obviously outside the terms of anything that could be considered 'just measure' and a 'fair deal'.[9] Macha appeals for justice, but Conchobor has no interest in justice and fairness, and the gawking spectators laugh at her. By forcing Macha to run they make a mockery of the principle of fairness and do a grave injustice, and by doing so, by inverting equity to iniquity, gift exchange to theft, they risk scrambling all exchange relations and put at risk the original gift. Macha wins anyway, proving her supernatural primordial power. But those who disrupt the economic-political system of fair exchange and justice by forcing an unfair deal, and who cause Macha to deliver her gifts prematurely and in suffering (Macha and her twin babies shriek in pain), and who cause her to deliver not for the good of her own household but for the pleasure of Conchobor and the amusement of the crowd, place their civilization at risk for nine generations.

Schismogenesis: the trouble begins

The *Táin* follows, an epic of schismogenetic[10] and mimetic violence culminating in slaughter, poverty and darkness. The story begins with pillow talk in the affluent household of Ailill and Medhb. In the classic pattern of Bateson's

(1958) formulation of symmetrical schismogenesis – competitive rivalry between equals – Ailill and Medhb, King and Queen, aristocratic tyrants and individually wealthy plutocrats, are boasting to one another, counting out, comparing and bidding up the wealth that each has brought to their marriage: one's gold, the other's jewellery, one's chariots, another's finery; your BMW, my Mercedes; your shares in Anglo Irish Bank, my property portfolio. At one, relatively innocuous level this is the pecuniary emulation of the global plutocracy and the local leisure class and their rivalry for status through competitive consumerism (Veblin, 1994). The marriage relationship between Ailill and Medhb resembles a consortium of possessive individuals bound in a decadent potlatch. As well as their grasping and over-reaching for money and power, competing against their peers and against one another, they compete sexually and they are promiscuously adulterous. Their whole way of life, having no sense of limits, is fundamentally excessive and unsustainable, though they are not yet aware of the dangers intrinsic to their ploenexia. At another, darker and more sinister level Ailill and Medhb exemplify the violent potential in mimetic desire (Girard, 1976). Mimetic desire to have what the other desires reciprocally amplifies, escalates and intensifies mutual desire for the same objects; imitated desire generates rivalry and potential for violent conflict. This is a powerful formula for economic growth, but a dangerous one, for it is economic growth at the constantly increasing risk of social conflict. Things escalate. Their respective herds of cattle? Ailill has a blond bull that Medhb cannot trump. But there is a brown bull in Ulster, under the protection of a minister called Dáire (his name derives from *dáir* (animals – specifically cattle – copulating) or *aire* – 'care', or 'minister'). As cattle were the most important resource, the basis of wealth (the words 'chattel' and 'capital' are etymologically derived from 'cattle' in Indo-European languages), Dáire is the Irish Bronze Age equivalent of the Minister for Resources and Finance. Medhb sends her consultants to broker a deal. 'Let us lease your bull to develop my herd, and you will get in return fifty heifers, a new chariot, a site of land, and – as a sweetener – Medhb's friendly thighs on top of all that.' 'I don't care what the Ulstermen think', Dáire says, 'I'll take my treasure.' The wine flows freely in the legendary equivalent of Buswells hotel.[11] "Twas a good job you agreed to our terms', says one of the consultants, 'for we'd have taken the bull anyway!' Sleeveen though he is, Dáire is offended. The deal is off. (His modern counterparts have perhaps even less honour, but that's another story!) ... The story unfolds ... Medhb, along with Ailill and Fergus (Medbh's lackey and occasional bedmate) sets off with her mercenaries and equipment to take the bull. Cúchulainn represents a lone minority amongst his weak and sleepy people. (As we have been shown already in the *réamhscéala*, Conchobor's people are superficially prosperous but feckless and lacking virtue, and now their hour of greatest need is upon them.) Cúchulainn commences a campaign of skirmishing and guerrilla tactics, progressing to formal duels fought at every fording point of the rivers along the way – obstructing machinery; planning hearings; court cases – Cúchulainn alone fighting against greater and greater odds, meeting treachery and dirty tactics, for Medhb 'knew well how to stir up strife and dissention' (Kinsella, 2002: 169). Each river ford, like every stage of the gas pipeline, is a threshold, a liminal situation where it seems to be only a skirmish, but what is at stake is the dissolution of order and the transformation of the world (Szakolczai, 2009a). Cúchulainn is at a disadvantage in the moving water; mostly he wins, often he switches, rushing to defend another fording point. Each battle is important but none is decisive. Medb's theft machine rolls onwards, and things go from bad to worse.

Mimetic violence: conflict spirals into mutual destruction

In conflict things become exaggerated and weirdly distorted. The dogs of war are unleashed and run amok on the fields of Mars and Badhb; madness, demonic fury, intensity, 'laughing, ecstatic destruction' (Yeats, 19343: 103), represented in the *Táin* by the

> warp spasm that seized Cúchulainn, and made him into a monstrous thing, hideous and shapeless, unheard of. His shanks and his joints, every knuckle and angle and organ from head to foot, shook like a tree in the flood or a reed in the stream. His body made a furious twist inside his skin, so that his feet and shins and knees switched to the rear and his heels and calves switched to the front. ...
> His face and features became a red bowl: he sucked one eye so deep into his head that a wild crane couldn't probe it onto his cheek from the depths of his skull; the other eye fell out along his cheek. His mouth was weirdly distorted. (Kinsella, 2002: 150)

As conflict intensifies everything gets turned inside out and people tear themselves apart in terrible demonic and inhuman ways. We cannot see properly, or speak, or hear one another; we are lost in furious ecstasy. In the intensifying spiral of mimetic violence, Girard says, the object is lost sight of and escalating violence becomes an end in itself, and indeed the bulk of the *Táin* depicts a Hobbesean nightmare of 'a perpetual and restless pursuit of power after power ceasing only in death' (Hobbes, 1985: 161). Slaughter ensues: the sons of Ulster are butchered; the daughters of Connaught are slain in retaliation. 'A hundred are killed, then two hundred, then three hundred, then four hundred, then five hundred ... they fell sole to sole and neck to headless neck, so dense was the destruction ... a bed of them six deep in a great circuit ... this slaughter of the *Táin* was given the name *Seisrech Bresligi*, the Sixfold Slaughter' (Kinsella, 2002: 154–155).

Medhb next tricks Ferdia into fighting Cúchulainn, who is his foster brother and lifetime friend, just as now Shell and the consortium stakeholders watch the duel from a safe distance: the political and legal battles between the state agencies and the protesters, the local community splitting into several factions, and the political parties – all the persons involved are relations of one sort or another in the same Irish extended family. 'We have done well out of this anyhow,' Ailill says. 'It is all the same to us if they both die' (Kinsella, 2002: 177). Eventually the brown bull is taken. That theft should have doubled the wealth of Ailill and Medhb, but no sooner are they brought together then the brown bull and the blond bull gore one another. First the blond bull is killed, and then, after a brief period of furious stampeding, the brown bull also falls exhausted, dead. Thousands have died, families and friendships have been torn asunder, order has been destroyed, once prosperous households are all in ruins. A fundamental injustice has been done, fair trade has become daylight robbery, and only evil and disaster can come of it. The *Táin Bó Cuailnge* ends abruptly. The scribe in Clonmacnoise signs off: FINIT. AMEN.

'The darkness drops again'

One possible history of the not-so-distant future of the global planetary present is already written in microform on the local deep historical landscape of Mayo. Thirty miles or so from Rossport and the developing sites of the pipeline and refinery, overlooked by Neifinn mountain, legendary home of the *Cailleach* and her sacred herds (O'Crualaoich, 2003: 107), lies the archaeological remains of the Céide Fields, the most extensive Neolithic ruins in the world. Dating from the fourth millennium BC, four and a half thousand years before the *Táin* was transcribed from oral lore, the archaeological remains of Céide Fields extend for several square miles under a thick blanket of bog (Cooney, 2000). The ruins testify to the presence, once upon a time, of a large, highly organized community who worked together to clear forests and to develop and divide land into an extensive field system. They were skilled craftspeople who built elaborate dwelling houses, who had a complex religion and culture, a system of government and order. Their wealth was based on cattle. As well as trading there may have been inter-regional cattle raiding, though no fortifications or other evidence of warfare have been identified. Why did this ancient civilization collapse? Archaeologists hypothesize that these people first settled in a temperate rainforest landscape with a rich floor under the canopy. They cleared trees to make arable land, extending their prosperous settlement outwards for more land and for building material and fuel. Eventually, at the very height of the development of their community, they exhausted their fuel supply and the forest canopy, thereby helping to bring about a local microclimate change and a regional ecological disaster. Soil became leached of nutrients and arable land perished. Over the relatively short period of a few hundred years a blanket bog encroached over the area, smothering and obliterating the community for forty centuries of stony sleep. Modern civilization, 250 years young, unsustainably ecocidal and self-destructive, may be, as in Yeats's vision of darkness dropping in 'The Second Coming', sliding like the Céide Fields under the blanket bog of a new dark age.

Conclusion: restoring normative principles of justice and fairness

But this is not the only possible ending. The *Táin* is signed off 'It is Finished. So Be It.' But the book in which it is written is a lamp from a golden age that dawned after the dark age following the *Táin*. The book contains other stories, crucially the radiant ideals of Christianity with its emphasis on redemption and atonement (at-one-ment) with the cosmos through *agape*, through loving one's neighbour as the realization of divine love; that is, for(e)giving the sin of iniquity and restoring the principles of justice and fairness as the earthly realization of the Good Life.

The sociological, philosophical, theological or political anthropological search for foundations on which we can ground ourselves to understand and interpret our contemporary society and suggest how we might make it better, whether in paleo-anthropological and ancient Ireland, in Classical Rome or in contemporary Ireland in the new mythic age of globalization, will lead us invariably to the authoritative community of agape interlocutors who share a deep need to understand one another and so who are speaking and listening; gathering, settling, dwelling, conversing, making sense together. We have always been, and we remain, 'all Livia's daughter-sons' playing our roles in 'a tale told of Shaun and Shem', as James Joyce (1995) tells us in *Finnegans Wake*, an eternally recurring self-disclosing story of Civilization re-told by Joyce for us on the eve of civilization-destroying world war. This making sense together in the face of the encroaching forces of barbarism is what Seamus Heaney (1988) has in mind to remind us of when he speaks of 'the government of the tongue'.

Telling stories about Shell, like all storytelling, seeks communication with the mythic powers the stories address and orient towards. Storytelling speaks to the normative horizon of a shared ideal of mutuality – a common world. Conflict between Shell, the state, Shell-to-Sea protesters and other community groups does not necessarily mean that they are absolutely opposed to one another, that their conflict is irresolvable. Certainly they are not indifferent – the only non-social relation. Conflict, Simmel (1964a) says, is ultimately a positive form of engagement that seeks a higher truth. The narrative that participates in the universal storytelling already acknowledges and speaks to an already presupposed and envisaged horizon of shared conventions and understanding. Speech acts may presuppose an ideal speech situation of normatively binding reasoned agreement – but equally they mark the great distance of the realization of that ideal, and how it is receding, and part of the work of storytelling is to chart the course of that receding while never giving up on the goal of its recovery and realization. Following Laclau and Mouffe (1985) we could say that storytelling is the hegemonic articulatory practice that in mustering its powers of communication so that it may better engage with the giant powers that it faces – and in so articulating and constituting itself – simultaneously clarifies and articulates and formulates the parties that, having begun as merely political antagonists in the Schmitian sense of implacable friend/enemy distinctions, become in the process members of the same community of interlocutors in agonal political discourse (Mouffe, 2005). The politics of storytelling may be best understood as that *phronesis* identified by Arendt (1990) and exemplified by Socrates in terms of a *maieutucs* – midwifery – assisting in enabling the antagonistic parties to mutually give birth to a new truth.

This brings our story not to a close but in a full circle and back to the beginning, for the new truth can only be the remembering and rebirth of an old one, the restoration of the principle of fairness and justice as the fulcrum of our exchange relations. Marcel Mauss leads us to the same place in his famous essay on the gift, leaving us with this story:

> There is no other morality, nor any other form of economy, nor any other social practices save these. The Bretons and *The Chronicles of Arthur* tell how King Arthur, with the help of a Cornish carpenter, invented that wonder of his court, the miraculous Round Table, seated around which the knights no longer fought. Formerly 'out of sordid envy', in stupid struggles, duels and murders stained with blood the finest banquets. The carpenter said to Arthur: 'I will make you a very beautiful table, around which sixteen hundred and more can sit, and move around, and from which no-one will be excluded. ... No knight will be able to engage in fighting, for there the highest placed will be on the same level of the lowliest.' There was no longer a 'high table', and consequently no more quarrelling. Everywhere that Arthur took his table his noble company remained happy and unconquerable. In this way nations today can make themselves strong and rich, happy and good. Peoples, social classes and individuals will be able to grow rich, and will only be happy when they have learnt to sit down, like the knights, around the common store of wealth. (Mauss, 1990: 106)

Notes

1 This story, our retelling of it, is made up of bits and pieces from many sources, including but not limited to: Leonard (2007); Connolly and Lynch (2005); McCaughans (2008); Garavan *et al.* (2006); various reports and opinion pieces from Ireland's top journalists, especially Fintan O'Toole and Vincent Browne; bits and pieces also by bottom feeders from the gutter press; headlines, snapshots, footage and sound

bites from radio, tv and internet; but especially it's made up of conversations, discussions and stories told by people associated in some way or another with the issue. It is an incomplete and partial story, as all stories are.

2 The comment plays cleverly on a phrase coined by *Táiniste* (Deputy Prime Minister) Mary Harney (2000) of the neoliberal Progressive Democrat Party, in which she remarked that whereas Ireland may be geographically closer to Berlin (i.e. to Europe and to the Rhinish social model) the development strategy of the so-called 'Celtic Tiger' has been 'Spiritually ... a lot closer to Boston' (i.e. to global-American neoliberalism).

3 Davitt founded the Irish National Land League, a nineteenth-century social movement dedicated to tenants' rights in Castlebar, Mayo. The word 'boycott' comes from the eponymous Captain Charles Boycott, a notorious Land Agent who was forced to leave Ireland by a campaign of social and economic ostracism organized by the Land League.

4 The full extent of oil and gas resources in Irish territorial waters is estimated at 2 billion barrels, at current market prices approximately 2 trillion euro (Shell to Sea, 2012).

5 Our method of theorizing the story of Corrib gas follows the methods – the paths – broken by others, including the journal *International Political Anthropology*, by locating contemporary political issues in contexts of the *longue durée*, interpreting events of the moment in terms of the deep histories of civilization, archaeology and mythology, tracing pre- and proto-political relations of meaning-formation. Irish scholars have produced some of the most relevant materials for our purpose, namely Michael Cronin's (2000) work on language and translation and Gearoid O'Crualaoich's interpretations of Irish folklore, particularly *The Book of the Cailleach* (2003). Here we gratefully follow their lead, in the original and true meaning of 'method', not as mere technique of analysis that breaks things asunder but as *(met)hodos*, a pathway leading towards understanding the whole as integral. This *methodos* shows how a dense text of the present (in this case the story of Corrib gas) can become illuminated when read through/translated into other languages and sign systems, including obscure texts from the past, from deep history, folklore and mythologies of other civilizations. This method of theorizing involving intertextual translation and mutual illumination is neither new nor restricted to sociological or literary theory. In the tradition of Rabbinical hermeneutics for example, the sacred texts are interpreted with continuous reference to Yiddish folklore. It is by such means of intertextual translations that one may approach the purported forty-nine levels of meaning in each passage of the Torah.

6 *Seanchaí* – 'storyteller'; *bean feasa* – 'wise woman' – are the bearers and transmitters of lore in non-literate, oral, traditional community, the Irish equivalents of the Shaman in other anthropologies. In this context it is noteworthy that three of the most prominent figures in the Rossport campaign against Shell are retired local primary school teachers.

7 Serres' investigation is into the foundations of Rome, but his *Book of Foundations* is more generally a work of epistemology, arguing that there can be no definitive empirical ground of historical fact, but only a dense web of discourse and interpretation.

8 Adapted from Kinsella's (2002) translation of the *Táin*. Etymologies of names and so on are from standard Irish dictionaries – Dineen (1996), Ó'Dónaill (2010) and O'Crualaoich (2003).

9 For a full exposition of the relation between justice and fairness, reciprocity, equivalence and equity, and their centrality to the institutions of economy, politics and law, see Comte-Sponville (2003: 60–85).

10 For a full exposition of 'schismogenesis' see Horvath and Thomassen (2008).

11 A hotel situated opposite the Irish government buildings in Dublin, reputedly the scene of wheeling and dealing between businessmen-politicians and their cronies during the Celtic Tiger years.

5

Political theologies in the wake of the Celtic Tiger

In the wake of the sudden death of the Celtic Tiger Irish business leaders called for the suspension of normal partisan democratic politics and the formation of a one-party government with the will to make crucial decisions necessary to deal with the 'exceptional circumstances' occasioned by this 'national emergency'. The government, they charged, was drifting aimlessly, unable to clarify what needed to be done and unwilling to rule. What was needed, Ireland's businessmen claimed, was 'an all party government ... for a three year period, with the possibility of extending it. ... [A] new national government [with] exceptional powers ... to insulate it against the unpopularity of the decisions that have to be made' (Corcoran, 2009: 1, 2). Such a model, business said, would provide the necessary leadership and vision to identify clear principles, and compel the country to adhere to them. These principles that we must be compelled to adhere to are the economic laws of the Market: now, more than ever, free enterprise must be championed and supported; labour must be forced to be more competitive; public expenditure must be radically cut back.

At the same moment a leading Irish left-wing academic called for the crisis to be taken as an opportunity for a radical political realignment, a clarification and re-ordering of the Irish political field by polarizing the right and centre-right parties as neoliberal champions of the Economy and the left and centre-left as repudiating rule by market principles and defending the interests of society (Kirby, 2012). In short, what we saw emerging in Ireland in the wake of the Celtic Tiger is the formula of 'authoritarian liberalism' and sharpened 'friend–enemy' distinctions that Carl Schmitt advocated in the 1920s as an antidote to Weimar Germany's economic depression, cultural decadence and political drift; a 'political theology'[1] that culminated in fascist totalitarianism.

Ireland, the success story of neoliberal globalization, was amongst the first and worst casualties of the global depression. In the wake of the death of the

Celtic Tiger, Ireland, which led the race to the bottom away from the post-war model of Social Europe, is one of the first places in which we catch a glimpse of historical recurrence when 'the centre cannot hold', as Yeats (1920a: 10) said of Schmitt's times. The question now, as then, is: 'what rough beast / its hour at last come round/ slouches toward Bethlehem to be born?' The intervention of the EU/IMF/World Bank Troika superseded one particular local national moment of danger, but the Troika represents a contemporary form of post-national politics where sovereign institutions of democratic government are subsumed and replaced by technocratic powers of financial institutions.

'Political theology' is a term coined by the legal and political theorist Carl Schmitt, who says that 'all significant concepts of the modern theory of the state are secularized theological concepts not only because of their historical development – in which they were transferred from theology to the theory of the state, whereby, for example, the omnipotent God became the omnipotent lawgiver – but also because of their systematic structure' (Schmitt, 2006: 36). There is a similarity of form between core elements of theology and politics – a crucial example for Schmitt is that 'the exception in politics is analogous to the miracle in theology' (Schmitt, 2006: 36). Schmitt argues that there is a limit to the Enlightenment's secular-rational project. Just as the 'miraculous' (i.e. 'transgression of the laws of nature through an exception brought about by direct intervention' by divine agency) cannot be theologically rationalized without evacuating religion of what is essential to it, sovereign decisionism, 'the sovereign's direct intervention in a valid legal order' in dealing with the exceptional case, cannot be replaced by rationalized procedure without evacuating that which is essential to the political (Schmitt, 2006: 36). While up to the seventeenth century 'a continuous thread runs through the metaphysical, political and sociological conceptions that postulate the sovereign as a personal unit and primeval creator' – 'the engineer of the great machine' – after the Enlightenment the place of the sovereign 'has been radically pushed aside. The machine now runs by itself' (Schmitt, 2006: 48). The modern democratic state and supra-state formations such as the EU/IMF/World Bank Troika come to resemble 'a huge industrial plant' (Schmitt, 2000: 65), 'an expression of a relativistic and impersonal scientism' (Schmitt, 2006: 47), wherein 'the political vanishes into the economic or technical-organizational' (Schmitt, 2006: 65). This evacuated immanent order reached an apotheosis, Schmitt said, in the Weimar Republic's blend of 'positivism and normativism … a formless mixture, unsuitable for any structure, which was no match for any serious problem concerning state and constitution' (Schmitt, 2006: 3). The alternative to this torpid stasis, Schmitt argued, is the restoration of the sovereign decision-maker, which historically has meant the dictator.

We now have the recurrence of a moment in which religion re-enters the political as a florid symptom of the lack of, and desire for, a transcendental principle and a sovereign decision-maker; conditions anticipated by Nietzsche and Weber as one of those moments when the spirit of capitalism confronts its inner nihilism:

> the Enlightenment seems to be irretrievably fading, and the idea of duty in one's calling prowls about in our lives like the ghost of dead religious beliefs. ... The fulfillment of the calling cannot be directly related to the highest spiritual and cultural values. Where this cultural tendency is most fully developed ... the pursuit of wealth, stripped of its religious and ethical meaning, tends to become associated with purely mundane passions, which often actually give it the character of sport ... a nullity that imagines that it has achieved a level of civilization never before achieved'. (Weber, 1958: 182)

Faced with psychosis-inducing nullity modern people may desire to be 'born again' in the political-theologies of 'entirely new prophets' proclaiming 'a great rebirth of old ideas and ideals' (Weber, 1958: 182). In Weber's time this meant nationalism and militarism alloyed with religious beliefs and charismatic messianic leaders of fascist and communist totalitarianisms that emerged after Weimar and the Great Depresssion (and which are again, now, the governments-in-waiting throughout Europe, from Scandinavia to Italy and Greece, from the Ukraine to the UK). But Weber also means the born again nineteenth-century political theologies of Utilitarianism, Liberalism, Positivism; dogmas that on being questioned – as they are now – are reaffirmed with evangelical zeal.[2] What has presented itself since 2008 as a rational, neutral alternative to political extremism of Left and Right, namely intervention by a non-partisan, post-national, post-political Troika of the EU/ECB/IMF technocracy, is far from being ideologically neutral. Rather, rule by the Troika means that the institutions of democratic politics in sovereign national states are over-ridden by technocratic dictatorship of the Market; authoritarian neoliberalism as a political-economic theology.

A genealogy of neoliberalism as a religion

Paraphrasing Schmitt (2006: 36) segueing from politics into economics, all significant concepts of modern economic theory are secularized theological concepts. In their historical development they were transferred from theology to the theory of the economy, whereby, for example, the omnipotent God becomes the omnipotent Market. The divine lawmaker in politics is analogous to the 'invisible hand' in economics: an objective, abstract, divine power transposed into the Market.

In an obituary written on the eve of the financial crisis in 2008 Nobel Prize winning economist Paul Krugman assesses the legacy of fellow Nobel Laureate Milton Friedman, the most influential neoliberal economist of the second half of the twentieth century. Making a parallel between economics and religion, Krugman explicitly formulates neoliberalism as an economic political theology. For two centuries before the Great Depression, Krugman says, economic liberalism had the status of an unquestionable orthodoxy: let the natural forces of supply and demand do their work – literally *laissez faire* – and the invisible hand of the Market will deliver as it must, as it ought, producing an objective, impartial social order that is fair, and just, and right, and good. But, Krugman says, 'classical economics offered neither explanations nor solutions for the Great Depression', and in the context of that crisis of faith 'Keynes played the role of Martin Luther. ... Keynesianism was a great reformation of economic thought. It was followed, inevitably, by a counter-reformation. ... If Keynes was Luther, Friedman was Ignatius of Loyola, founder of the Jesuits. And like the Jesuits, Friedman's followers have acted as a sort of disciplined army of the faithful' (Krugman, 2007: 27).

The genealogy of neoliberalism as an economic theology is that it was born (and has been successively born-again) in circumstances of crisis and responses to emergencies. Conditions of emergency call for the sovereign decision-maker, Schmitt says, just as for neoliberals an emergency is a 'crisitunity' for the heroic entrepreneur. The world became familiar with Hayek and Friedman during the Thatcher–Reagan era, the collapse of the Soviet Union and the 'end of history', when their ideas had been taken on board and systematically put into practice as public policy. Their legacy has been the guiding political-economic theology of late twentieth- and twenty-first-century globalization. But Hayek's and Friedman's political-economic theology had been formed decades earlier as a response to the crises of Weimar and the Great Depression, in exactly the same moment as Schmitt. Like Schmitt they saw the world in morbid stasis, underpinned by a latent tension between right and left totalitarianisms, a confusion that needed to be clarified, simplified and decisively resolved. Hayek was the scion of an elite family whose status and security were rocked by the break-up of the Austro–Hungarian Empire and the influx of Polish and Slovak Jews to an impoverished, demoralized Vienna. Friedman graduated in 1932, in the trough of the Depression. And later, at another moment of crisis, Nozick wrote *Anarchy, State and Utopia* during 1971–1973, at the height of civil conflict about conscription for Vietnam.[3]

The same states of emergency that are so important in the genealogy of twentieth-century neoliberalism have, in turn, historical antecedents in the cases of the 'founding fathers' (and grandfathers) of Liberalism. The ideas of Hobbes and Locke were born in the circumstances of the English Civil War. In the raging conflicts between Catholic and Protestant, monarchy and parliament, Natural law was posited as an alternative to institutional religion as the basis for cosmic and social order. Crisis and conflict at another level of experience underpinned the work of J. S. Mill. Mill suffered a nervous breakdown that he himself attributed to the fact that his moral sentiments were neglected in the natural science Utilitarian education in which he had been indoctrinated under Bentham. His father, he said, 'made Reason a religion and always deprecated sentiment and feeling' (Mill, 1956: x). *On Liberty* was written as he was recuperating his mental health, supported by his co-author Harriet Taylor, as they grappled with the moral contradiction in their adulterous relationship. Human beings, by virtue of their reason, should be free to pursue their free will, so long as they do no harm to others, they argued – as though an affair caused no harm to a third party!

The young Adam Smith at first pursued a conventional religious vocation, but he became a deist, and his religious worldview remained essential to his economic theories (Heilbroner, 1999). Deism emerged from the Enlightenment, democratic and industrial revolutions, in the circumstances of a paradigm shift from Religion to Science, from a divinely ordered cosmos to a Natural order, as an attempt to find a mid-point between religious dogmatism on the one hand and positivist atheism on the other. Deists believed that God made the universe and the laws of Nature that govern it, but, having set things up, God does not intervene any further with the Natural order. The universe unfolds as it should, as it must, guided by an invisible hand; that is, in accordance with the laws of Nature that God created. God's laws of Nature constitute a cosmic order, a transcendent reality, morally neutral and objective; simply the way things are, and are meant to be.[4] The laws of Nature can be analysed by the scientific method, apprehended as simple principles, and articulated in terms of reason.

In this vein, Hayek (1991) argues that the market is a spontaneously ordered social institution that has evolved naturally from human behaviour. Spontaneously ordered institutions are analogous to crystals, or snowflakes, or solar systems in the natural universe. While the market is the result of countless human actions and patterns of behaviour over many generations it is not something of human – or indeed any other – intelligent design, but a fundamentally simple Natural order. Friedman locates his neoliberalism within this paradigm of Natural order as a transcendental economic theology. 'Positive economics is in principle independent of any particular ethical position or normative judgment' (Friedman, 1953: 4). Economics is a science with a positivist epistemology that analyses an order of objective ontology, matters of empirical facts of Nature, and discerns therein laws that are absolute; that have transcendental and universal validity. Friedman, with Hayek, argues – believes – that spontaneously ordered institutions are in a state of equilibrium; that left alone to evolve without interference, rational economic behaviour will produce market equilibrium –its perfect, 'natural' condition. Natural systems in a state of equilibrium should not be the subject of human interference, Friedman says, except when government acts as rule-maker and umpire (1962: 25) to guide and restore them to such a condition, as when a government enforces market conditions by privatization, deregulation and austerity. Why the purportedly natural institution of the Market should not be subject to human interference while in every other dimension we must 'hound Nature in her wanderings', apprehend and subdue her, 'command her by action', after Francis Bacon's manifesto of the scientific method (Bacon, in Adorno and Horkheimer 1992: 4), is an ideological blind spot in evangelical neoliberalism.

For Friedman, economics is a science that makes things simple. 'A fundamental hypothesis of science is that appearances are deceptive and that there is a way of looking at or interpreting or organizing the evidence that will reveal superficially disconnected and diverse phenomena to be manifestations of a more fundamental and relatively simple structure' (Friedman, 1953: 33). Friedman's belief in a fundamentally simple order of the cosmos, a naturalistic paradigm of basic facts that can be discerned, grasped by empirical scientific method and the individual cognitive faculty of reason was 'impressive'. A former student remembers: 'I was impressed with his ability to get so much mileage out of an extremely simple view of the world.'[5]

Friedman's worldview rests upon an equally simple political anthropology, represented by the figure of *homo economicus* – Economic Man.[6] Political economy, Mill says, 'is concerned with [man] solely as a being who desires to possess wealth, and who is capable of judging the comparative efficacy of means for obtaining that end'. *Homo economicus* is 'a being who inevitably does that by which he may obtain the greatest amount of necessaries, conveniences, and luxuries, with the smallest quantity of labour and physical self-denial with which they can be obtained' (2008: 108). Even though Smith and Mill acknowledge that human beings have motives other than individual self-interest, the anthropological figure of *homo economicus* became taken-for-granted: a hypothetical person who acts rationally, logically, prudently, on the basis of complete knowledge, represented by the price mechanism, out of individual self-interest and the desire for wealth. Successive generations of orthodox liberal economists' mathematical models of 'rational choice theory' rest on the shoulders of *homo economicus*, a puny Atlas.

Homo economicus, a concept of the human being so reductive as to be a caricature, flies in the face of anthropology, psychology, history, philosophy, all of which show how human beings are not motivated solely by instrumental-rational self-interest but more often as not by higher substantive and communicatively rational reasons; reasons of reciprocity and solidarity; sympathy and empathy; love and affection; moral obligations of loyalty and duty. The human being is more than individual *homo economicus*. The person is part of a larger whole, a normative universe; the person is a member of society. Easily refuted empirically, *homo economicus* and the obfuscating mathematical castle in the air that is rational choice theory was the Achilles heel of neoliberalism. Neoliberalism needed a better foundation in moral philosophy. It acquired this by leveraging on the strongest fulcrum of Enlightenment humanism.

The fundamental principle of Enlightenment humanism is that Reason is a universal quality common to all human beings. The person, by virtue of Reason, is simultaneously united with universal humanity and is also a unique and autonomous individual who can freely choose to act. Nozick emphasizes the separateness of persons, the dignity of the individual, in Kant's formulation; that is to say (in the secular Enlightenment equivalent translation from the previous religious worldview), to Nozick the individual is 'sacred': 'individuals are ends and not merely means; they may not be sacrificed or used for the achieving of other ends without their consent. Individuals are inviolable' (Nozick, 1974: 31). By virtue of this Kantian maxim Nozick argues that social goals have an unacceptable cost, namely to individual dignity and personal liberty. Nozick is the originator of the neoliberal principle that 'there is no such thing as society': 'There is no *social entity* ... there are only individual people, different individual people, with their own individual lives' (1974: 33). So strong and far reaching are the rights of the individual that any entity that acts in a collective capacity (a group of individuals, a state, a society) violates the individual's dignity. Taxation, Nozick argues, is tantamount to bonded labour. This resonated with an American public of the late 1960s and early 1970s, especially with a generation whose taxes were spent to fund the Vietnam war, and that was variously disgruntled by conscription, civil rights and affirmative action.

Neoliberalism now is not only value free, objective and morally neutral, as Friedman and Hayek claimed,[7] but, through Nozick, neoliberalism is born again as the evangelical economic-political and moral theology for an anarcho-capitalist utopia: the anarchy of the market enforced by a minimal state stripped down to its authoritarian core:

> The minimal state is morally legitimate; ... no more extensive state could be morally justified, that any more extensive state would (will) violate the rights of individuals. ... The minimal state treats us as inviolate individuals, who may not be used in certain ways by others as means or tools or instruments or resources; it treats us as persons having individual rights with the dignity this constitutes. Treating us with respect by respecting our rights, it allows us, individually or with whom we choose, to choose our life and to realize our ends and our conception of ourselves, insofar as we can, aided by the voluntary cooperation of other individuals possessing the same dignity. How *dare* any state or group of individuals do more. Or less. (Nozick, 1974: 334)

In the genealogy of neoliberalism as political–economic–moral theology we can see a three-fold dialectic of Enlightenment. First, in the metanarrative of modernity, the paradigm shift from religious to secular order entailing the substitution of the former transcendental authority of the divine by Natural law, as revealed by science and Reason; and of foremost importance in this paradigm shift – which is as much a continuity as a shift – the abstract power of the Market as an 'invisible hand' assuming the role of a divine power. Second, modernity's tendencies of disenchantment and nihilism redeemed by political theologies that re-sacralize the profane, secular world by identifying spirit in the immanent order, whether in the people (the nation, *volk*, or the proletariat), articulated by and embodied in the person of the charismatic messianic leader, first as demagogue, later as tyrant demigod. Third, the appropriation of the Kantian principle of Enlightenment humanism as containing the seed of its own destruction: the faculty of Reason by virtue of which people are individuated as the dignified, autonomous citizens of a rational society becomes extrapolated to the point of being inverted and turned inside out to repudiate society as such, leaving only the individual as the subject of anarcho-capitalism.

Towards alternative theologies

Presently we are in a period of intense liminality similar to the period of the 1920s and 1930s. Already we have a transcendental principle and totalitarian power, a power not so much this time around embodied in the person of *il Duce, der Furher* or the Great Leader, but the dictatorial decisionism of the Market – 'let the Market decide' – which is everywhere articulated in anthropomorphic terms as a mythic power – 'the Markets reacted badly today to news of renewed protests in Greece'; 'the further stimulus package approved by Congress has pleased the Markets'. The first commandment in the political theology of neoliberal Market fundamentalism is monotheism: 'There Is No Alternative.' As it is questioned, the truth of the Market is proclaimed even more sternly. This is the political theology of authoritarian neoliberalism. To begin to imagine an alternative to authoritarian neoliberalism and the dictatorship of the Markets we look back to an alternative to Schmitt's project represented by the work of James Joyce.

Schmitt and Joyce, contemporaries, writing from the heartland of Europe in the inter-war years, exemplify two paradigmatically alternative responses to the crisis of modernity. Schmitt stands for the re-assertion of Apollonian logocentrism – naming, defining, clarifying and simplifying the political cultural field: restoring primacy of authority to the decisionism of the sovereign whose word is Law. But Apollo's law-giving *logos*, while it clarifies and simplifies like blazing sunlight, can become an anti-life political theology, just as neoliberalism obliterates the society it purports to serve. In Joyce's work we see the antithesis of Schmitt's. Against the singular *logos* Joyce resurrects a more fundamental *muthos*; a Dionysian gynocentric celebration of *Zoë*, singularity dissolved by the chthonic forces of indestructible life. Whereas Schmitt seeks to end the flux and slippage of discussion through determination by the *logos*, Joyce stands for the over-determination of *muthos*; he destabilizes the *logos*, disassembling, re-combining and generating polysemy; restoring and celebrating the irreducible plurality and inexhaustible fecundity of the social.[8]

The antinomy between Schmitt and Joyce exemplifies problems addressed by Nietzsche in *The Birth of Tragedy* and throughout his work: the need to transcend the rationalism and nihilism of modern civilization by relocating the primordial, mythological and political-anthropological substratum of a human will to power, the source of vital energy that would enable a transvaluation of values and the emergence of 'beyond man'.[9] Nietzsche's central thesis is 'the antithesis of the Dionysian and Apollonian – translated into the realm of metaphysics; history itself as the development of this idea' (Nietzsche, in Kaufmann, 1968: 395). Schmitt and Joyce exemplify history developing this idea in terms of antitheses, alternatives: the Apollonian (ultimately simple) and the Dionysian (always complex and multiple). Socrates, for Nietzsche, is the original synthesis: a 'beyond man' who takes one 'in contact with those extreme points … where he stares into the unfathomable. When to his dismay he here sees how logic coils around itself at these limits and finally bites its own tail' (1995: 54). Socrates surpasses himself through reason and thereby gives birth to new art. This is the *daemonic* or 'musical Socrates', 'dissonance in human form', an embodied synthesis of antitheses, 'chaos in one', hallmarks of the characters of Socrates, Nietzsche and Joyce who gave birth to their respective 'dancing stars' (Nietzsche, 1986: 46). But not Schmitt, whose star, containing only the Apollonian principle of simplification and singularity, implodes into a black hole of deathly gravity.

Ulysses employs myth to achieve clarity against the prevailing chaos of modernity. The dense and formless anomic pluralism of modern mass urbanism is reorganized by Joyce in mythic form so that the significance of mundane contents of modern day-to-day life are grasped from the stream and articulated into a meaningful whole so that the experiences of people in an ordinary day are redeemed as recurrences in an eternal heroic mythic historical cycle. The formlessness of modern existence, whether in Dublin, Trieste or Paris, was the background of political, economic and cultural chaos that reached an apotheosis in Schmitt's Berlin. Schmitt's interventions, *Of the Political* and *Political Theology*, were intended, like Joyce's, to clarify transcendental/fundamental principles upon which order and meaning could be restored. In Schmitt's case the chaos and decadence of 1920s Berlin, fed by many sources, had its political correspondence in Weimar's 'degenerate decisionism ... clinging to the normative power of the factual' (Schmitt, 2006: 3), a government that administered but that did not rule – as today the national governments of Ireland, Italy and Greece do under the Troika, and where the language of politics has been replaced by the technical jargons of economics; all decisions being determined by what are purported to be 'the simple economic facts of the matter'; the 'bottom line'; the reviews, audits, reports, forecasts and 'necessary measures' determined by the Troika's economic technocrats and communicated by local politicians as puppets. There are no alternatives to be debated democratically; simply the normative power of the factual decides; the purportedly natural laws of the Market, to which there is no alternative.

Against this, Schmitt sought a re-vitalized politics by identifying the principle of the political, making the friend/enemy distinction (Schmitt, 2007: 26) and by asserting transcendent sovereignty in terms of the ability to decide 'on the exception' to the routine application of rules and procedures. 'The exception confounds the unity and order of the rationalist scheme. ... In the exception the power of real life breaks through the crust of a mechanism that has become torpid by repetition' (Schmitt, 2006: 15). Sovereign is he who 'decides whether there is an emergency as well as what must be done to eliminate it' (Schmitt, 2006: 7). Such sovereign leadership restores the transcendent religious and mythical core of moral authority that had become hollowed out by the disenchantment of the world so that the modern liberal state, epitomized by Weimar, had become a headless, formless empty shell operating only by the blind automatism of its own bureaucratic instrumental-rational legalistic processes, much as juridified technocratic administrative procedures today substitute for politics and leave both nation states and the supra-states of the post-national constellation such as post-republican Ireland under the Troika and more generally the whole EU in a condition of chronic legitimation crisis and democratic deficit.

Cyclops/sovereign/dictator

We are presently tyrannized by a headless, formless empty shell operating by the blind automatism of its own instrumental-rational legalistic processes – hammering on the principles of the Market, a return to growth by cuts and austerity, an enormous rough beast with 'a gaze blank and pitiless as the sun' (Yeats, 1920a: 11) insisting that 'there is no alternative'. To look for alternatives we will begin with the famous episode of *Ulysses* wherein the Cyclops appears as the archetype and prototype of the sovereign: an autochthonous 'son of the soil', the monstrous primal father, the primordial One, a singular vision unclouded by the complexities of civilization, whose word is law and whose decisive action fixes the political in terms of friend/enemy distinctions.

The Cyclops as sovereign is powerful and dangerous, and Joyce understood this ambivalence better, and earlier, than did Schmitt, so after *Ulysses* Joyce keeps his other giant, Finnegan, asleep, whereas Schmitt wants to reawaken the giant to restore rule over the confused and decadent liberal democratic age of men.

In Vico's (1999: 244) interpretation the Cyclops is a mytho-poetic representation of logocentrism. His singular eye represents the clearing burnt in the forest: nature subdued by fire and hostile enemies defeated in combat. The giant clears the ground and constitutes the original settlement: kith and kin, family and friends under the protection of the sovereign within the territorial circle; hostile enemies and strangers outside. This is the primordial form of the political. This paleo-anthropological literalism in the mytho-poetic imagination is in turn a figurative and metaphorical representation of the 'settlement' in the forest of symbols that is achieved by the primal father's *Logos* – his naming, his law, his truth. The Cyclops is the sovereign dictator, man and god con-fused in the giant; the singular primal Father before he becomes differentiated, abstracted and symbolically transfigured into deified attributes such as the collective representations of Apollo and Dionysus. The clearing and settlement represented by the Cyclopean giant is the logocentric *point de capiton* that anchors and fixes the field of differences and the flux of the social; the point around which the construction and institutionalization of the symbolic order begins. Rule in the singular field established by the sovereign Cyclops would be liberal, permissive in the Dionysian sense of giving free rein to passionate instincts, but only within the parameters of filial loyalty to the Apollonian Father. In political theology the Father appears as the Dictator; in economic theology he appears as the Market. Schmitt would reawaken this giant. In Germany this meant Hitler, the primal Father as the incarnated/sublimated will of the *volk*; the Fuhrer as the sovereign mythico-religious, man-giant-hero-god whose decisionistic leadership restored rule to a singular political field clarified and polarized by unambiguous friend/enemy distinctions. In our present age of authoritarian neoliberalism this means the agency of the self-interested political-anthropological ideal-type subject of *homo economicus*, whose liberty is ensured by the state as upholder and enforcer of the natural law of Market.

Politics seeks to establish a logos as *point de capiton*, a capital/captain/ quilting point, the stamp of the Father's authority so that action is ordered 'in the name of the Father' in the field of difference around which diverse individual subject positions can be articulated in a chain of equivalences that identifies them in terms of their opposition to an enemy Other as constitutive outside. This is what is at stake in Bloom's encounter with Dublin's Cyclops – Nelson, hero of the British Empire on the one hand, and the subaltern Irish nationalist Citizen on the other.

Britannia ruled the waves because Nelson waived the rules[10] and imposed his will on the rolling chaos that is battle conditions – battle conditions being the quintessential Schmittian state of exception, 'a case of extreme peril ... that cannot be circumscribed factually and made to conform to a preformed law' (Schmitt, 2006: 6). In a celebrated incident at the battle of Copenhagen Nelson 'turned a blind eye' to a signal to withdraw from the Admiral of the Fleet, placing the telescope to his blind eye saying 'I see no signal' and pressing ahead with his attack. 'Never mind about manoeuvres, always go straight at 'em' he famously advised his own Captains when he became Admiral himself. On another front, recuperating in Naples after the battle of the Nile, Nelson flouted convention by openly having an affair with the wife of the British Envoy. By these exceptional decisions Nelson made himself more sovereign than the Sovereign, as it were. This was the source of his tremendous charismatic authority.[11]

Nelson is a prototypical modern Schmittian leader-*cum*-dictator because he incarnated an authority superior to the law by his will to power in deciding on the exception and by his relentless clarity in defining his enemy.[12] Nelson's captaincy was defined by a characteristic articulatory practice of uniting the multiple and divided English – the officers and men under his command, the Admiralty and the Ministry, the Aristocracy, Parliament and the popular masses: all should be prepared to die in the name of an England, a name of the Father that he not merely represented but embodied: 'England expects that every man will do his duty' was his famous signal commencing the battle of Trafalgar.

Nelson's Column stands in Trafalgar Square, a clearing at the geographical centre of London.[13] Four lions representing dominion over Nature and disciplined ferocity sit at his feet facing north, south, east and west. Piccadilly, the National Gallery and the commercial heart of the city shelter safely at Nelson's back. Down the Mall to his right is Buckingham Palace. Before him lie Whitehall, the War Office, the Admiralty, Scotland Yard, the Foreign Office and the Home Office – the imperial military and security apparatus; and beyond that, overseen by his gaze, Downing Street and Westminster; to his left, the east, the banks and financial houses of the City. Nelson is the *point de capiton* that quilts this vast historical tapestry of modern England. He stands at the centre of the world-conquering civilization that is assembled around him. Nelson–Cyclops–Apollo holds this symbolic place of honour because he made the world open for nineteenth-century globalization –the expansion of British capitalism, industry and finance, trade and commerce, science and engineering, culture and language across a whole globe cleared by British naval power.

Ulysses' other Cyclops, the Citizen, is diminutive compared with Nelson. Nelson structures the whole city without saying a word. Nelson's name is only mentioned in passing a few times in *Ulysses*, but the hallmark of power, the Law of the Father, is that 'it goes without saying'; whereas the Citizen, though verbose, has only idle words.[14] The citizens of Dublin live under the baleful gaze of this powerful Cyclops.[15] And the nationalist citizen is not an antinomy or an alternative to Nelson – an Other – but the smaller Cyclops is a subaltern mime of the greater, as today it is not that a national sovereign government would in any way be an alternative to the Troika. The lesser Cyclops is fully possessed by the spirit of the greater.

Cyclops Schmitt

We can see Schmitt's identity with the Cyclops in their logocentrism: that form of life wherein the giant's word, his *logos*, is Law. Logocentrism is the desire for a centre; an original guarantee of all meanings. Logocentrism, Derrida (1991) claims, has characterized Western thought since Plato; in Judeo-Christian scripture, for instance: 'In the beginning was the Word: the Word was with God and the Word was God.' According to Vico (1999) for the Greeks *logos* (the Greek term for speech, thought, law or reason) appears through the mytho-poetic metaphor of the Cyclops as the primordial form of sovereignty, the original name of the Father.[16]

There is an affinity between logocentrism and proto-fascistic authoritarianism, whether conventional political tyranny or the post-political tyranny of the Market as lawmaker. The Law as understood by Schmitt is more than legal positivism: it has what Derrida calls a metaphysical surplus. Schmitt's Law is founded upon a 'Metaphysics of Presence'; metaphysical in that 'it bases itself on certain assumptions, for example the founding notions of Greek philosophy: *ousia* (substance), *nous* (reason), *logos* (thought/speech), *telos* (goal), and so on' (Derrida, in Hart, 2004: 55). Moreover, this 'Metaphysics of Presence' presupposes and relies upon a 'Transcendental Signified', or ultimately self-sufficient meaning, 'a pure intelligibility tied to an absolute logos: the face of God. This history of the sign, of the Law, that is coextensive with the history of logocentrism is essentially theological' (Derrida, 1991: 32). Thus, according to Derrida, logocentrism is onto-theological. Schmitt's onto-theological logocentrism is a political theology that systematically deprecates and repudiates difference in favour of identity and presence, and seeks the eradication of polysemy, mixture and ambiguity in favour of the singular, the certain, the identical and the pure: – *ein Volk, ein Reich, ein Fuhrer*. Logocentrism is the elementary foundation of fascism and other authoritarian totalitarian discourses. Neoliberal market fundamentalism is the current idiom of logocentrism.

Day into night: from *Ulysses* to the *Wake*

Against a backdrop of chaos and anomie Joyce's aesthetic political project was to restore order and coherence by constructing a new, 'reasonable' myth, the Modern Ulysses. But no sooner had *Ulysses* appeared, in 1922, the year Mussolini came to power, than Joyce confronted a new problem. Myth was increasingly becoming the new ordering principle of modern life. We saw the 'intensification of myth' in the phantasmagorias of consumerism and mass culture (Benjamin, 1999; Horkheimer and Adorno, 1992) and the systematic political deployment of myth by Mussolini, Hitler, Stalin and indeed by de-Valera, leaders as supermen, as demigods, leading their people on divinely ordained paths. This meant that after *Ulysses* the aesthetic/political use of myth could no longer be to restore order to chaos, but, as Benjamin also realized, to use myth against myth, to tell dialectical fairy tales to awaken Europe from its collective dream sleep. Between the day book and the night book Joyce engaged in an entirely opposite aesthetic-political project: where previously he sought to restore order to chaos through myth, now he sought, through *Finnegans Wake*, to deliberately dis-order the new mythoscapes of totalitarian singularities. Anticipating Fascist and other totalitarian authorities and their singular identities and certainties, like today's theology of the Market, Joyce 'declared war in language and on language and by language, which gave languages' (Derrida, 1984: 146). Joyce subjects 'each atom of writing to fission in order to overload the unconscious with the whole memory of man: mythologies, religions, philosophies, sciences, psychoanalysis, litera-tures' (Derrida, 1984: 149). Joyce asserts the multiplicity and plurality of forms of life, the irreducibility of difference and the infinities of interpretation and discussion by writing a book that would not submit itself either to the Enlightenment's panoptical principle of Reason and transparent legibility, to the dictator's prerogative of the last word, or to the divine Market's 'invisible hand'.

Joyce reinvented modern literature twice. *Ulysses* mythologizes to restore order to chaos: modern urban mass society's people of no consequence or qualities are restored to their full humanity, an utterly realist and reasonable book in which people's outer lives and inner processes are attended to with scrupulous care. But whereas *Ulysses* is an Apollonian book that 'represents the most arduous attempt to give physiognomy to chaos' *Finnegans Wake* is Dionysian; it 'defines itself as chaosmos and microchasm and constitutes the most terrifying document of formal instability and semantic ambiguity that we possess' (Eco, 1982: 61). Whereas *Ulysses* may correspond to Freud's *Interpretation of Dreams* with its Apollonian promise of clarity through systematic reflexive self-analysis, in *Finnegans Wake*, by that same self-analysis the unconscious (the Real) returns to its place as the Dionysian kernel that resists analysis and reconciliation and remains the source of discontented fission underpinning the libidinal economy of Civilization: 'one continuous present tense integument slowly unfolded all marryvoising moodmoulded cyclewheeling history (thereby, he said, reflecting from his own individual person life unlivable, transaccidentated through the slow fires of consciousness into a divisual chaos, perilous, potent, common to allflesh, human only, mortal)' (Joyce, 1995: 186).

Against calls for Apollonian simplicity Joyce insists that 'every honest to goodness man in the land of the space of today knows that his back life will not stand being written about in black and white' and it is only through 'putting truth and untruth together a shot may be made at what this hybrid actually was like' (Joyce, 1995: 169). The dictator's singularity appears in the *Wake* linked in a chain of equivalences that includes Wellington (the Iron Duke), *Il Duce* (Mussolini), Bismarck (the Iron Chancellor), Stalin (the Man of Steel), the tribal giant Finn McCool and the old FearyFather – *Fuhrer*, Finnegan. The shadow of 'the great Finnleader himself on his high horse' (1995: 214) frightens the washerwomen; we hear his bombastic radio broadcasts (1995: 593). The coming catastrophe is foretold by Joyce as Shem the Penman: 'sniffer of carrion, premature gravedigger, seeker of the nest of evil in the bosom of good word, you who sleep at our vigil and fast at our feast, you with your dislocated reason, have cutely foretold ... death with every disaster, the dynamitization of colleagues, the reducing of records to ashes, the leveling of all customs by blazes ... (O hell, here comes our funeral!)' (1995: 189).

Anticipating the *anschlauss* of authoritarian levelling machines Joyce wrote an unreadable, unfinishable book that as it ends it begins-again, a machine to generate ambiguity and polysemy: 'a vicoclycometer, collideoscope, prototeifoem graph, polyhedron of scripture, meanderthale, a work of doublecrossing twofold truths and devising tail-words' (Joyce, in Eco, 1982: 66). To see how Joyce's gift might help us to survive what was – and what is coming again – we must approach it theologically, as Joyce intended: his model and inspiration was the Book of Kells:

'Ho, talk save us!':[17] God's gift of democratic speech

> And the earth was of one tongue, and of the same speech. And when they removed from the east, they found a plain in the land of Sennaar, and dwelt in it. And each one said to his neighbour: come, let us make brick, and bake them with fire. And they had brick instead of stones, and slime instead of mortar: And they said: Come, let us make a city and a tower, the top whereof may reach to heaven; and let us make our name famous before we be scattered abroad into all lands. And the Lord came down to see the city and the tower, which the children of Adam were building. And he said: Behold, it is one people, and all have one tongue: and they have begun to do this, neither

will they leave off from their designs, til they accomplish them in deed. Come ye, therefore, let us go down, and there confound their tongue, that they may not understand one another's speech. And so the Lord scattered them from that place into all lands, and they ceased to build the city. And therefore the name thereof was called Babel, because there the language of the whole earth was confounded: and from thence the Lord scattered them abroad upon the face of all countries. (*Genesis*, 11: 19).

The Tower of Babel is the prototype totalitarian form of singularity. It is a construction based on Apollonian logocentrism, built by one people united under a tyrant-king, of one tongue and the same speech. Their unambiguous and singular symbols – bricks baked in fire – enable them to suture the social, despite the slipperiness of language, so that they can close the cosmic gap between Heaven and Earth. They are driven to this quest for security out of their fear and vulnerability, of their being scattered. The hubristic singular quest for fame, certainty of identity, one people under one name, united by singular ideas and perfect forms, can only be accomplished by the tyrannical elimination of ambiguity and polysemy. Then the city and the tower can be built systematically and completed – a final solution, a *Reich* that will last for a thousand years; a workers' Utopia fulfilling the immutable laws of History; a futurist technological sublime; the panoptical, fully enlightened Earth that radiates disaster triumphant; the end of History; a global Market wherein all social relations are commodified; an Olympian world ruled by Platonic philosopher-kings illuminated by eternal ideas. It is at the point where the quest is well underway that the Lord intervenes. 'The Lord' here is a collective representation of the power of society, as in Durkheim's (1974: 52) classic formulation – 'divinity is society configured and expressed symbolically'. In this case the 'Lord' that intervenes is the Dionysian aspect of society as infinite field of differences, the inexhaustible presence of lively multiplicity that persists against the tyranny of Apollonian logocentrism, that confounds the tongues, subverts understanding, prevents the construction of the city and the tower, and from there the people are scattered abroad to all lands, and the whole cycle begins again. The Tower of Babel stands for the archetype of the fascist form that collective life tends towards under the singular rule of Apollonian logocentrism: *ein logos, ein langue, ein volk*. God's gift is the Dionysian scattering, the confusion of tongues. The Fall (into language and history) that is the collective, transcendent power of the multiplicity and diversity of the social, just as it protects us from the fascism of Market totalitarianism, also prevents the realization of the perfect communication of Enlightenment Reason, but while it is anti-Utopian in both directions, paradoxically, the lack generates the desire to build the Tower of Babel. Theological amnesia, forgetting God, losing our ability to apprehend the transcendent idea of collective life in terms of the tension and equilibrium between Dionysus and

Apollo is one of the conditions of possibility for political theology, and underpins the libidinal economy, the fear of confusion and the desire to restore order. By virtue of God's second gift, the gift of a Dionysian confusion of tongues, desire for communication and understanding is reintroduced into the world in a way that reproduces the constitutive antagonism of the social, the conditions of possibility for human being together and learning again how to build and to dwell with one another. The confusion of tongues, God's gift, is a political-theological gift that Joyce seeks to remind us of and restore to us in *Finnegans Wake*.

Political theology and the arts of politics

As darkness is falling over Europe and the hawks of war are circling, the washerwomen on the riverbank tell the eternal tale of Shem and Shaun (Cain and Abel; Gilgamesh and Enkidu; Michael and Lucifer; Black and White; Man and Woman; Aryan and Semite; Irish and English), enemies who are 'All Livia's daughter-sons. Dark hawks hear us' (Joyce, 1995: 215). Friend and enemy do not stand dichotomously opposed to one another, but, as Joyce shows, dialectically and communicatively, as mutually sustaining constitutive outsides they incorporate and contain one another within each other – the other is the Other in my interior. In the *Wake* the One, 'Shem the Penman', Semitic, effeminate, creative, artistic; the Other, 'Shaun the Post', Aryan, rigid, bully-German-speaking model of the petty-bureaucrat functionary in the power/knowledge/communication nexus – the Post Office – cannot be understood in terms of the reductive polarity of either friends or enemies. Shem and Shaun are joined to each other through an irrational complex of emotions of which they are not in control. This is the model of all relations between human beings, for Joyce. All human relations have this coloration of uncertainty, jealousy, hostility and affection: the usual name for this hodge-podge is 'friendship' (Ellmann, 1982: 312).

Contemporary social and political thought is in the grip of desire for clarification and transparency, separation and re-ordering, for simplification, re-regulation by post-national dictatorial powers like the EU/IMF/ECB Troika. But the lesson to be learned from Schmitt is that the assertion of Apollonian logocentrism to re-order the political field in terms of singularity can become conjoined with Dionysian atavism, so that the form that emerges is an intensified, authoritarian neoliberalism; regulation, not *of* the market *by* the state, but *by* the market *with* the state. The growing form is global authoritarian neoliberalism: the rough beast supported by the riot squad, the police force and the army.

Notes

1 A recent compendium (deVries and Sullivan, 2006) describes the field of 'political theology' in terms of the re-emergence of religion into politics and public life, both as resistances to globalization and as responses to internal crises and exhaustions of Enlightenment-derived institutions and discourses, the absence of higher values and transcendent meaning. Political theology refers to a proliferation of zones of cross-over between the spiritual/religious/theological and the political, realms that had been conventionally taken to be separate spheres of value and action. But this mapping of the field of usage is perhaps too general and inclusive, and the reluctance to decide what fits within and what falls without the field of discussion is itself symptomatic of the conditions that gave rise to the term in the first place. That modern political and legal principles are secular rational reformulations of what were originally religious ideas is not exclusively Schmitt's insight. Durkheim had noted that all modern institutions have their foundations in religion and that religion 'is an essential and permanent aspect of humanity' (1995: 3). The return of the theological in contemporary politics should be of no surprise, for it had never gone away.

2 In the 2012 US Presidential election both Obama and Romney professed themselves economic neoliberals; the only minor difference between Democrats and Republicans being Obama's espousal of generic utilitarianism and Romney's (and Ryan's) explicit Aynn Rand 'objectivism'.

3 Nozick, a thirty-year-old Harvard philosophy prodigy, surfing on the wave of youth culture, issued a moral challenge: 'How dare they,' he said, infringe on the right of the person not to be conscripted by the state and sent to war.

4 Mill and Smith were strongly influenced by Hume's theory of human nature. The matrix, the womb, as it were, within which Hume's (amongst others') theory of human nature gestated, is the larger paradigm of Natural law. Natural law is the paternal discourse of the natural rights of individuals. The laws of Nature govern the universe, fundamental principles that can be apprehended and analysed by the scientific method and articulated in terms of reason. Human beings are creatures of nature, endowed with reason; as such their actions are governed by reason. Morality is grounded in human nature, and universally valid moral principles can be analysed and discovered by reason and positive scientific method. Antithetical to the divine right of kings, Natural law is the basis of natural rights, rights that are not contingent on the beliefs, customs or traditions of any particular society or form of government, but are, like the laws of Nature, essentially simple: universal, transcendent, inviolable and inalienable.

5 Leonard Rapping, cited in Klamer (1983: 220).

6 Autobiographically, Friedman saw his own life experiences and historical events as factual evidence that people are rational and autonomous, that economic and social systems are inherently stable and self-stabilizing. Friedman was the child of first-generation Hungarian–Ukrainian Jewish immigrants who ran a small shop in New Jersey (like a grocer's daughter in England who became a fervent believer in his economic theology). He worked throughout his student years, 'pulling himself up by his own bootstraps', as it were, by maximizing utility, pursuing his own individual rational choices (though enjoying the benefit of scholarships to cover his fees). He also ascribed much of his success in life to 'just plain good luck!'

7 By this time the metaphysical baggage of deism had been mostly discarded in the paradigm shift from religious to naturalistic cosmology, but science's transcendental

claims had become morally threadbare in the aftermath of the Holocaust and during the cold war nuclear stand-off.

8 Joyce is the father of *écriture féminine, avant la lettre* as it were, while at the same time, in Schmittian fashion, he establishes himself as the singular and supreme sovereign authority!

9 Nietzsche's work is infused with a deep ambiguity, and he has been taken up ambivalently by Zionists, National Socialists, Anarchists and Modernists alike. Nietzsche's influence came to Schmitt indirectly, through Weber, and later, corruptly, through the selective appropriation of Nietzsche by the Nazis. Joyce read some Nietzsche as early as 1903 (probably through Yeats's influence). *Dubliners* may be read as an indictment of the world of 'last men', and Nietzsche's celebration of Jewish intellectuality in European civilization may have given Joyce some of his inspiration for Leopold Bloom. But neither Schmitt nor Joyce could be called Nietzscheans. The point is not the explicit connections between Schmitt, Joyce and Nietzsche, but rather the ways in which Schmitt and Joyce are implicated in the dialectical drama of modern European civilization of which Nietzsche provides such a rich formulation.

10 In contrast to Wellington, a conservative aristocrat and a cautious commander who purchased his military commissions, Nelson's advancement in the Royal Navy was meritocratic – despite (or rather because of) his insubordination. As a teenage midshipman on a mission to the Northwest Passage he went AWOL to shoot a polar bear, saying his father would like the pelt; as Master and Commander he frequently set sail in advance of orders, and returned to port without waiting to be recalled if he felt a mission was futile; as Captain he often broke formation from the ships of the line to engage the enemy on terms that he chose rather than by following the orthodox strategies.

11 Nelson considered standing for Parliament on a number of occasions, and were it not for his untimely death at Trafalgar it is possible that history would remember him as a political leader rather than as a military hero.

12 At Trafalgar Nelson refused advice to disguise himself; as his decorations were all for military valour he said it was important that they should be seen by the enemy, a display that cost him his life as he was singled out and shot by a sniper.

13 A similar (smaller) Nelson's Column stood at the centre of Dublin, overlooking the subaltern city. Wellington was born in Dublin and is memorialized there by an obelisk. But as in London, where the Wellington monument is at the rear of the Palace (attesting to his second-rate stature in the symbolic order of the Empire), in Dublin similarly Wellington stands far from the city centre.

14 But the Citizen is a subaltern giant in his own right. Joyce's model for the Citizen is Michael Cusack, founder of the Gaelic Athletic Association, an organization now 125 years old, with 3000 clubs, several hundred thousand members and millions of fans, a core Irish social institution. Cusack may legitimately claim to have imposed his sovereign mark on the political-cultural landscape too. Like Nelson, Cusack was a Captain, in this case not on the battlefield but on the playing field. A formidable athlete, Cusack, like Nelson, was willfully insubordinate and uppity. A show-off, he dressed in the anachronistic manner of an Irish tribal chieftain, his sporting medals pinned to his chest, and he introduced himself 'I'm Citizen Cusack from the Parish of Carron in the Barony of Burren in the County of Clare, you Protestant dog!' (Ellmann, 1982: 61).

15 As much as seeing Cyclopes like Nelson and the Citizen as villains, dictators-in-the-making, Joyce identified with them. Like Nelson and Cusack Joyce saw himself in

Schmittian terms as singular, sovereign and exceptional. An abiding concern, bordering on an obsession, with differentiating between friends and enemies and identifying moments of betrayal as decisive moments in historical, autobiographical and fictional narratives runs as a red thread throughout Joyce's work, and is for him a *leitmotif* of Irish political culture; and like Apollo, Joyce flayed his enemies alive in the pages of his books. Like Nelson and Cusack Joyce was of modest origins, but wilful and combative. He consistently refused to know his place and in the face of indifference and hostility he persevered, confident always of his own genius. Joyce's whole project, as Lacan (1975) has argued, was to become a God-like Father to himself, to take command, overturn and reinvent the entire literary canon. He would 'keep the Professors busy for three hundred years', he once laughed, and in full seriousness at the climax in his own *mein kampf* (the *Portrait*) Joyce declared that he sought nothing less than to re-create Adam: 'to forge in the smithy of my soul the uncreated conscience of my race'. (Joyce, 2003: 217) One-eyed like Nelson, single-mindedly determined in his artistic cause as Cusack was in his, flouting his scandalous union with Nora, a Vichian giant who was sovereign ruler of the clearing that he cut out for himself in the forest of modernity, the Cyclops for Joyce is not a figure of deprecation, but on the contrary one to be admired and emulated, a sovereign god-like authority who makes decisive actions that shape the historical, political and cultural landscape by virtue of his will to power.

16 Developing Derrida, Cixous (1976) says that 'phallogocentrism' is the operative principle of culture that is male-dominated. Just as the phallus is implicitly (or explicitly) assumed to be the only significant sexual organ, the masculine is accepted as the central point of reference, the only source of validity and authority. Women and others are defined only in terms of their relation to men, only in terms of what they lack.

17 Joyce (1995: 215).

6

Conversion: Turning towards a radiant ideal

Love as a mediating and unifying power between neoliberal *eros* and political-theological *agape*

> The interests of rulers require that their subjects should be poor in spirit, and that there should be no strong bond of friendship or society among them, and love, above all other motives, is likely to inspire this, as our Athenian tyrants learned by experience, for love ... had a strength that undid their power. (Plato, 1892: *Symposium*, 10)

In a post-Catholic, materialist, secular-cynical Ireland, if we are interested in what kind of power we might hope to set against the contemporary tyrannies of authoritarian neoliberal political-theologies we might do well to begin again with Plato's *Symposium*, the first formulation of the power of love. The discourse begins with Phaedrus' celebration of the body and the joys of erotic love in terms of the power of love as 'the eldest and noblest and mightiest of the gods, and the chiefest author and giver of happiness and virtue' (Plato, 1892: 8). Next we hear Pausanias' argument for a higher form of love – of the soul – mind, reason, but also and in the interests of that higher form of love, for the strict limitation of carnal *eros*: 'Evil is the vulgar lover who loves the body rather than the soul, and who is inconstant because he is a lover of the inconstant' (1892: 11). Eryximachus, anticipating a principle developed later by Aristotle, now moderates the conversation, arguing for a harmonious balance between passionate and disinterested love, mediated by temperance and justice: 'in all other things human as well as divine, both loves [love of the body and of the soul] ought to be noted as far as may be, for they are both present'. Such a considered and temperate moderation 'is the source of all our happiness and friendship' (1892: 14).

But just as we are getting somewhere the conversation takes a regressive turn, towards an alluring image that we are still in the grip of today, namely

Aristophanes' famous metaphor of love in terms of individuals pursuing their lost soul-mates:

> We are disunited halves of what was once a united whole, and we go in search of our original unity. And when one of them finds his other half ... the pair are lost in an amazement of love and friendship and intimacy ... for human nature was originally one and we were a whole, and the desire and pursuit of the whole is called love. ... If all of us obtained our love, and each one had his particular beloved, thus returning to his original nature, then our race would be happy. And if this would be best of all, that which would be best under present circumstances would be the nearest approach to such a union. (1892: 17, 18)

Modern romantic love and its discontents are here anticipated by Aristophanes in terms of individualized searching for 'the nearest approach to such a union'; an elusive life-partner soul mate through whom and in whom one may find true love and fulfilment: an erroneous pursuit, of course, for it is premised on a fantastic conceit of identitarianism (the wholeness of a primordial singular identity that can be recovered), whose conditions of possibility of realization, however implausible in other historical and anthropological forms of life, are, under the conditions of modernity, intensified and amplified. Aristophanes' formulation eschews society. Love is an entirely private individualistic, psychologistic matter for the subject as existential monad pursuing his/her individual self-interested actions in an unlimited market of possible partners. In this Aristophanes' formulation anticipates the mass psychology of neoliberalism, the utilitarianism of our 'present circumstances' – that 'the nearest approach to such a union' would be 'best for all'. Recent sociology's investigations find love in modernity very much in the grip of Aristophanes' premises: Giddens's (1992) account of the intensified search for true love under contemporary conditions of 'transformation of intimacy', the emergence of 'plastic sexuality' and the search for the 'pure relationship'; Beck and Beck-Gernsheim's (1995, 2002) 'individuation' thesis and Bauman's (2003) account of 'liquid love', 'semi-detached relationships' contingent on the existential conditions of modernity's liquefaction of social institutions – 'no long term', no stabilization structures that would enable character formation and life-long relationships – are all contemporary elaborations of Aristophanes' thesis: modernity is an amplification and intensification of the liberal utilitarian formulation of romantic love identified (in passing, and quickly passed over) in the *Symposium*.

The liberal individualized autonomous subject's free pursuit of their desire in a marketplace of relationships as ideology and mass psychology of neoliberalism reaches an apotheosis in what Taylor (2007) identifies in *A Secular Age* as the existential ethics of an entirely de-transcendentalized and immanent ontological and epistemological order wherein the subject in the name of emancipation and authentic self-actualization deliberately seeks out and transgresses whatever remaining taboos exist. Contemporary neoliberalism under the banner of the search for authenticity values what amounts to no more than a decadent recurrence of fornication. In our contemporary cities of Sodom and Gomorrah there are fewer and fewer repressive constraints – the incest taboo and control of violations of childhood sexuality being amongst the last remaining – and the anxiety surrounding children, violence and protection is itself indicative of the weakening of social prohibitions (Jenks, 1996: 136). The result of this is the diminution of the conditions of possibility of 'aim inhibited love' that Freud (1961) argues are the very foundations of civilization, that is, strong social superego injunctions on *eros* that, its aims thereby inhibited, become repressed, returning either in distorted form or, more importantly from the point of view of our present concerns, *eros* is not redirected and sublimated into higher forms of *philia* and *agape*. If the discontents of our civilization were, previously, characterized typically by neuroses and frequently by perversions – *eros* distorted by the power of repression, exemplified by child sexual and physical abuse in the church and church-run state institutions – the discontents of our contemporary civilization appear as *eros* liberated and discharging itself extravagantly, but formlessly and insatiably, and at the expense of the stunting and atrophy of institutions of *philia* and *agape*. And even as *eros* flourishes at the expense of *philia* and *agape*, it only appears to flourish. With other forms of love underdeveloped, all of the weight falls upon *eros'* puny wings. Contemporary people place all of their hopes and dreams of friendship and solidarity, purpose in life and even its ultimate meaning in their erotic intimate romantic relationships. Suffering under such disproportionate expectations *eros* cannot bear the weight, and contemporary relationships frequently collapse in mutual disappointment and resentment.

The social processes identified in terms of sexuality's 'plasticity' and the search for the 'pure relationship', 'individuation' and the turbulence and flux of institutions in liquid modernity can only end in frustration and disappointment. Of the three sociologists – Giddens, Beck and Bauman – Bauman has by far the darker view of what the malaise of modern love is symptomatic of – not as the birth pangs of a new level of emancipation in the form of the democratization of intimate relations (Giddens) for a reflexively self-actualizing subject (Beck), but, on the contrary, the contemporary subject unhappy in love as like the refugee: the isolated non-person of a post-social order existing as vulnerable monad without the support of institutions, without community and solidarity, without the protection of law and citizenship, harbinger of the general human condition in an age of global liminality. Pursuing *eros* even further cannot get us out of this predicament, for we are blinded to higher forms of love by our contemporary version of Aristophanes' conceit. Bauman redirects us back towards a higher road, echoing Hannah Arendt's (1955) call in *Men in Dark Times* for a reactivation of philanthropy as the necessary basis of recollecting humanity.

Meanwhile, back at the Symposium ... Agathon speaks next, stepping over Aristophanes' liberal-individual reductionism, reviewing and modifying some of what has been said already by others, though now drawing attention to love's affinity with grace, beauty, justice and temperance, evidenced by love's power in resolving and preventing conflict. The attribute that defines love over any other 'is his grace, which is universally admitted to be in an especial manner the attribute of Love ... force comes not near him neither does he act by force. For all serve him of their own free will, and where there is love as well as obedience, there, as the laws which are the lords of the city say, is justice' (Plato, 1892: 21). *Eros'* individualistic pursuit of egoistic self-interest can only take place within the context of the institutional order of the city as a whole to which individual egos are subordinate; an institutional order whereby conflict has been resolved or ameliorated by love's mediating power. Love appears now as a higher form than *eros*, the fraught pursuits of individuals, namely in the form of *philia* manifested in the social institutions that transcend individual egoism and selfishness, the transpersonal normative order of society in which philanthropy is manifested in graceful reciprocity, recognition and due consideration, equity, fairness, and justice in individual interactions and social relations.

Eventually we hear Socrates' famous formulation of *philosophia* – love of the beautiful, and through beauty love of the true and the good. One proceeds from recognition of another's beauty to appreciation of Beauty as it exists apart from any individual, to consideration of divinity, the source of Beauty, to love of Divinity, the transcendent plane and source of the ideas upon which social institutions, the laws of the city, rest; that they partake of and aspire towards. This level of love corresponds to *agape*: love as abstraction to pure and universal forms of Beauty, Truth and the Good, radiant Ideals that transform those who turn towards them and whose actions are guided by them. Socrates tells us that this is not his own original wisdom but that he is passing on the wisdom of Diotima, a wise woman whom he says was his instructress in this and many other things. Socrates' passing on something handed down from another emphasizes the social nature of wisdom; that these are not individuals' ideas but collective representations. Collective representations, as Durkheim says, are 'the product of an immense cooperation that extends not only through space but also through time; to make them a multitude of different minds have associated, intermixed and combined their experience and knowledge. A very special intellectuality that is infinitely richer and more complex than that of the individual is distilled in them ... ingenious instruments of thought which human groups have painstakingly forged over centuries, and in which they have amassed the best of their intellectual capital' (Durkheim, 1995: 15). In collective representations the experience of previous generations is distilled and handed down as tradition – 'tra dere' 'to give': that which is gifted and handed down from generation to generation, institution-alized as norms and shared conventions and expressed in the doxai, the opinions of ordinary people, represented in Symposium by Socrates' drinking companions. The collective ideas that constitute the city thereby transcend and govern the individual, and love is to be understood as that unified and unifying power that reconciles individual interests with the collective life of the city by constituting mediating normative institutions. Love, Diotima explains, Socrates relates, is neither a god nor a mortal, but is 'in a mean between them ... he is a great spirit and like all that is spiritual he is interme-diate between the divine and the mortal ... [Love is] a spiritual power ... which interprets and conveys to the gods the prayers and the sacrifices of men, and to the men the commands and the rewards of the gods ... [Love is] a power [which] spans the chasm which divides them ... [so that] all is bound together ... through this power all the intercourse and speech of God with man ... is carried on.' Love appears here as an anticipation of a contemporary formulation of a normative communicative power oriented to mutual under-standing. Love 'is the child conceived from the union of Poros [plenty] and Penia [poverty]'; the spirit of a mean between extremes, working hard to find equity and equilibrium to resolve the dilemmas, ambivalences and paradoxes of collective life (Plato, 1892: 522–524ff).

Love formulated in terms of its being a unifying power that seeks a mean to moderate and mediate between extremes of immanence and transcendence, individual and society, poverty and plenty helps us to address the challenge posed by Charles Taylor's A Secular Age (2007). Taylor formulates the source of the malaise of contemporary secular civilization in terms of a lost sense of transcendence and ultimate meaning. The source of this lack, and what is necessary to restore spiritual fullness, Taylor argues, is divine (specifically the Christian version of) agape, a unifying divine love emanating from a transcen-dental plane, something repudiated by the secular age and its immanent orders, but something that cannot be substituted for by human eros – espe-cially a specifically modern form of eros that in the name of authentic self-realization and in search of a missing sense of deeper meaning and higher purpose has made a value of erotic excess and normative transgression as ends in themselves. Modernity is that form of life that imagines itself to be a civi-lization while its highest value, authentic self-realization, is realized only by the deliberate and systematic repudiation, transgression, and destruction of tradition; that is, by undermining and dismantling the inheritance of Civilization in the name of civilization; but while imagining itself to be heroic and emancipatory this pursuit leads to neo-barbarism and nihilism. Tradition, that which has been given down to us, as we have heard from Socrates, is the bearer of beauty, truth and the good, though these ideals may be obscured and dissimulated and in need of being brought to light again for us. But seen in the light of *Symposium*'s formulation of love as a mediating power, *eros* and *agape* are not so different from one another as Taylor presents them as being. Rather than belonging to two different planes of being – *eros* to the immanent order and *agape* to divine transcendence – they both belong to the immanent transcendent order of society.

Sorokin's thesis in *The Crisis of Our Age* (1992) and *The Ways and Power of Love* (2002) is remarkably similar to Taylor's (2007) *A Secular Age*, in that Sorokin then, just as Taylor now, diagnoses the central malady of contemporary neoliberal global Western Enlightenment/Modernity in terms of the sterility, emptiness and decadence of a culture that eschews a divine 'supra-consciousness' (Sorokin) or 'transcendence' (Taylor) in favour of an ontology and epistemology of a 'sensate' order (Sorokin) or 'immanent' order (Taylor). It thus suffers from what Baudelaire (1999: 19), writing a century previously in the turbulence between the Second Empire and the Third Republic, formulated in terms of a morbid insatiability, a hunger from lack of spiritual fulfilment, 'an appetite for the infinite'. In the immediate aftermath of World War II Sorokin established at Harvard the Research Centre in Creative Altruism. Launching the Centre, Sorokin said: 'At the present time there seems to exist no power but creative love that can prevent future suicidal wars and revolutions; and there seems to be no effective defense against the Apocalyptic methods of destruction but the Sermon on the Mount practiced in human behavior, incorporated into our social institutions, and incessantly articulated by culture. '[Unselfish love is] a life-giving force, necessary for physical, mental, and moral health ... only the power of unbounded love practiced in regard to all human beings can defeat the forces of inter-human strife, and can prevent the pending extermination of man by man on this planet' (2002: xii).

Looking across all the major religious and ethical systems of thought, Sorokin says, love is identified with goodness itself, inseparable from truth and beauty, three unified aspects of absolute value or God. This is the ontology of love: 'a *unifying, integrating, harmonizing, creative energy or power*'. The substantive unity of love, that quality which must be preserved and respected by any theological or sociological analysis of love that would artificially disassemble it, is that love is a unifying principle in the 'holy trinity' of Beauty, Truth and the Good. *Eros* and *agape* are inextricably inter-related to one another, and one form grows from/into/merges with others in Oriental as well as Occidental ethico-religious and philosophical conceptions. *Eros*, domesticated through the institution of marriage, can become *philia* (friendship, fidelity, fondness), the stable foundation of familial relations that may then be extended outside of the household to friends and neighbours, community and fellow countrymen; and *eros* and *philia* can, and sometimes do, become further generalized to *agape* – unlimited, wilful benevolence towards society broadly conceived and to humanity and the world as a whole.

From this theoretical formulation of love as a unified and unifying power by means of which we make our way from the profane, immanent, sensate, material world towards the eminent transcendent realm of the higher Ideals of Beauty, Truth and the Good, a reality that is both immanent and transcendent, Sorokin proposes that love can be meaningfully gauged and compared in terms of five variables: intensity, extensivity, duration, purity and adequacy. He believes it can be empirically demonstrated (in diametrical contradiction to Parsons' affirmative sociology which was triumphant at the time Sorokin was writing) how Western sensate civilization has become severely impoverished; its love relations, concentrated overwhelmingly at the level of *eros*, are becoming increasingly shallow, privatized and empty, lacking the fullness that only the meaning-giving power of more extensive and enduring forms of love – *philia* and *agape* – can provide. And having empirically historically and sociologically shown the problem – the diminution of *philia* and *agape* and the increase in egoistic *eros* – might also suggest wherein solutions may lie: socially institutionalized and sustainable reservoirs of *philia* and *agape*: health care for all in need of care; housing for all in need of shelter; security and dignity for the elderly, the poor and the vulnerable; education for children, and so on – the Sermon on the Mount translated into the infrastructure of recognition and redistribution funded through the collective Treasury as institutional forms of *philia*; political, social, civil and human rights institutionalized in national and international law as forms of *agape* – that is, the power of love put into practice and extending as the integrating institutions of society as a whole. Sorokin gives us the basis on which we can respond to Taylor's condemnation of modern civilization's secular liberal individualism: the cult of the individual may be the only form of religion that modern society has; a barbarous cult to a savage god of egoism, narcissism and the Market, but, in its worship of the individual as sacred, protected by severe taboos, enshrined as Human Rights, it is the keystone of what keeps our contemporary form of life still something of a Civilization. If we were to imagine modern life without the cult of the individual it would be then that it would become truly a new dark age of Hobbsean barbarism.

Conversion

We want now to address subjective and collective moral transformation, 'conversion', or 'turning around', and in particular the conversion experience of the artist or the poet to which Taylor gives particular attention in the closing chapters of *A Secular Age*. One such convert, though in the opposite direction, that of a repudiation of Catholicism, is James Joyce, and his conversion experience is of interest because it is explicitly the subject of one of the masterpieces of modern literature, *A Portrait of the Artist as a Young Man*. The conversion away from institutionalized Catholicism and towards an eminent, transcendent realm but manifest in and accessible through mundane immanent reality is the central and sustained theme of all of Joyce's work. *Dubliners* begins with the simony of the priest with a false vocation, going through the motions of a meaningless charade until his nervous breakdown, paralysis and death. Simony stands for the general predicament not only of the modern Irish, but Modernity as whole that has sought to exchange spiritual goods for material advantage. *A Portrait* explores the artist's long dark night of the soul, where he rejects a Jesuit vocation that he comes to see as a sterile mimetic repetition in a dead church. But Joyce's apostasy does not throw the divine child out with the bathwater of Irish Catholicism. Instead, the *Portrait* is an account of a spiritual transformation wherein the artist, awakened by *eros*, becomes a secular priest of *philia* and *agape*, whose true vocation is to grasp and express transcendent divinity, as it is manifest in the immanent order of society and everyday life.

A *Portrait of the Artist* exemplifies the conversion experience in terms of the structure of a *rite de passage*. It begins when the Director of the Jesuits at Belvedere invites Stephen to his office for a solemn conversation, asking Stephen to consider carefully whether he has a vocation. Stephen has been preparing himself, working hard to be a pious and devout boy. He has fasted, prayed, confessed, and trained his will to be one with the will of God. 'I have transformed my life, have I not?' he says to himself, the rhetorical form expressing his uncertainty: he has completed the preliminaries, but is this the right transformation? He may well have an authentic vocation to holy orders, but perhaps not to this church. Stephen is standing on the threshold: 'At the heavy hall door the director gave his hand to Stephen as though he were already a companion in the spiritual life.' Outside, Stephen became 'conscious of the caress of the mild evening air'.

> Towards Findlater's church a quartet of young men were striding along with linked arms, swaying their heads and stepping to the agile melody of their leader's concertina. The music passed in an instant, as the first bars of sudden music always did, over the fantastic fabrics of his mind, dissolving them painlessly and noiselessly as a sudden wave dissolves the sandbuilt turrets of children. Smiling at the trivial air he raised his eyes to the priest's face and, seeing in it a mirthless reflection of the sunken day, detached his hand slowly which had acquiesced faintly in that companionship. (Joyce, 2003: 173)

The group of friends striding along the street merrily playing music is alive, a Dionysian celebration heading towards a different church, one that Stephen too might 'find later', the church that joyfully celebrates the gift of an inexhaustible life, whereas the spiritual retreat he has just attended – a sermon on hell and eternal damnation – was not about celebrating divine *agape*. The Redemptorist Missionary's interpellation of the boys in terms of love – 'my dear little brethren in Christ' (Joyce, 2003: 99) – is a deeply hypocritical empty rhetoric. His actions, deliberately calculated to terrify the children, betray fear, hatred and contempt for life.

In the next section Stephen has broken from the parental institution of Catholicism but he has not yet found his new vocation. He is suspended in a frightening condition of liminality, represented by his wandering through the lanes and alleyways of the city. He crosses a footbridge over the river Tolka.[1] He passes a squad of grim Christian Brothers, heavy-booted, black-draped, with red-shaven gills, tramping across the bridge against him. Joyce recognized them then for what they would later prove themselves to be in Ireland and the world over – a dark and dreadful menace. He shrinks aside and lets them pass. On the other side, Stephen finds himself still in a liminal zone, the desolate seashore, and even though it is a fine day the endless horizon of the ocean and the dome of the sky at first leave him feeling empty, cold and uneasy. His mood first begins to turn when some acquaintances who are swimming off the rocks hail him, calling out his name. This unwelcome but friendly personal interpellation to *communitas* Stephen feels as 'the call of life to his soul ... not the inhuman voice that called him to the pale service of the altar' (Joyce, 2003: 184) but the voice of *eros* – sensual life, and *philia* calling to him in companionship and sociability. He becomes aware of an epiphanic scene as it unfolds and fills up the emptiness that had previously surrounded him. 'He was alone and young and wilful and wildhearted, alone amid a waste of wild air and brackish waters and the seaharvest of shells and tangle and veiled grey sunlight and gayclad lightclad figures, of children and girls and voices childish and girlish in the air.'

> A girl stood before him in midstream, alone and still, gazing out to sea ... and when she felt his presence and the worship of his eyes her eyes turned to him in quiet sufferance of his gaze, without shame or wantonness. Long, long she suffered his gaze and then quietly withdrew her eyes from his ...
>
> – Heavenly God! cried Stephen's soul in an outburst of profane joy. ...
>
> He turned away from her suddenly and set off across the strand. His cheeks were aflame; his body was aglow; his limbs were trembling. On and on and on he strode, far out over the sands, singing wildly to the sea, crying to greet the advent of the life that had cried to him. Her image had passed into his soul forever and no word had broken the holy silence of his ecstasy. (Joyce, 2003: 186)

Stephen's glimpse of Aphrodite in the person of an ordinary girl on a Dublin beach awakens his true vocation: to perceive the divine as radiant ideals of beauty, truth and goodness incarnated in beautiful moments of human life and to work to reveal it and proclaim it, like Dante's *Commedia*, in the eloquence of ordinary language. Stephen now systematically sets about developing his aesthetic/evangelical methodology, which he describes as 'applied Aquinas'. This is Joyce's explicit statement of method; of what it is to be an artist/priest engaged in the sacred ministry of revealing radiant transcendental ideals in the mundane immanent world, how to re-sacrilize modernity – and especially modern Ireland – with the help of St Thomas:

> An aesthetic image is presented to us either in space or in time. What is audible is presented in time, what is visible is presented in space. But, temporal or spatial, the aesthetic image is first luminously apprehended as selfbound and selfcontained upon the immeasurable background of space and time which is not it. You apprehend it as *one* thing. You see it as one whole. You apprehend its wholeness. That is *integritas*. ... Then ... you pass from point to point, led by its formal lines; you apprehend it as balanced part against part within its limits; you feel the rhythm of its structure. In other words the synthesis of immediate perception is followed by the analysis of apprehension. Having first felt that it is *one* thing you now feel that it is a *thing*. You apprehend it as complex, multiple, divisible, separable, made up of its parts, the result of its parts and their sum, harmonious. That is *consonantina*. ... When you have apprehended [beauty] as one thing and have then analysed it according to its form and apprehended it as a thing you make the only synthesis which is logically and aesthetically permissible. You see that it is that thing which it is and no other thing. The radiance of which [Aquinas] speaks is the scholastic *quidditas*, the *whatness* of a thing. ... The instant wherein that supreme quality of beauty, the clear radiance of the aesthetic image is apprehended luminously by the mind which has been arrested by its wholeness and fascinated by its harmony is the luminous silent stasis of aesthetic pleasure, a spiritual state ... the enchantment of the heart. (Joyce, 2003: 178–179)

Stephen's (Joyce's) method of the artist/priest is that of cultivating abilities for apprehending the *integratis*, *harmonia* and *claritas* of the radiant ideal as it appears in epiphanic beautiful moments of immanent transcendence, a method that he systematically applies in *Ulysses* and *Finnegans Wake*. This *methodus* is the path to salvation, 'for once the mind is illuminated by a knowledge of what is highest, it will lead the spirit to choose what is best' (Vico, 1999: 136). The graces of the artist-priest are gifts of the 'Holy Spirit' (corresponding to the inheritance bestowed by the society of which the artist is a member – the multiple traditions within which the subject is formed that constitute an inheritance, that can be worked with as repertoire) that enable him to see and to hear the divine (the unifying and vivifying *esprit des corps* of the collective social body; the transcendent ideals to which the collective is beholden and espouses), and, especially well developed in the case of James Joyce, the evangelist's 'gift of tongues' with which to give voice and to spread the good news. By revealing the power of love to the world the artist performs the service of the priest. Whereas the institutional church is ministered by 'priested peasant[s] ... who [are] but schooled in the discharging of a formal rite ... [the secular artist would be] ... a priest of eternal imagination, transmuting the daily bread of experience into the radiant body of everliving life' (Joyce, 2003: 240).

That artist/priest carries out his mission in *Ulysses* by faithfully recording epiphanies of *philia* in the networks of reciprocal relations that constitute Dublin as a unified collective form of life despite its glaring divisions and conflicts and the subordination of its people to gigantic powers, thereby transubstantiating the bread of everyday life – immanent content – into everlasting supra-individual form, redeeming the lives of common people from the fall into obscurity and meaninglessness of modern hyper-individuated urban existence. Like Dante's *Divine Comedy*, Joyce intended *Ulysses* to be a modern secular 'gospel'; a book for the common people, written, like Dante's, as *commeida*, in the vulgar vernacular, that would teach us how to live better lives (Kiberd, 2009). This is exemplified in the model life of the central protagonist, Leopold Bloom, an ordinary man who strives to turn around from the various circles of hell in which he and his contemporary Dubliners are swirling, to transcend his carnal and egoistic appetites, and to reach outwards and upwards from the darkness towards luminous, transcendent ideals. Joyce intends that Bloom's life, like the lives of the saints, would serve as a model life for the people of modern secular society to emulate. Bloom's actions, grounded in *eros*, institutionalized in *philia*, reach upward and outward towards realizing the ideal of *agape*. The moral grammar of *Ulysses* is structured around the pathways towards redemption, for instance Bloom's performing 'corporal works of mercy':[2] he feeds the cat; he pays his respects at a funeral and assists in the financial affairs of the widow and children; he helps a blind man across the street; he extricates a young fellow from a drunken fracas, takes him home and gives him food and shelter, and so on.

At the heart of *Ulysses* is the promise of redemption: the flock can be saved from the rough beast. In the Cyclops chapter, to focus again on one exemplary episode, the run-down bar becomes a theatre of demonic possession. The giant immanent orders of empire, nation, church and commerce that rule over the life of the city here take over and possess the bodies and souls of the bar's customers who are subjectivized and animated by the demonic spirits of the ruling powers: one is a nationalist-chauvinist, another a paranoid litigationist; others are enthralled variously by the prestige and authority of science, by the glamour of arts and cultural scenes, fashion, publicity and celebrity, and so on.

The 'nameless' narrator at first seems a neutral and objective commentator, but he is a soulless, empty cipher, a husk of a man reduced to a nobody, but possessed by a legion of demons. The spirits of various authoritarian figures pass into and out of his body metempsychotically – a policeman, an informer, an 'agent': a collector of bad debts for banks and moneylenders. They are all intoxicated, not just by Guinness and Jameson, Dublin's giant brewers and distillers whose premises are near the scene of the action and which stand for the market forces more generally that rule the city, but they are possessed by spirits and enthusiasms swirling around and animating the wider culture. Bloom himself is not immune to these metempsychotic demonic powers, and, while usually calm and measured, he finds himself being led into temptation, into a dangerous conversation that at first seduces him and begins to draw him towards the darkness, until he turns around again towards the light:

> – And I belong to a race too, says Bloom, that is hated and persecuted. ... Robbed, says he. Plundered. Insulted. Persecuted. Taking what belongs to us by right. At this very moment, says he, putting up his fist, sold by auction off in Morocco like slaves or cattle.
>
> – Right, says John Wyse. Stand up to it then with force like men. ...
>
> – But it's no use, says he. Force, hatred, history, all that. That's not life for men and women, insult and hatred. And everyone knows that it's the very opposite of that that is really life.
>
> – What? Says Alf.
>
> – Love, says Bloom. I mean the opposite of hatred.
>
> ... A new apostle to the gentiles, says the citizen. Universal love. Well, says John Wyse. Isn't that what we're told. Love your neighbours.
>
> ... Love loves to love love. Nurse loves the new chemist. Constable 14A loves Mary Kelly. Gerty McDowell loves the boy that has the bicycle. M.B. loves a fair gentleman. Li Chi Han lovey up kissy Cha Pu Chow. Jumbo, the elephant, loves Alice the elephant. Old Mr Verschoyle with the ear trumpet loves old Mrs Verschoyle with the turnedin eye. The man in the brown mackintosh loves a lady who is dead. His majesty the King loves her majesty the Queen. Mrs Norman W. Tupper loves officer Taylor. You love a certain person. And this person loves that other person because everybody loves somebody but God loves everybody. (Joyce, 1998: 319)

In tune with Socrates' formulation in *Symposium* of the substantive unity of all three aspects of the power of love, *eros, philia,* and *agape,* constituting a divine holy trinity, Bloom is animated by *eros*, though his relations with Molly have matured into loyalty and respect. Erotic and carnal desires are still vitally present in his life, but he is not ruled by them, as other characters are. Bloom is equally animated by the spirit of *philia*, not only at home, where he is a caring husband and father, but proceeding from his private realm in the family home and returning to home in the evenings, Bloom's *philia* extends outwards. He is an active presence in Dublin's *agora*: he conducts all of his dealings – business, social and personal – in the city's streets; he is friendly to various groups and interests in the city, acquaintances, professional contacts and colleagues, networks of friends and their families to whom he is loyal and solicitous, ranging from sporting, music and cultural scenes, to current affairs and politics, and to their respective knowledges and causes which he supports and advises but without getting caught up in prevailing enthusiasms. And combining and incorporating the spirits of *eros* and *philia*, but without either ascetically repudiating *eros*, or denigrating *philia*, without deprecating or subordinating but rather by extrapolating and synthesizing these aspects of the power of love, Bloom exemplifies the quality of *agape* as a self-transcending wilful benevolence that exceeds philanthropy and cosmopolitanism by a divine gesture of forgiveness: fore-give-ness being an intentional response to promote well-being when confronted by that which generates ill-being by repaying – or rather by pre-paying (fore-giving) evil with good.

The artist-priest finally attends to the *Wake*, a representation of *agape* written as darkness fell over Europe. (Arendt (2006) says that the banality of evil was not fascism or communism but the moral failure of European civilization as a whole, its fall to immanence and nihilism and the genesis of a new kind of non-thinking subject). In that context Joyce appears as a contemporary of the monastic scribes and scholars of Iona and Clonmacnoise on the outer fringes of collapsing Roman civilization, producing the illuminated sacred scriptures. Joyce's model for *Finnegans Wake* was the *Book of Kells*. In the *Wake*, Lacan (1981) says, the word is 'full', overdetermined, by Joyce's beautifully wrought linguistic puns, portmanteaus and semantic proliferations. The *Book of Kells'* scribes sought to express the austere, absolute *Logos* of the Father and to harmonize the Word with the vulgar, contingent word of mankind, a unification, by virtue of beauty, of the transcendent and the immanent realms. In the beautiful illuminations of the *Book of Kells* the word is overflowing with convoluted patterns of astounding intricacy and subtlety, representing meanings within meanings in infinite regress and yet balanced and ordered to form a coherent whole. In the *Wake*, as in the *Book of Kells*, the infinities of the text serve to protect and preserve the immanent human word as transcendent divine Logos against the encroaching powers of the new dark age. The *Wake* preserves and celebrates the creative and transcending power of language and the authority of the *agape* network of interlocutors seeking to understand one another to wake us from the dream sleep into which Europe had fallen – totalitarianisms, but also the immanent orders of Progress and Scientism, repressive desublimated unthinking mass consumerism and market nihilism. The *Wake* shows how by the power of *agape*, like Finnegan, everything begins-again. The central reversal of the secular age, Taylor says, is that Christian incarnation – the Word made flesh – has been displaced by secular excarnation – disembodied Reason. The *Wake* seeks nothing less than the reincarnation of the Word, re-embodied reason as the epistemic authority of the *agape* network of interlocutors who share a deep need to understand and communicate with one another.

'All valid ideals are already anchored in a deep tradition, in ways of life which have already been lived. They cannot enter history like a newly invented plan that sweeps reality aside or shapes it from above. The validly new is a recreation of a tradition' (Taylor, 2007: 748). This is exactly Joyce's formulation, 'imagination is nothing but the working over of what is remembered ... imagination is memory' (Joyce, in Ellmann, 1982: 661). This is how Joyce works with the traces of deep memory that find expression in the everyday speech of ordinary Dubliners to cultivate imaginative resources for a new future. The artist attunes to the fullness of the prosaic word, which incarnates the spiritual reality of the *agape* network. Joyce exemplifies the artist who strives in his vocation to listen for the divine word that is incarnated in the mundane immanent reality as it is encoded in deep traditions and expressed in the ordinary language of everyday life, and who works to proclaim the transcendental wisdom accumulated in the deep history of collective life and to bring it into the light to illuminate the coming – already present – dark age.

Plato and Joyce (and Sorokin and Taylor too) give us love lights for dark ages. The tissue of lies that constitute the ballad of Persse O'Reilly – *perce oriole*, the earwig – a tiny 'rough beast', a monstrous, terrifying thing to have in one's ear, a thing that can only be lured out by shining a light outside the ear so that the insect crawling in the darkness of the labyrinth is drawn towards the light, turns around and leaves peacefully by its own accord. Addressing the relation between the voice, the story and the ear in the *Wake*, Erzgraber traces how the ballad relates an event in Earwicker's life that happened in Phoenix Park, where a stranger asks him for the time. Earwicker misunderstands – thinking it to have been a homosexual overture towards him he begins to speak hesitantly, to stutter, and to protest that he is not a homosexual. The anonymous stranger, misunderstood and somewhat mystified, later recalls, half aloud and not very exactly, what he remembers of Earwicker's talk. His wife overhears what he is saying and confides it to a Jesuit priest, who in turn passes it on in a modified form to a teacher of agriculture and orthophonetics. Again, this report of the story is accidentally overheard by other persons, one of whom repeats fragments of the story while sleeping off his hangover, which is now taken over by an unsuccessful poet, Hosty (hasty). Hosty gives Earwicker the French name 'Perce Oreille', which he then transforms into an Irish name, Persse O'Reilly. The Ballad of Persse O'Reilly presents a tissue of lies about HCE. It is the sum of all the rumours and slander that have been put into circulation about him, the gradual distortion of the originally question-able word-of-mouth reports on HCE's character (Erzgraber, 1992: 161ff). But the ballad does have some informative value (and paradoxically some truth content) in that it allows us to recognize the fictitious picture of the protago-nist that has arisen in the consciousness of the Dubliners on the basis of rumour, gossip and unscrupulous chatter. The scurrilous ballad against HCE is countered by a letter written by his wife ALP, which, though purporting to be 'reasonable', the 'sober' 'truth' about what 'really' happened, 'setting the story straight' as it were, like the ballad it enjoys no exalted status; it is scratched in the dirt by a mother hen. The *Wake* is the language of the fallen world, of the public and of politics, a language that 'stotters' (Earwicker has a speech impediment, a stutter) around the unspeakable; for something did – seemingly – happen in the Park, but Reason (the letter) will not get to the bottom of it. The *Wake* is ultimately indecipherable or, rather, it is generative of a multitude of new interpretations, but this non-rational polysemy is more true to the wholeness of life than the singular clarity of Reason, an ideal speech situation (desire for which springs from the confusion of tongues) and may save the world from the final word of the Dictator.

Plato's *Symposium* and Joyce's *Finnegans Wake* are works of art and labours of love. They are composed of reported speech; pieces of remembered stories and conversations, passed along hand to hand and by word of mouth, 'transaccidentated through the slow fires of consciousness' (Joyce, 1995: 186) with all of its ellipses and confusions, and misremembering and distortions, well lubricated with alcohol, humour and ribaldry, for the *Wake* and the *Symposium* are both parties, occasions of gregarious celebrations of life even in the face of death; defiant sociability against the backdrop of encroaching tyranny, living on and surviving through the night until the light of a new dawn. *Finnegans Wake* and the *Symposium* are not exemplifications of rational discourse. *Symposium* appears the epitome of the clarity of reason in Socrates' dialectic method, but it is presented as a conversation about half-remembered conversations that some others had at a party some years previously held by two men who meet in the street, and the kernel of that conversation – Socrates' speech as recollected by these unreliable witnesses – is Socrates' recollection of his own earlier conversation with a mysterious woman, Diotima. Similarly, to decode *Finnegans Wake*, to clear up the mystery of the text, is to miss the point, for the *Wake* and the *Symposium* are works of art as generative normatively oriented stories that grasp and express the unity of the beautiful, the true and the good in poetry and philosophy: they present us with the gift of the need for interpretation and the occasions for discussion and conversation.

The *Symposium* and the *Wake* are two texts that on the face of it are worlds and eons apart from one another. Two and a half thousand years separate them. One is brief, succinct, a handful of interlocutors, a seemingly elevated conversation amongst poets, soldiers, doctors and philosophers; the other runs to 1000 pages, a veritable babble of voices, some forty different languages, speaking in altered states of consciousness, including the voices of rocks, trees and rivers. But they are transaccidented stories – a tale told of Shaun and Shem, of 'broady'[3] and 'skinnny', from Thom to Jim and as Charlie took it from Pete. And we overhear these conversations and pass them along as garbled messages that may contain the gift of a scrap of truth: that the divine *logos* resides not outside and above the fallen world but within it: the transcendent is nowhere else but immanently within the words of the *agape* community of speakers who, in their everyday lives and their ordinary speech, give voice to the unity of beauty, truth and the good life through their love of working out the puzzle of being with one another through our sociable conversation.

Notes

1 *Tolcadh* means a sudden flood or torrent.
2 The corporal works of mercy, Christ states explicitly (Matthew 41), enumerate the actions that the good person ought to perform and which will be criteria used on the Day of Judgment. They are: (1) to feed the hungry and give drink to the thirsty; (2) to clothe the naked; (3) to give shelter to the homeless; (4) to give alms to the needy; (5) to care for the sick; (6) to visit the imprisoned; (7) to bury the dead (Gill, 1963: 17–21).
3 'Plato' is a nickname meaning 'broad-faced' (like a plate) or perhaps 'big-head'.

Part III
POLITICAL ECONOMY

Part III
POLITICAL ECONOMY

7

Pleonexic tyranny in Plato's *Republic* and in the Irish republic

You eat what you kill

'You eat what you kill' is a phrase coined (as it were) in the City, where its usage articulates the principle of remuneration in the financial sector, amongst bankers, fund managers, traders and brokers, whereby individuals who are responsible for particular lines of business within financial organizations personally get the full financial reward accruing to that business. 'You eat what you kill', the ethic of the City and of Wall Street, the ethic of the developer and the financier as 'shark' or 'lone wolf', came into general disrepute after 2008. A fundamental source of the crisis according to commentators in the newspapers of record, including the *Financial Times*, *The Economist* and the *Wall Street Journal* as well as our own local press and mass media, was the insatiable greed, over-reaching ambition and hubris that characterized bankers and those in the financial sector, developers and politicians, and even the general public. Some particularly greedy individuals have been identified and scapegoated – New York's ponzi schemer Bernie Madoff, Anglo Irish banker Seanie Fitzpatrick, and Ireland's once-richest, Sean Quinn; but during the boom years we had all 'lost the run of ourselves', as we say in Ireland; 'we had all become too greedy'; 'we were all responsible', Bertie Ahern said. Is this the case? How are we all implicated in a culture of greed?

'You eat what you kill', like 'greed is good' and a cluster of cognate usages associated with the representation of the market as a 'jungle' governed by the rule 'the survival of the fittest', is an anachronism echoing nineteenth-century Liberalism's political-economic theology of *laissez faire*. More particularly it resonates with evolutionary theory as it was taken up and developed by Herbert Spencer's social Darwinism and subsequent socio-biology. It is worth noting in passing that contemporary zoology very significantly refutes the nineteenth-century notions that animals act as singular hunter-killers. Wolves and lions and similar top predators, the heroes of 'you eat what you kill' mythology, are in fact gregarious social animals, they hunt cooperatively and they share what they kill. A pride of lions or a pack of wolves may have an alpha male who takes a 'lion's share' but the kill is divided and shared. The principles of distribution amongst animal species remain obscure to humans, of course, but the practice wherein cubs, females, younger males, and weak, injured and elderly members of the animal group take care of one another and all receive their fair share is empirically well established.

The tyranny of pleonexia

As we have seen, the world falls into darkness when Pluto abducts Persephone, keeps her captive and rapes her. Pluto's rapacity is an archetype of the problem of 'pleonexia' – excessive and insatiable greed, raging ambition and envy combined with distributive unfairness of money, power, honour and of all divisible social goods. Three millennia of religious, ethical, philosophical, political and even medical discourse identify pleonexia as a social pathology, as being *the* problem of the Classical city, paradigmatically Athens, where its greatest minds, Socrates, Plato and Aristotle, all identify it as the cause of the collapse of civilization, a theme repeated by the historian Thucydides and by Livy in the case of the decline and fall of Rome. But neoliberalism makes a virtue of pleonexia – 'greed is good'.

Pleonexia is an excessive desire to get more than one's fair share of something which one already has, violating canons of distributive fairness within self-conscious political communities. Pleonexia cannot be contained by discourse when there is no certainty, no consensus on the principles according to which distribution should take place. Whereas Pluto's rape of Persephone represents the problem of pleonexia in cosmology and mythology, in philosophy the problem of pleonexia is analysed in Plato's *Republic*. The character Thrasymachus in Plato's *Republic* is a 'wild beast', a wolf, who articulates the principle of 'you eat what you kill'. Socrates' reasoned philosophy tries to call Thrasymachus to heel, but he persists. He will, he says, nod along to Socrates' discourse as he would to the tedious talking of an old woman. Pleonexia assumes that it will have its way anyway, despite any reasonable argument made against it: 'the powerful do what they can, and the weak suffer what they must', as Thucydides says. This means that pleonexia is a fundamental and perennial problem of political anthropology, as much an issue in the contemporary Irish republic as it was in Plato's Greece.

Pleonexia is *the* problem addressed by Plato's *Republic* and Aristotle's *Ethics*. How could the Greeks manage the threat of grasping, over-reaching and insatiable greed that flouts norms and conventions, boundaries and limits and that undermines and overwhelms collective life? Zeus restores order to the cosmos by establishing just measure, a 'fair deal', whereby no-one gets all that they want, neither Pluto, nor Demeter, nor Persephone is entirely satisfied with the arrangement, but the new deal – Hermes's free market, regulated by Zeus's wise government – mediates and moderates the desires of all parties and allows balanced, dynamic and harmonious exchanges with which everyone can live.

As money can be used to acquire other goods such as honour and safety, education, social security and well-being, pleonexia is often conflated into greed for more money, but in Plato and Aristotle's more expansive understanding, pleonexia 'focuses on a potentially wide range of objects, which are desired either individually, in shifting combinations, or all together' (Balot, 2001b: 33). Civic strife results from perceptions of proportional inequality in a community's distribution of divisible goods, and stasis is the symptom of the internal conflict, the blockages and morbid immobilities arising from pleonexia. In this context it is important to note that a radical equalization of material goods will not necessarily solve the problem of civic strife, Aristotle says, as material inequality is neither the deep source of pleonexia nor its singular focus, though it is an important locus at which pleonexia becomes manifest. For this reason Aristotle argues for the moderation of disparities in wealth, that is, a reduction of extremes of wealth inequality rather than the equalization of wealth, for, 'even if one prescribed a moderate level of property for all it would be of no advantage; for it is more necessary to level desires than properties' (Balot, 2001b: 35). If a radical programme of material equalization will not solve the problem of pleonexia (as contemporary Marxists and anarchists imagine it would) neither would a programme of general education (as contemporary Liberals imagine), for Aristotle is quite explicit that education of a certain sort may very well intensify the desire to get more money, power and honour. The emphasis in contemporary societies on liberal education premised on the cultivation of the individual, and especially on encouraging entrepreneurship, enterprise and innovation, for instance, which Ireland's secondary, tertiary and 'fourth level' education all explicitly promote, all amplify rather than ameliorate pleonexia.

Pleonexia is a highly generalized but also quite specific problem. It is general in that it is diffuse, dispersed and widespread throughout the body politic. It manifests and expresses itself differently in the various social strata, having a characteristic coloration amongst elites (who, for instance, may want distinction, honour and status more than merely more money); amongst citizens, an already advantaged cohort of land-owning men who were descendants of citizens (who may want more power and political influence, or recognition, or respect, manifest in the quality of the services and care that they feel are due to them as citizens); amongst the demos, the general population, who typically want more material goods; and amongst would-be tyrants who 'want it all'.

Pleonexia can be understood in the context of the Greeks' conception of citizenship as a form of sharing in the political, economic and religious life of the community. Greek citizens perceived themselves as possessing in common all the divisible goods of the community. 'Justice' meant to have a 'just share' of these goods, that is, to have an 'equal share' not in the sense of the 'same' share, as in that everyone would have an identical amount, but a share on the basis of agreed-upon principles of distribution; in other words, people are equal and receive their equal share by virtue of their agreed-upon principles. This allows for such internal variations as, for instance, a 'lion's share' being the agreed-upon fair share of a member of the community who makes a major contribution, a businessman, for instance, who creates wealth and employment, or a heroic general, or certain shares to be allocated for children, the elderly or whatever category to receive their due. Injustice would have meant violating that principle by 'taking more', as in 'taking more than what the community agrees to be each one's fair share'.

What counts as 'fair share' depends upon what the agreed-upon principles of distribution are amongst the community, and that varies from community to community and from time to time. Justice is a historical-sociological and political-anthropological question. Questions of justice and fairness cannot be answered on an abstract and *a priori* basis. But that does not mean that justice is arbitrary and idiosyncratic. Rather, it means that questions of justice and fairness arise, and are answerable, only within the prevailing conventions, practices and traditions of the particular community. And neither is this to say that justice is static, for conventions and traditions are themselves living and dynamic. To translate this into the contemporary languages of sociology and political theory, it means, as Durkheim (1974) says, that morality is the property of the collective, that every society has its own specific morality and it is on the basis and within the terms of that morality that tribunals condemn and prevailing opinion judges. As Chantal Mouffe (1988: 39) argues, 'Tradition allows us to think of our own insertion into historicity, the fact that we are constructed as subjects through a series of already existing discourses, that it is through this tradition that forms us that the world is given to us and all political action made possible.' If tradition is the set of discourses and practices that form us as subjects, then politics, Mouffe says, is the pursuit of intimations within those prevailing discourses: 'the creation of new usages for the key terms of a given tradition and of their use in new language games that make new forms of life possible' (1988: 40).

Like Durkheim and Mouffe, Aristotle says that every polis lays claim to some sort of justice, but the particular principle of distributive fairness in any given polis depends on the prevailing notion of proportional equality according to which citizens receive differential shares in collective goods depending on their relative worth and merit in promoting the common good.

Justice is the prerogative of the authoritative political community of inter-locutors who are self-consciously working within their own traditions which have formed them, from which they have inherited their conventions and political-cultural practices, including the principles by which they govern themselves. It is the traditions that form them and by which their world is given to them that make their political action possible and within which they make arguments of the justice or otherwise of particular cases of distribution of goods.

Pleonexia is always latent, as it is anchored in appetite and desire, but it becomes a manifest problem only under certain conditions. Pleonexia, ordi-narily managed and mediated within the collective morality, becomes a problem at times of historical, social and political change and transformation, revolution and liminality, when there are mutations of the symbolic order, when evaluative principles are susceptible to dissolution, re-evaluation and reinvention. People tend to become extravagantly acquisitive, over-reaching in their ambitions, suspicious and aggressively envious of others when the normal constraints and limits that govern and contain individual appetites and desires are loosened and become uncertain. When the individual is not beholden to previously prevailing norms and conventions and there is lack of answerability to collective principles, when the social superego is lacking, pleonexia is a social pathology of unrestrained egoism and narcissism that can tend towards psychosis.[1] The accelerated modernization of Ireland's Celtic Tiger period and the chaos and free-fall experienced since the crash of 2008, like Athens at the time of Plato's *Republic*, are quintessential examples of such periods of dissolution and uncertainty of principles, and it is in exactly these circumstances that 'we lose the run of ourselves'.

In Plato's *Republic* the threat to Greek civilization is less so from barbar-ians, war against whom (the Persians for instance) helped to unite the Greeks into the Delian league; nor is it conflict amongst Greek cities, such as that between Athens and Sparta, which is the immediate context of *Republic*. Thucydides' *History of the Peloponnesian War* tells how thirty years of conflict had demoralized the Athenians, desensitizing people to atrocity, injustice and hypocrisy, just as familiarity with mediatized violence and scandals of corrup-tion in business and politics and abuses and cover-ups in religious institutions blunts our sense of moral outrage today. But, Thucydides says, pleonexia preceded the war and was in fact a root cause of it; the demoralizing effects of the war feeding off and amplifying pleonexia even further, leading to a general morbidity in all of Athens' social and bodies politic, a plague of stasis (Fleiss, 1959).[2] Stasis – 'civil war' – is antagonism internal to the city, conflict between aristocratic, oligarchic and democratic factions.

As the son of an aristocratic family directly implicated in tyranny (his uncle and his grand-uncle were amongst the oligarchy of the Thirty Tyrants, which also included several of Socrates' associates), internal conflict, strife and antagonism was something with which Plato was personally very familiar. Following the crisis and Athens' loss of sovereignty the Tyrants, backed by a garrison, imposed a Spartan 'programme of austerity' and set about purging Athens of leading democrats, severely limiting citizens' rights so as to consolidate their power, and confiscating the assets of rival leading citizens. Plato's solution (at least in part) is that in his ideal, utopian Republic a caste of aristocratic noble 'guardians' – the philosopher-kings – would have their pleonexic tendencies curbed by a regimen of education in the virtues of temperance, prudence and justice, and, because fragmentation and dissent amongst and between members of the castes of guardians, auxiliaries and artisans are caused by individual disparities of wealth and sexual success, overall harmony would depend upon a Spartan communalism of the guardians – that they would have no private property and their sexual relations would be carefully managed so that they embodied ideals of a measured, tempered, orderly life of chastity and fidelity that all others would emulate. One may consider here a contemporary parallel in the emblematic figures of Dominique Strauss Kahn and Silvio Berlusconi as the necessary scapegoats of the neoliberal world order, purged, and replaced by a caste of Spartan technocrats, who, when they visit Dublin, travel by taxi and on foot to the Central Bank and the offices of the Minister.

In such a city governed by noble guardians, assisted by loyal auxiliaries who manage and oversee the lower orders of artisans, women and slaves, when individuals' desires are self-governed and the general libidinal economy is well regulated, the market would not need to be regulated. Plato has Socrates ask Glaucon:

> as to those common business transactions between private individuals in the market, including if you please the contracts of artisans, libels, assaults, law-proceedings and the impannelling of juries, or again questions relating to tariffs, and the collection of such customs as may be necessary in the markets or in the harbours, and generally all regulations of the market, the police, the custom-house and the like; shall we condescend at all to legislate on such matters?

No, says Glaucon. 'It is not worth while to give directions on these points to good and cultivated men: for in most cases they will have little difficulty in discovering [for themselves] all the legislation required.' Yes, my friend, says Socrates. But that all depends upon one very important condition: 'if god enables them to maintain the laws which we have already discussed' (Plato, 1997: 425b–426c). Therein lies the problem, for the *Republic* is an ideal and hypothetical model city, hypostatized by Plato to contrast with the way things actually are, more often than not, and as they stood at the time of his writing. The realpolitik of Athens is an oligarchic plutonomy, as Thrasymachus represents it, and he laughs scornfully at Socrates' naiveté for imagining that it could be otherwise.

Thrasymachus is a sophist who has made a career of being close to power; a speechwriter and coach of rhetoric, he is the contemporary equivalent of a government press secretary or a 'spin-doctor'. At the moment in which *Republic* is set Athens is defeated, demoralized and is under Sparta's proxy management by the Thirty Tyrants. The dialogue is set in Pireaus, the port, at the outer margin of the city, at the house of Polemarchus and Cephalus, who are amongst the leading Athenians whose property has been confiscated. Thrasymachus, as a foreigner, is also on the margins of the current regime, but as a professional sophist in the service of whatever ruling elite, not only does Thrasymachus know very well the mindset of the Thirty Tyrants, the ways powerful, wealthy people think and act, he personally represents and embodies the same values. Like them, he lives by the rule 'you eat what you kill'. Listening in on Socrates' conversation, Thrasymachus 'could restrain himself no longer, but gathering himself up like a wild beast, he sprang upon us, as if he would tear us in pieces. ... I was astounded, and gazed at the speaker in terror; and [Socrates likening Thrasymachus specifically to a wolf, says] I think that if I had not set eyes upon him before he eyed me, I should have been struck dumb.'

'Wake up! Get real!' Thrasymachus says to Socrates; and, because 'there is no such thing as a free lunch', 'besides being instructed, you must make me a payment'. Our praise for your good argument is as much as we can offer, says Socrates, so let's hear it. Wolf-like Thrasymachus is an ethical nihilist and a cynical realist. 'My doctrine is that justice is simply the interest of the stronger,' Thrasymachus states: 'The interest of the stronger is everywhere just.' In retort to Socrates' dialectical anthitheses Thrasymachus simply ups the scale of injustice:

I am speaking of the case ... of an unjust man who has the power to grasp on an extensive scale. To him you must direct your attention, if you wish to judge how much more profitable it is to a man's own self to be unjust than to be just. And you will learn this truth with the greatest ease if you turn your attention to the most consummate form of injustice, which, while it makes the wrong-doer most happy, makes those who are wronged, and will not retaliate, most miserable. This form is a despotism which proceeds not by small degrees, but by wholesale, in its open or fraudulent appropriation of the property of others, whether it be sacred or profane, public or private; perpetrating offences which if a person commits in detail and is found out he becomes liable to a penalty and incurs deep disgrace; for partial offenders in this class of crimes are called sacriligious, men-stealers, burglars, thieves and robbers. But when a man seizes not only the property of his fellow citizens but captures and enslaves their persons also, instead of those dishonourable titles he is called happy and highly favoured, not

only by the men of his own city but also by all others who hear of the comprehensive injustice which he has wrought. ... Thus it is, Socrates, that injustice,
realized on an adequate scale, is a stronger, a more liberal, and a more lordly
thing than justice. (Plato, 1997: 344a–345a).

Injustice is a virtue, Thrasymachus says, 'I call it good policy.' It is wise and
good when the unjust 'are able to practice injustice on the complete scale and
reduce whole cities and nations of men to subjection' (Plato, 1997:
348c–349b). Thrasymachus is the Classical ancestor of contemporary neoliberals like Hayek, Friedman and Nozick, whose revolutionary moral and
political-economic formula is that the free market is a jungle where the only
law is survival of the fittest, where 'private vice is public virtue' and where
'greed is good'. The more extensive and total the injustice, the further out the
unjust man can push the boundary of the practice of injustice: 'when he takes
it upon himself to go beyond all and in everything', the better it becomes. 'The
best city,' Thrasymachus says, 'is the one that is most completely unjust.'

Socrates tries to refute this doctrine by arguing that the better city will be
the one that can pursue a common cause or course of action, whereas
'injustice breeds divisions and animosities and broils between man and man,
while justice creates unanimity and friendship' and that 'if the working of
injustice is to implant hatred wherever it exists, will not the presence of it,
whether among freemen or slaves, cause them to hate one another and to form
parties, and disable them from acting together in concert?' (Plato, 1997:
351a–e). Thrasymachus seems to concede these points, though reluctantly,
while perspiring and blushing, but not changing his mind at all, for his is not
an argument and this is not a discussion as far as he is concerned, he is merely
stating the amoral doctrine of the rich and powerful. 'If you are not convinced
by my statements, what more can I do for you? Must I take the doctrine and
thrust it into your mind?' (Plato, 1997: 345a).

As far as Thrasymachus and the plutocratic oligarchs that he speaks for are
concerned this is simply how the world works: 'might makes right'; these are
the bald facts of life, and so they will remain until they are made to change, not
by force of Socrates' better argument but by force of arms, as indeed was the
fate of the unjust and rapacious regime of the Thirty, overthrown by a guerrilla
army of returning Athenian exiles who restored a fraught and flawed
democracy imbued with a conservative religious revivalism, a democracy that
in turn had Socrates executed, and, already falling, from then Athens fell
precipitously.[3] For the time being Thrasymachus treats Socrates' reasoned
argument as a frivolous entertainment, and, as his contemporary equivalents
would do with a Habermas today who claims that the force of the better
argument ought to win: 'I will do with you as we do with old women when
they tell us stories: I will say "Good," and nod my head or shake it, as the
occasion requires' (Plato, 1997: 350c–351a).

Republic unfolds thereafter as Plato's elaboration of an educational programme for a caste of noble guardians, for the cultivation and institution-alization of the virtues of temperance and reason in the light of eternal ideals amongst an ideal Republic ruled by philosopher-kings. Plato wrote *Republic* when he was in his fifties, having lived through the convulsions of the fall of Athens through a rolling chaos of successive forms of governance: from being the hegemonic military and naval power of the Delian league that had success-fully defended Greece against Persia; through that timeocratic order of noble warrior heroes sliding into an arrogant and overweening plutocratic oligarchy with imperial ambitions that alienated lesser city states, leading to a long war with Sparta; the hardships and privations of wartime contributing to the over-throwing of oligarchy by democracy; and two oligarchic *coups d'etat* that overthrew democracy again; eventual defeat, collapse and the subsequent imposition of tyranny; each regime morphing, metamorphosing and hybridiz-ing into the others, each one in turn as bad or worse than the others. Against this backdrop of historical experience Plato favoured rule by a sober and disci-plined nobility.[4] But whereas it was written in the wake of historical events and experiences of political turmoil and civic strife in Greece, *Republic* was written before Plato took up an invitation to go to Sicily to become the advisor to the heir to the throne there, who, having inherited power from a despot, aspired instead to become a philosopher-king of the kind Plato recommended. Twice Plato became advisor and pedagogue to Dionysius II but on each occasion the mission ended badly. Syracuse was a tyranny; Plato was a consultant, a courtier, a hireling paid to lend philosophical legitimation to power, the very thing that he had repudiated the poets and the sophists for doing in Athens. He was eventually made a prisoner. Plato escaped and fled back to his Academy in Athens, and, disappointed and disillusioned, he stayed away from politics for the rest of his life.

We cannot cover all of the themes of *Republic* here, of course, but we will focus on how Plato formulates the various forms of government that arise and become institutionalized and are in turn undermined, destabilized and degen-erate by the perpetual recurrence of pleonexia. As we shall see, the patterns and pathologies that Plato identifies in *Republic* resonate strongly with current patterns and problems in our own republic.

As a general rule, Plato says, 'there is such a gulf between wealth and virtue, that when weighed, as it were in the two scales of a balance, one of the two always falls as the other rises. ... Consequently when wealth and the wealthy are honoured in a state, virtue and the virtuous sink in estimation.' As what is honoured is practised and what is dishonoured is neglected, noble and heroic leaders who begin by 'being contentious and ambitious ... end by becoming lovers of gain and covetous; and while they commend and admire and confer office upon the wealthy they despise the poor' (Plato, 1997: 551a).

The dynamism of glory-seeking rule by state-founding heroes – 'soldiers of destiny' or 'soldiers of the gael', trading on the charismatic residue of father figures and fallen heroes (de-Valera and Collins are Irish examples) – tends to degenerate towards a plutocratic oligarchy, that has its own internal and fatal flaws. The ruling caste's practices of looking after their own – 'cronyism' – mean limited meritocratic social mobility so that the city tends towards mediocrity. 'Such a city must necessarily lose its unity and become two cities' (Plato, 1997: 551c). In this divided city 'some persons are extravagantly rich while others are utter paupers' (Plato, 1997: 551e) and the city is fiscally impoverished because the oligarchs' 'love of money renders them unwilling to pay taxes' (Plato, 1997: 551b). Plutocratic oligarchy is a form of parasitism because the plutocrat, 'though he seemed to be one of the government is really neither governor nor servant of the state, but only a consumer of its resources' (Plato, 1997: 552a). Likening the city to a beehive, Plato says that while many people are drones who work to make the plutocrats wealthy in this kind of hive there grow up 'stinging drones' 'that become a plague of the state' (Plato, 1997: 552b). These gangsters and criminal classes are kept down by force while 'the cause which produces such persons therein is want of education and bad training, and a bad condition of the commonwealth' (Plato 1997: 552e). Meanwhile, at the top of the social hierarchy, amongst the oligarchs themselves, their appetites for money-making and covetousness become, as it were, 'an eastern monarch, adorned with diadem and collar and with a scimitar by his side' (Plato, 1997: 553c); an oriental despot that subjects and subordinates all other rational and high-spirited capacities, 'forbidding the former to investigate or reason about anything, save how to multiply riches, and forbidding the latter to admire or esteem anything save wealth and the wealthy, or to be ambitious after a single object save the acquisition of riches and whatever else may conduce to this' (Plato 1997: 553d). If one wishes to see the evil of this kind of society, Plato says, 'you must look to occasions where they are the guardians of orphans, and to any similar accidents which put it completely in their power to act unjustly' (Plato, 1997: 554b). In other words, Plato says, the proof of plutocracy can be seen in how a state takes care of the needs of its children, the elderly, the ill and the vulnerable.

While neglecting the vulnerable, plutocratic oligarchs 'by their reckless admission of unrestrained license' also prey upon one another, creating additional enemies from within their own number, for 'whenever one of the remainder yields them opportunity, they wound him by infusing their poisonous money, and then recover interest many times as great as the patent sum, and thus make the beggar and the drone multiply in the state'. Thus plutocratic oligarchy generates internal enemies, lurking in the city, 'some owing debts, and others disenfranchised, and others labouring under both misfortunes – hating and plotting against the new owners of their property and against all who are better off than themselves, and enamoured of revolution'. One ameliorating measure that could be taken, Plato says, would be that if 'it be enacted that voluntary contracts be as a general rule entered into at the proper risk of the contractor, people will be less shameless in their money dealings in the city and such evils as we have just now described will be of less common growth therein'. But plutocratic oligarchs 'nursed in luxury and surfeited with abundance ... cannot make up their minds to extinguish this great evil' (Plato, 1997: 555a–556d, *passim*). When their money-making schemes fail, rather than suffering the consequences they transfer their debts on to other people in the city. This city thereby, Plato says, sows the seeds of its own destruction, and like a diseased body degenerates, making way either for conquest and takeover by a stronger and more vigorous external regime, or else by an internal revolution. Democracy arises, Plato says, whenever the poor win the day.

Democracy appears initially to be very much a better form of life than plutocracy, but pleonexia persists here too and will eventually undermine it, paving the way for tyranny. At first sight, 'liberty of act and speech abound in the city and a man has licence therein to do what he will, and every citizen will arrange his own manner of life as suits his pleasure'. There is great diversity of character, so that 'it may be thought of as beautiful as a coloured dress embroidered with every kind of flower' (Plato, 1997: 557c) ... 'an agreeable, lawless, parti-coloured commonwealth, dealing with all alike on a footing of equality, whether they be really equal or not' (Plato, 1997: 258b). All is not as well as it seems, though, for democracy not only liberates the appetites but 'maintains that all appetites are alike and ought to be equally respected' (Plato: 1997: 561c). The typical subject of liberal democracy

> lives from day to day to the end in the gratification of the casual appetite, now drinking himself drunk to the sound of music, and presently putting himself under training, sometimes idling and neglecting everything, and then living like a student of philosophy. And often he takes a part in public affairs, and starting up, speaks and acts according to the impulse of the moment. Now he follows in the footsteps of certain great generals, because he covets their distinctions; and anon he takes to trade, because he envies the successful trader. And there is no order or constraining rule in his life, but he calls this life of his pleasant and liberal and happy, and follows it out to the end. (Plato, 1997: 562a)

Living without constraint, without rules, 'living in the now', all of this sounds great, Plato says, but being ill-disciplined the social body tends towards falling out of shape, paving the way for sickness in the body politic. Democracy, eventually, 'is destroyed by its insatiable craving for the object which it defines to be supremely good' (Plato, 1997: 562b). That single object that democracy pursues to the disregard of all else is Freedom.

The democratic city, thirsting for freedom, 'falls under the influence of toastmasters and quaffs the wine of liberty untempered far beyond the due measure and proceeds to arraign its rulers as oligarchs unless they become submissive and supply it with freedom in copious draughts' (Plato, 1997: 562d). Inversions of order and transgression of limits become the rule. Everything is permitted under the banner of liberty and equality, confusing 'disorder as freedom, and licenciousness as magnificence, and shamelessness as bravery' (Plato, 1997: 560d). The prevailing anarchy steals into private houses and spreads on every side, so that gorged with freedom, 'the hound becomes the mistress of the house' and becomes intolerant of anything that casts the shadow of a master (Plato, 1997: 563d). Thus, Plato says, 'that same disease [pleonexia] which broke out in oligarchy and ruined it, appears in democracy also with increased strength and virulence', a contagion that spreads throughout the body politic, so that 'the most intense freedom lays the foundation for the heaviest and fiercest slavery' (Plato, 1997: 563e–564a).

Democracy accelerates into decadence and paves the way for tyranny. A wealthy, greedy elite persists in democracy, and finding greater latitude and licence can become even wealthier. There is no principle or power to oppose or to constrain them, except for 'a class of idle and extravagant men' (Plato, 1997: 564c) – politicians and bureaucrats – which separates from the mass society beneath and from the elite above. This class becomes, 'with few exceptions, the sole presiding body; and its keenest members speak and act, while the residue sit on the benches round and hum applause, and will not brook any opposing statement: so that all the concerns of such a commonwealth are, with some trifling exceptions, in the hands of this body' (Plato, 1997: 564d), a political class that while depriving the moneyed class of their substance, and making division of it among the numerous masses, manage, if possible, to keep the largest share of it for themselves' (Plato, 1997: 565a). The moneyed elites respond by evading taxes and buying political favour, so that democratic political parties are corrupted by the influence of elites from above and the demands and expectations for greater freedoms and benefits from below. Amongst the three strata, moneyed elites, government and the popular masses, political antagonism intensifies in the form of 'impeachments, prosecutions and trials, directed by each party against the other' (Plato, 1997: 565b), generating a morbid condition of chaos and stasis. Out of such conditions tyranny is born.

The first face of the tyrant is of a popular champion of the masses who promises to break the stasis and impose a new order on the chaos. But the popular champion, who in the beginning explicitly repudiates tyranny, 'has a smile and a greeting for everybody that he meets, is mild and gracious, and makes large promises, cancels debts and redistributes land', eventually 'stands in the chariot of the state, metamorphosed from a champion into a consummate tyrant' (Plato, 1997: 566a–556d, *passim*). Specifically, Plato says, he is 'metamorphosed into a wolf' (Plato, 1997: 565d). The cause of the lycanthropy of the popular champion and the emergence of tyranny from the decrepit body of democracy grown decadent is that in the course of the revolution that he leads there is civil bloodshed. The tyrant gets a taste for blood – the blood of his own people. There are those members of the city who have presided over the previous corrupt and decadent state of affairs, the perpetrators of its worst excesses and injustices, whom the champion must necessarily have killed or have banished, whose debts are cancelled, whose land is seized and redistributed. But amongst those necessary victims of the revolution are also people who are also integral members of the community. It is during this dimension of revolution as civil war that, according to legend, human entrails are minced up and eaten with the entrails of other sacrificial victims, an un-holy cannibalism, that however unintentional or unavoidable is the source of lycanthropy. 'Thenceforth the inevitable destiny of such a man is either to be destroyed by his enemies, or to become a tyrant, and be metamorphosed from a man into a wolf' (Plato, 1997: 566a).

Having relieved himself of his enemies, destroying some and reconciling with others, the tyrant 'excites wars so that the people may stand in need of a leader'. He imposes heavy taxes and austerity so as to constrain people to devote themselves to the day-to-day requirements of getting by; he keenly monitors those 'who are manly, who high-minded, who prudent, who wealthy, for he is compelled to be the enemy of all these, and to plot against them, til he has purged them out of the city', until he has left himself not a friend nor an enemy who is worth anything. The opposite of a physician who cares for the body politic by removing what is bad and leaving what is good (Plato, 1997: 566d–568b), 'the tyrant removes the good and leaves the bad'. The body politic becomes progressively corrupted and diseased. The tyrant employs a local bodyguard of lackeys backed by foreign mercenaries; poets and dramatists and all the agencies of culture – 'fine, loud persuasive voices' – are paid to puff and to proclaim that all is well. He expends the sacred property of the city to pay his retainers, and as revenues from taxes on an increasingly impoverished citizenry decline, the tyrant 'will draw on his parents' estate' – the assets and the natural resources of the commonwealth of the state, the inheritance that ought to be the legacy to future generations. And supposing, Plato says, that the people grow to resent this notion, that the child they had begotten – their one-time champion – had turned out badly:

> They had begotten and installed him not with the intent that when he was grown big they should be made the slaves of their own slaves, and maintain him and them with a mob of others, but with the intent that under his championship they should be emancipated from the rich men of the state, and the gentlemen, as they are called; and suppose they now bid him to depart out of the city, together

with his friends, like a father expelling a son from home along with some riotous boon-companions? What then? (Plato, 1997: 569a)

Well, unfortunately, the people soon discover that they have grown feeble while he has grown strong, that the tyrant has disarmed his parents, and that the tyrant child will beat and kill them, and that from now on government will be an open and avowed tyranny. People will discover that they have gone from the frying pan of the vast and unreasonable liberty of democracy into the fire of the harshest and bitterest of all slaveries.

Plato eventually turns to the question of the genealogy, the political psychology and the political anthropology of the subject of tyranny. The tyranny of the future – perhaps in fact the present tyranny suffered by the citizens of contemporary republics like Ireland – is not necessarily the familiar historical figure of a Hitler, Stalin, Mao or Mugabe, though there is a possibility that a native son, local hero, popular charismatic leader who turns out to be a wicked trickster may very well emerge from the liminal conditions of unfolding crisis, under the banner of resurgent nationalism; or, just as likely, under the banner of liberty a champion of an even more radical free market. The tyranny that Plato identifies, our tyranny, may be one of 'indwelling tyrant passions' (Plato, 1997: 573c–574b), frightful appetites that abound in wants shoot up day and night, so that 'a tyrant is in truth a slave to passions that cannot be satisfied; his life is loaded with terrors' and full of convulsions and pangs, resembling the state over which he rules (Plato, 1997: 579d–580c). The tyrant's passions are fierce and raging. Those pleonexic passions that tyrannize the common people are banal, but no less bestial. Plato identifies them specifically as the ruling passions of bovine ruminants:

> After the fashion of cattle, always looking down and with their heads bent to earth and table, they feed, fattening themselves, and copulating: and for the sake of getting more of these things, they kick and butt with horns and with hoofs of iron, killing each other because they are insatiable. (Plato, 1997: 385e)

How are we to represent a society and its people that are slaves to passions, prone to devolve into wolves, cattle and other brutes? Drawing from figures that Greek mythology is brimming with – Chimera, Scylla, Cerberus and a host of other monsters where 'several generic forms have grown together and coalesced into one' – Plato gives us the poetic image of another one: think first, he says, of a form 'of a motley many-headed monster, furnished with a ring of heads of tame and wild animals which he can produce by turns in every instance out of himself'. These heads stand for the passions and the appetites that the elderly businessman, Cephalus, in whose house the discourse is staged, at the very beginning of *Republic* refers to as 'a multitude of furious masters'. He thanks old age for abating their frantic and savage appetites; they stand for the demon whose name is legion; the multiple, various hybrid morphology of Pazuzu; the 'rough beast' of Yeats's 'Second Coming'. Next, Plato says, as part of the same composite, monstrous being, think of the forms of a lion, and of a man. The multi-headed monster is by far the strongest of the three, the lion second, and the man the weakest. The three are combined and grown together into one being, but externally having the form of the man. If we were to depict the unjust man and the unjust society it would be as if one were to 'feed and strengthen the multifarious monster and the lion, and to starve and enfeeble the man to such an extent as to leave him at the mercy of the guidance of either of the other two, without making any attempt to habituate or reconcile them to one another, but leaving them together to bite and struggle and devour each other' (Plato, 1997: 588e–589d). Such is an image of the *spiritus mundi* of pleonexia in the de-regulated, un-moderated, de-sublimated, neoliberal new world order; a world ruled by a savage god in which the rough beast of market forces and animal passions tears asunder limb from limb the social body of which it forms part; market society as a body politic demonically possessed by wild, raging passions that (like Pazuzu's possession of Regan) lurches forwards and backwards and careens from side to side, turning itself inside out, wrenching its head from front to back, fluxing, morphing and wildly alternating between grotesque and bizarre forms of plutocracy, democracy and tyranny; authoritarian populist anarcho-capital-ism. As it was for Plato's Athens, this is the present sorry state of the Irish republic.

Is there no alternative? Contrary to the neoliberal doctrine that 'there is no alternative', Plato says that there certainly is an alternative. Just as Zeus saves the cosmos from Pluto's rapacity, a wise and just society would be one in which the inner man is enabled to have a firmer control over the entire being, 'and with the lion as his ally, to cultivate, like a husbandman, the many-headed beast – nursing and rearing the tame parts of it, and checking the growth of the wild; and thus to pursue his training on the principle of concerning himself for all jointly, and reconciling them to one another and to himself' (Plato, 1997: 589a).

Sounds great! says Glaucon, but the only problem is that things remain pretty much as Thrasymachus said at the outset, that the rich and powerful will do as they have always done and the ideal 'city whose outline we have now just completed . . . is confined to the region of speculation, for I do not believe that it is to be found anywhere on Earth' (Plato, 1997: 589a). Indeed that may be so, Plato concludes, but what we have sketched is a blueprint that may be known only in heaven, an ideal form, 'a pattern for him who wishes to behold it, and beholding it organizes himself accordingly, with it and the question of its present or future existence will be redeemed and superseded because he will adopt the practices of such a city, to the exclusion of all others (Plato, 1997: 592b).

Plato's *Republic* can be read as a treatise on the social pathologies of contemporary civilization in general and the contemporary state of the Irish republic in particular. In the diseased city questions of justice and the good society are undermined by the recurrence of pleonexia. *Republic* is Plato's political science, political economy, political psychology and political anthropology. The only possible resolution that Plato can see is what Foucault would in our own time take up in terms of a 'care of the self'; education as the cultivation of capacities that would enable people – or, for Plato, at least, an ideal-type caste of people – to master their appetites and their passions so that they may be moderated and sublimated, and thus constitute a model that others may emulate and subjectivize, thereby becoming self-governing and 'each one governing their self correctly being the best possibility of realizing the well-being of the whole' (Foucault, 1998: 7).

Pleonexia – greed, hunger, society degenerated to the 'hunger games' – is an excess of appetite and desire and a lack of empathy and judgment. Always latent, pleonexia emerges and becomes de-contained when laws are weakened and virtues cannot be formed. Pleonexia is amplified and intensified in the wake of crises. Pleonexic greed is therefore most decidedly not 'good', as neoliberalism proclaims it to be, but a social pathology of civilization, pathogenic to social and bodies politic, and with a corresponding idea-typical pleonexic subject – wolf-like, amoral, isolist, narcissistic-psychotic. A system built predominantly upon unrestrained greed, anger, envy and pride will not, by definition, be virtuous, but degenerative, unstable and ultimately self-destructive, if not put down by its victims first.

Notes

1 An example is to be found in the university. Egocentric conceit, narcissistic self-regard and jockeying for recognition and position are quite common throughout the ranks and offices of the university. Weber identifies such power games as the specific and peculiar pathology of academic life, and we are all familiar with it. It is, in the unique little world of the university, a 'normal' pathology. It becomes abnormal and pathological, however, under particular conditions, as when the traditional standards measuring 'academic excellence' become unstable and uncertain, and when they are de-symbolized and re-symbolized and translated into a new currency; when the quality of scholarship is rendered into countable, quantitative terms, the number of pages published and the quantity of research monies 'captured'. Under such circumstances – exactly the circumstances of the university under the neoliberal revolution – mediocre people who publish much but of little genuine value in terms of scholarship or originality, or whose research finds favour with funding agencies, imagine themselves to be prodigious talents, people of genius deserving universal acclaim and accelerated promotion, and the clamouring to become Professor intensifies to a fever. This is often misrecognized as vitality in our universities, but in fact these intensities are flurries and death-rattles, symptoms of a mortally sick collegiate body.

2 Thomassen (2013: 607) synopsizes Thucydides' diagnosis as follows: symptomatic of this pathological state was the total subordination of the common welfare to the satisfaction of the private aspirations of factional leaders 'aiming at the seizure of power as good in itself without regard to any genuine political end'. Politics had become reduced to a question of means, and a central element of those 'means' involved a rivalry over the emotions of the masses. True patriotism was gone; it had been replaced by empty populist slogans. Politics and social life had dissolved into obtuse friend–enemy categories, eliminating all possibility of toleration and mutual trust. The situation was marked by a devastating loss of values: 'General indifference toward everything except money and power, rejection of higher values, and lack of concern with moral self-perfection had of necessity produced a loss of respect for law and religion' (Fleiss, 1959: 607). As leaders were concentrated on seeking the emotional support of the masses, reason itself was vanishing. Anti-intellectualism was spreading; status was gained by entertaining the masses with easy slogans; lies were accepted as true; neither honesty nor wisdom were of any importance in the faction-ridden *poleis*; in this state of affairs, the intelligent citizens were excluded from political influence (ibid.). The social disintegration was even visible via a complete confusion of language and concepts: words and concepts were losing their meaning, preventing the communication of truth, 'without which no order can endure' (Fleiss, 1959: 608).

3 Many of Plato's most radical and innovative proposals seem to be intended as a compliment to his new Spartan overlords, such as the discipline, asceticism and anti-materialist communalism of the philosopher-kings, and especially the egalitarianism between the sexes, an idea unthinkable in Athens but long the norm in Sparta.

4 Plato represents political history in terms of a cycle, degenerating from aristocracy through timocracy–oligarchy–democracy–tyranny: and then the cycle recurs again, in reverse: revolutionary and anarchic radical democracy, to oligarchy, to plutocracy, and so on. The sequence in this cycle of degeneracy is not necessarily linear: rather than being overthrown by tyranny, democracy often reversed into oligarchy, as was the case in Plato's time. Democracy was overturned by oligarchy twice by what were overt *coup d'etats* in rapid succession, in 409 and 411, and numerous times democracy reverted into oligarchy less overtly, whereby while Athens was a democracy *de jure* it was *de facto* ruled by oligarchy, whether aristocratic elite or plutocracy, which for the most part amounted to the same thing. This pattern bears comparison with our contemporary experience and in our own time by the 'quiet coup' of the global financial plutocracy.

8

Anamnesis for a new Ireland

The construction of any human dwelling requires an *anamnesis*, a 'naming', the calling of a divine power instituting a centre of the world. That is why the place on which it is built cannot be arbitrary or even 'rationally' be chosen by the builders. It must be 'discovered' through the revelation of some divine agency. Anamnesis is achieved by incanting a *verba concepta* that interrupts the ordinary passage of time and by repeating the archetypical gesture of the mythical hero. The *Leabhar Gabála* has it that when the Milesians, the first invaders of Ireland in about 2000BC, made their landfall on the Beara Peninsula, it was necessary for their bard, Amergin, to chant the land into existence so that they could set foot on shore. Similarly in modern Ireland we can identify precisely the place and time of the mystical inaugural rite that initiated the Mythic Age of Globalization. In this instance the *verba concepta*, repeated as a mantra ever since, is 'Tax-Free Zone' –and more recently 'Defend our low corporate tax rate'.[1] The *verba concepta*, the divine *logos*, states the law, the new commandment. In this case the incantation that was intended to bring prosperity to the community, provide a basis for society by inaugurating the free market, invokes a demonic power that tends to make society disappear. In the free market, as Margaret Thatcher famously declared, 'there is no such thing as society, only individual men and women'. The society that places itself under the rule of Hermes dissolves its boundaries and opens itself up to limit-lessness and insatiability.

The mythic age of globalization has one of its most important genealogi-cal moments in Ireland, specifically at Limerick's transatlantic sea-plane base at Foynes, later the airport at Shannon and its tax-free export processing zone, which were inaugurated at the historical, axial, liminal moment of the transi-tion of world empires from the British Empire to American imperialism. The two globe-spanning airlines, British Imperial Airways, which served the British Empire, the Middle East, Africa and India, and Pan American Airways, which served the American Empire in Latin America and the Caribbean, Hawaii and the Pacific, both used Foynes and then Shannon as their transatlantic hub. From the skies came the herald angels of the new gods of globalization, Humphrey Bogart, Gracie Fields, the glittering stars and celebrities of America's culture industry, flying between New York, London and Paris. The cargo cults of the South Sea Islands sprung up at exactly the same moment as Pan Am developed its trans-Pacific bases in the Philippines, Midway and Guam, and as the air-forces of the Japanese and American Empires gunned up for a clash of the Titans. Enraptured by the glamour of global superpowers, like the cargo cultists at the opposite side of the world, in Ireland we too prepared libations for the transatlantic gods – Irish coffee – and we gave small sacrificial gifts – duty free shopping – to attract the gods and to keep them coming, and when the jet age meant that the new gods might overfly us, we built the infrastructure for runaway globalization – a duty free export processing zone.

Cargo cults and sacred visions

In cargo cults world events and new ideas are assimilated into natives' traditional Holy Dreams. In one particular South Sea island's cargo cult, for example, cult members believed, as most religions do, that their Gods, their ancestors, were the source from which all good things were given to their people. After their contact with Whites, who had an abundance of wonderful things, it seemed to the natives that these missionaries and merchants must be emissaries from the natives' own ancestor Gods, and the 'cargo' was intended for them. For instance, in the case of the John Frum cargo cult, 'John', 'from America', was a Black serviceman whom the natives took to be their own ancestor sent from Paradise. The White men had, it seemed, intercepted the cargo that had been intended for Black natives. John Frum returned to the ancestors, but he will come again, this time bringing the natives their rightful gifts from the gods. Thus native cosmology becomes blended with the religion of European missionaries, merchants and soldiers (Harris 1989). Lawrence (1965: 75–78) and Worsley (1987: 146–169) trace cases in which the various influences of German Lutheran missionaries, Australian, English, Japanese and American colonists, administrators and soldiers amalgamated during the period between the late nineteenth century and World War II into a baroque phantasmagoria. Natives came to believe that the European's God created Adam and Eve and gave them cargo of food, tools, radios, guns and matches. He took the cargo back when they discovered sex and he sent a flood to destroy them. When Ham disobeyed his father Noah, his cargo was taken away and he was sent to New Guinea. White masters were divine beings, and the exploitation and forced labour they imposed on natives was a purgatory they must endure. Now all Noah's descendants (native, white and half caste) were being given a chance to reform and regain their cargo through Jesus Christ/John Frum. For many years the natives suffered, waited, worked and prayed, but after a while it seemed to some that the missionaries were lying; the natives had been good Christians and worked hard, but it was the foreign bosses who did no work that got all the cargo. To account for this they formed a new theory. Jesus Christ had been kidnapped by a combination of the European missionaries and a conspiracy of Jews. Their cargo and their saviour-ancestor-God were imprisoned in Australia, but he would escape and come in a plane with the cargo that had been intended for them all along. In the meantime they would build a runway and watchtowers and wait patiently for his second coming.

In the mytho-poesis of the cargo cult the new world does not necessarily refute and replace the original myth, but is alloyed with it so that it supports and affirms it, makes it more meaningful, and the new cosmopoiesis – creating a new world and making a new universe of meaning – contains the old world. This anthropological tale of a cargo cult from the South Pacific seems at first to be exotic and bizarre, and to have nothing remotely of relevance to an understanding of the development of modern Ireland. But 'cargo' stands for 'meaning', and the South Pacific Islanders who are waiting for cargo have in fact a great deal in common with their modern Western counterparts depicted by Beckett as 'Waiting for Godot', and even more in common with their antipodean contemporaries on a remote island in the North Atlantic, the Irish of the 1930s. As Berger (1976: 21) says, the cargo cult is 'a perfect metaphor for the myth of economic growth as a Holy Dream'.

A genealogy of the Holy Dream of 'economic development' and the Irish cargo cult

The language of Ireland's economic development used in the twenty-first century, replete with such terms as 'drivers' of 'progress', 'cultivating entrepreneurship and innovation' by providing 'infrastructure and services' within a 'business friendly' culture; 'strategies for recovery' that emphasize securing 'foreign direct investment' by 'protecting' our 'low corporate tax rate', is a language that seems rational and sensible, that states the obvious and necessary. But languages and discourses that speak taken for granted truths have origins and courses. They have a genealogy. By 'genealogy' we mean their conditions of emergence or 'birth'. 'The manner in which a particular entity comes into being really matters. Political institutions and social practices that come into being at a certain moment are concrete and specific responses to the conditions prevailing at that moment, and they gather their "justification" over time' (Szakolczai, 2013: 461). Genealogy means also that the circumstances of the birth of ideas and practices have lasting effects, so that even once a particular institution has ceased to function its ways of acting and thinking may be carried over for a considerable time. The genealogical conditions of emergence are 'stamping experiences' whose indelible mark is borne by subsequent generations (Szakolczai, 2013). The holy dream of Irish economic development was born in the 1930s within a liminal moment of transition between two world empires: the inter-war era, the decline of the British Empire and the rise of the global American Empire, and it grew to maturity during the Cold War. We are still speaking that language, a language that has become clichéd and vacuous, and we are living in a holy dream that has become a nightmare.

Coinciding with the rise of the global American Empire was a 'golden age' of American Anthropology. In the South Seas this generated such canonic works as Franz Boas' (1975) studies of the Pacific North West, notably the institution of the Potlatch, essential to Mauss's formulation of *The Gift* (2002); Malinowski's *Argonauts of the Western Pacific* (1924); Margaret Mead's *Coming of Age in Samoa* (1928); Gregory Bateson's *Naven* (1958); and later Clifford Geertz's studies of Java/Bali (1993). Mirroring anthropologists' interests in the paradise islands of the South Pacific was American anthropologists' interest in the enchanted island of the North Atlantic, the Ireland of the Harvard Irish Mission 1931–1936 led by Conrad M. Arensberg, whose books *The Irish Countryman* (1937) and, with Solon T. Kimball, *Family and Community in Ireland* (1940) were for many years the classic social science texts on Irish society. The anthropologists' interest was complemented in popular culture by iconic Hollywood depictions of romantic dreams in paradise and in fairyland, 'South Pacific' and 'The Quiet Man'.

In Ireland, the enchanted isle, Yeats had already said that the Fairies 'are still alive, giving gifts to the kindly and plaguing the surly'.

Have you ever seen a fairy or such like?' I asked an old man in Co. Sligo. 'Amn't I annoyed with them,' was the answer. 'Do the fishermen along here know anything of the mermaids?' I asked a woman of a village in Co. Dublin. 'Indeed, they don't like to see them at all,' she answered, 'for they always bring bad weather.' 'Here is a man who believes in ghosts,' said a foreign sea-captain, pointing to a pilot of my acquaintance. 'In every house over there,' said the pilot, pointing to his native village of Rosses, 'there are several.' Certainly that now old and much respected dogmatist the Spirit of the Age [The Enlightenment] had in no manner made his voice heard down there. (Yeats, 2003: xxiv)

Conrad Arensberg and his Harvard anthropologist missionaries found that 'the Good People' were still a powerful force in Ireland of the 1930s:

The chief of these powers is usually called the 'fairies'. The country people have many other names for them which they prefer. But, most often, they feel

no need for distinguishing them by particular names. They simply call them
'them'. In the pronoun they summarize both their nameless power and their
immanence. No greater specification is necessary where such powers crowd
so closely in upon one's life. The acts and rituals which spring out of this
belief are similarly broad in scope. They range from minor doings and turns
of speech of daily life to the most hidden practices of rare and deadly black
magic. (Arensberg, 1937: 184)

Whereas according to Weber 'the Puritan outlook stood at the cradle of
modern economic man', in Ireland the hand that rocked the cradle belonged
to a different order entirely:

> First one must notice that the Irish countryman is a very devout man. His life is
> ordered in his adherence to his religion. Much of his habit of mind and his view
> of the world responds to his Faith. He is a devout and practising Catholic. But
> he is also devout and practising in another direction too, very often. Just as there
> is room in his mind and heart for patriotic fervour as well as religious zeal, so is
> there room for fairy belief. Sometimes, of course, these devotions may conflict;
> but ordinarily they need not. They can intermesh and support one another.
> Thus in his daily life, one finds the countryman carrying out many acts which
> are related both to his Church and his fairy belief.... 'pisherogues' occupy... the
> border-line between the natural, profane, mundane world and that of the super-
> natural, the sacred and the religious. It is along this border-line that we must
> trace the Irish countryman. (Arensberg, 1936: 185)

If we listen closely to the moments when the *verba concepta* of Irish
modernity is ritually incanted we can discern the fairy influence and the cargo
cult mentality. The formal ritual moments wherein the *verba concepta* of
Ireland's holy dream of economic development was enunciated and subsequently incanted as a sacred mantra include the Opening Ceremonies by Sean
Lemass of the Foynes Atlantic Flight Terminus on 23 March 1936, and the
inauguration of the first 'Duty Free' sales at Foynes shortly afterwards; the
announcement of the *Shannon Customs Free Airport Act* (1947), 'an Irish
invention, the world's first...'; duty free shopping in Shannon in 1950, and the
International Mail Order Service in 1954; the declaration of the Shannon Tax
Free Zone, that is, the *Industrial Development (Encouragement of External
Investment) Act* (1958); the *Customs Free Airport (Amendment) Bill,* and
Finance (Miscellaneous Provisions) Bill (1958) 'to encourage location of
business [by abolishing Customs–border regulations] and tax exemption on
profits for 25 years'; and the *Shannon Free Airport Development Company
Limited Act* (1959).

> The Minister, with the concurrence of the Minister for Finance, may by order
> declare that, on and after a specified date, the land enclosed within the limits

defined by the order shall be the Customs-free airport for the purposes of this Act' (Lemass 1947a: 2). 'By This Bill we are making Shannon Airport the first free airport in the world. ... Even though the establishment of a customs free airport could be fully justified if it were designed solely for the convenience of transit passengers ... the people who should benefit most from the setting up of the free airport are merchants and transport companies engaged in international trade. For such people we are providing at Shannon a centre for international trade subject to the minimum restrictions'. (Lemass, 1947b: 2)

The government has reached a decision to reorganize Shannon Airport to meet freight and industrial developments. Freeport and tax concession encourage-ments will be given to industries which establish facilities at Shannon Airport. Beginning in March 1958 the Irish government will eliminate completely the income tax on profits derived from exports. As far as Shannon is concerned, this will mean that any firm which sets itself up in the Free Port to distribute its goods by freight from Shannon to any part of the world will have no income tax to pay on the profits derived from this business. In addition, free sites and grants of up to £50,000 will be made to firms to build factories and warehouses. Grants will also be made for the purposes of training operatives. (Lemass, in Callanan, 2000: 83).

The Antipodes of the 1950s were testing grounds for technologies of glob-alization. In the South Pacific a 10.4 megaton bomb, almost 500 times more powerful than the bomb dropped on Nagasaki only seven years previously, left behind a crater 2 km wide, and an island had been wiped off the face of the Earth. In the North Atlantic not a fission but a fiscal bomb had been detonated: 'It was like working in the middle of an explosion! ... There was tremendous excitement – everyone in the place was talking about develop-ment ... everyone wanted development to take place. There was a total appreciation that the place had to develop or else go back to the hares' (manager, Shannon Free Airport Development Company (SFADCO), cited in Callanan, 2000: 47).

One of Sean Lemass's right hand men was Brendan O'Regan, the charis-matic visionary hero behind developments at Foynes and later at Shannon.[2] The transatlantic sea-plane base at Foynes had only just been established, giving modern Irish visionaries like Lemass and O'Regan their 'taste for the infinite' when the danger that it might all move on again became apparent. Technological advances in the run-up to war indicated that planes of the future would be land based, so Lemass and O'Regan moved across the river to develop a runway at Rinanna (later Shannon Airport). But no sooner had they laid the runway and set up the tower there than the leap in technology during the war from propeller to jet engines meant that Ireland's beachhead of modernity might already be a thing of the past. Like the islanders of the South Pacific, Ireland too may be abandoned and overflown by the gods of globalization. O'Regan remembers: 'All our ideas at that stage were targeted on coping with the threat of the jet age. There were genuine fears that the airport would be by-passed. ... I became firmly convinced that the phenomenal success of the duty-free shop could be transferred to the industrial sector. ... 250 acres of airport land could be easily converted to an air-age, tax free industrial estate' (O'Regan, in Sweeney, 2004: 253). Ireland's cargo-cult of economic development was a mystical world in which 'We were selling a concept,' O'Regan says. They had to hold on to the holy dream at all cost:

> Things were regarded as impossible by many people. We had to get going quickly. Get some buildings up at all cost. We were in a desperate hurry. We were told that in a year the airlines were likely to remove Shannon from their schedules. We had a major public relations effort to convince the airlines that by leaving Shannon they were leaving a potential market. We had to talk people into believing the vision. (O'Regan, cited in Callanan, 2000: 84)

That vision was born of the cold war and the Marshall Plan. O'Regan had been a delegate sent by Lemass to Montreal for the conference that drew up the Marshall Plan. This was a moment of historical opportunity and O'Regan was the charismatic visionary who could see the emerging *spiritus mundi* and sense the zeitgeist. The future of the world was at stake as the two global superpowers faced off against one another, and the fortunes of the world's small nations would be determined by how they strategically aligned themselves. 'Though anti-communism had long been a feature of Irish life, George Garrett, US minister to Dublin, believed that Ireland was as vulnerable as any other European country to communist infiltration as a result of deteriorating economic and social conditions' (Whelan, 2000: 31). Motivated by the constant threat that Shannon would be overflown, O'Regan knew it was essential to create reasons to keep landing there. In 1950 O'Regan, Lemass, Whittaker and others set about implementing the ideas O'Regan first suggested in the Marshall Plan Trip Report. During the Cold War Ireland's strategy would be to make itself a hot spot for propagating 'the American way'.

Ireland's dreamtime turns to nightmare

In the summer of 1963 *Time* magazine ran a special feature on Ireland with the title 'Ireland: Lifting the Green Curtain' (*Time*, 2 July 1963). The cover pictured Sean Lemass, the urbane, cosmopolitan, post-de-Valera generation New Man who would usher in a New Ireland. There is 'a new spirit in the ould sod', *Time* declared. Lemass, in a well-cut dark suit, the modern uniform of international business, is depicted with a Leprechaun on his shoulder. The grinning Leprechaun is drawing back a curtain behind which we see a glimpse of the Ireland that is coming – a crock of gold consisting of factory chimneys and gleaming office towers. The Leprechaun holds the promise of riches, but there's always a trick! Celebrating this nascent moment of neoliberal global-ization, and at the same time as though sensing that the Leprechaun will get up to devilment in due course, the Editorial commences:

> The summer sky still breaks over the land in splinters of green, gold or lumi-nous waves of grey, staining the hills blue and purple and vermilion, heaping the valleys with shimmering veils of mist. In that weird, wet Atlantic light – or so they say – the swarthy chieftains and pale queens who once ruled the five kingdoms of Celtic Ireland still clatter across country. As the island's endless sleight-of-sky creates and dissolves horizons, the landscape seems dreamily unreal. The reality of Ireland is special: it lies on a border region where tragedy and laughter, jollity and gloom, hell and the happy isles converge. (Time 1963: 30)

Ireland's 'sleight of sky' that creates and dissolves horizons has its corre-spondence in sleight of hand in the political culture, for the Leprechaun's devilment always entails transgression of boundaries between the human world and the world of the fairies. Shannon Free Airport is the magical spot where the rainbow of dreams touches the earth. There the Leprechaun promises riches by jumping over the sacred boundary:

> For American merchants and manufacturers seeking bases in Europe, the free trade zone at Shannon Free Airport is an ideal location. It is a subtle springboard of trade. It helps you jump over the wall of taxes, regulations and other imped-iments that make it tough to do business in Europe from across the Atlantic. (SFADCO brochure, 1958)

The Leprechaun's trickery is well known to the Irish. A note of caution was aired in the Senate: 'The Minister in charge of such a development as the Shannon Free Airport where such extraordinary measures are taken to attract industries should be ultra conservative, ultra careful, to see that there are not any undesirable results from the arrival of such industries. ... What at first sight may seem to be an extremely logical and proper effort to employ labour and to make a profit may not be that at all. ... It may in fact turn out to be 'a chain hanky operation' [i.e. a magic trick, a con job]' (Donegan, 1961: 1653). But still, with the Leprechaun we are always willing to take the risk, and this is the tragedy of Ireland's development strategy, then, as it is still today. The demon of politics and the tragedy of development is, as Weber says, that 'the world is governed by demons and that he who lets himself in for politics ... contracts with diabolical powers and for his action it is not true that good can follow only from good and evil only from evil, but that often the opposite is true'. The tragedy is that good people, acting with good intentions, in good faith, with good ideas, heroic modern Irish visionaries like Lemass and

O'Regan: when they make a deal with the Leprechaun, their actions may have unintended consequences that undermine the good and turn out to be evil.

Surreal Ireland: *At Swim-Two-Birds*, again

One person who understood the strange ways in which the cargo cult dreams of modern visionaries can turn into nightmares was Brian O'Nolan/ O'Nuallain/ (aka Flann O'Brien, aka Myles na gCopaleen) whose *At Swim-Two-Birds* (1967) is a modernist-surrealist proto-postmodernist representation of the Irish idiomatic and idiosyncratic phantasmagoria of Progress. *At Swim-Two-Birds* is a book with several beginnings, storylines, narrative voices and temporalities, in which the action unfolds in a liminal zone between the Fairy-devil world of the Pooka McPhellimy, the mythic history of Finn McCool and mad King Sweeney, the cowboy world of wild west pulp fiction and the mundane realities of daily life in Dublin. It's a spectrum encompassing petty bourgeois respectability and conventionalism represented by the (purported) author's uncle and the pub-crawling pseudo-bohemian life of an undergraduate university student, played out against the backdrop of a capital city of an Ireland suspended in stasis between empire and nation, insular traditionalism and European modernism and cosmopolitanism, the dead hand of history and an emerging new world order teetering on the brink of World War II. All these various realities co-exist, collide and collude, conflate and confound and confuse one another. Recycled fictional characters revolt against their (fictional) author and recompose the text, while the author of the meta-text, O'Nolan himself, exists in pure liminality: he is Principal Officer in the Department of Local Government, a columnist in the *Irish Times* (writing under a pseudonym, Myles na gCopalleen, and several additional aliases) and a writer of fiction under other names again. The strange placename 'Swim-Two-Birds' is an actual place, *Snamh Dá Ein*, an island at a ford on the River Shannon at the geographical centre of Ireland; situated in the middle of floods and swirling currents; at the intersections of the mythic (Swim-Two-Birds is home to the Children of Lir), the legendary (St. Patrick and Mad Sweeney both rested there), the historical (the island is adjacent to the monastic site of Clonmacnoise, and more recently it was the site of an important English military base) and the modern (the German-built Shannon hydro-electric scheme is downstream). It seems plausible that 'Swim-Two-Birds' is also O'Nolan's cypher for the fairy cargo cult nexus of Foynes–Rineanna. In his 'Cruiskeen Lawn' column in the *Irish Times* Myles reports a typical moment from his contemporary surreal Ireland:

> History was again made at Rineanna when an enormous green-painted Skymaster touched down after making the Atlantic crossing. ... The plane was

the *Cruiskeen*, flagship of the Hiberno-American Air Lions Incorporated, gigantic menagerie operators who were making their first survey flight. (Myles, cited in Keown and Taafe, 2010: 219)

And this first survey flight is 'celebrated' by Myles with deep irony as a premonition of the brave new world of global American imperial neoliberalism:

The contemporary American technique of replacing the political and military sciences by the monetary: this involves the overt purchase by dollar bills of old and obsolescent nations – what one might call a global amercantile transaction aimed at the extinction of non-American cultures. (Myles, cited in Keown and Taafe, 2010: 219–220)

Erasing the sacred boundary

In Classical civilization by the ritual cutting of the *sulcus*, the first furrow, the city was founded; the sod for cultivation and crops for the future folded inside, the barren, fallow and barbarian turned outwards (Rykwert, 1998: 67). Today's ceremony of turning the first sod reiterates this ancient practice. The axial moment of Irish neoliberalism enacted at Foynes and at Shannon inverts the *sulcus* and re-founds the society as the city without boundaries, the 'Free Trade Zone', no taxes, indeterminable space; nothing folds into the *urbs*, the rich sod falls outwards. When the sacred boundary is erased, somewhere out in the sands of the desert the Sphinx, the Manticore, Pazuzu begin to stir. The tax free zone that provides employment and wages and the semblance of prosperity, like Pepsephone, who for her temporary freedom remains in thrall to Pluto, comes at a high price to be extracted in due course by the Dark Lord. 'No taxes' means that there is no *mundus*: no collective commonwealth, no store to appease the demons of the underworld – hunger, scarcity, sickness and ignorance. The commonwealth of the collective household, Central Revenue, though it benefits in the beginning, in the long run is systematically impoverished: schools, hospitals, housing, pensions are chronically underdeveloped and under-resourced. The Tax Free Zone was an Irish invention. The world's first. But the idea quickly grew legs, proliferated and metastasized. Mimicked and emulated it spread world-wide.

In 1960, Charles (Chuck) Feeney, born to a blue-collar Irish-American community in depression-era New Jersey, founded 'Duty Free Shopping Group' in Hong Kong. He quickly built up one of the world's largest retail empires, with Duty Free shops and malls in airports and cities and tax free zones throughout the Pacific Rim and Oceania, spanning Hawaii, Australia and the Middle East – Hong Kong, Hainan, Macau, Singapore, Kowloon, Bali, Okinawa, Abu Dabi, Sydney. A fraction of the billions of tax free profits skimmed from the revenue systems of national governments now finds its way back to Galway and Limerick, back to the spot where Lemass and O'Regan had first seized hold of the Leprechaun and learned of his money-making boundary-scrambling trickery. Through his Atlantic Philanthropies foundation Feeney now re-institutionalizes *philia*, but charity, being discretionary and arbitrary, is a poor compensation for the loss of the *mundus*.

There are presently over 3000 tax free designated development zones, so that it is no longer Ireland's Revenue that is initially enriched and subsequently impoverished, but the Central Revenue systems of European states and the EU. Ultimately the effects are felt at the centre of the global American Empire, where the Federal Government finds itself deprived of the revenue stream from American multinationals whose operations are located in such zones and whose profits are washed through off-shore banking facilities in magic castles built on virtual islands, in Dublin's International Financial Services Centre and the International Bank of the South Pacific. Tax Free Zones now compete vigorously with one another, fighting always lower and being unregulated they tend to become the bases for infernal commerce: Shannon became the base for laundering Apartheid blood diamonds, and more recently America's platform for global warfare and the rendition of its *homo sacer*, the human being denuded of human rights. The same 'Tax Free Zone' formula is repeated in Dublin's International Financial Services Centre, the money laundry of post-national capitalism. The power of incantation that reverses the founding of the city abandons the immortal gods in favour of global, mortal elites. Current political leaders defending Ireland's low corporate tax regime reiterate the fairyman's incantation that tries to draw down the magical cargo again, and repeats the foolishness for further generations.

Come build in the empty house of the stare

Yeats's anamnesis for a New Ireland is the ritual incantation 'Come build in the empty house of the stare' (1928). 'The Stare's Nest By My Window', a piece within a larger poem, 'Meditations in Time of Civil War', is like a bookend to Yeats's 'The Second Coming'. The centre cannot hold; the blood-dimmed tide has been loosed. Civil war is raging. Yeats looks out of his window as death is passing by the door:

The Stare's Nest By My Window

The bees build in the crevices
Of loosening masonry, and there
The mother birds bring grubs and flies.
My wall is loosening; honey-bees,
Come build in the empty house of the stare.

We are closed in, and the key is turned
On our uncertainty; somewhere
A man is killed, or a house burned.
Yet no clear fact to be discerned:
Come build in the empty house of the stare.

A barricade of stone or of wood;
Some fourteen days of civil war:
Last night they trundled down the road
That dead young soldier in his blood:
Come build in the empty house of the stare.

We had fed the heart on fantasies,
The heart's grown brutal from the fare,
More substance in our enmities
Than in our love; O honey-bees,
Come build in the empty house of the stare.

In October 1917 Yeats, who was then fifty-two years old, married Georgiana Hyde-Lees. She was twenty-five. He hardly knew her, but he felt an urgent need to marry, settle and raise a family. Only months previously he had proposed (again) and was rejected (again) by his muse Maud Gonne, and by her daughter Iseult, to whom he had subsequently – desperately – proposed.

On the honeymoon, Yeats brooding with doubt and regret, her four-day-old marriage shaping up to be a disaster, George began automatic writing in order to entertain and to capture the interest of her despondent husband.[3] Yeats was instantly enthralled, and with George acting as medium he gained access to a legion of voices and daemons. 'We have come to give you metaphors for poetry,' they said, and thus, through George, Yeats experienced a second birth and the full flourishing of his inspired and visionary art (Maddox, 1999). This liminal period in Yeats's biography – his marriage, his accessing the spirit realm, setting up home in the tower, the birth of his children and the death of his father – coincided with the most intense and liminal moments in the wider historical context (Ellmann, 1964: 257–259): the Bolshevik revolution in the month of his marriage; the end of the War; the global flu pandemic; the beginning of the Irish War of Independence in

January 1919, when Yeats wrote 'The Second Coming'; the rise of Mussolini in 1921; and the start of civil war in Ireland in 1922. 'The Stare's Nest' was written two weeks into the civil war.

The stare (starling) is a gregarious, garrulous bird. Flocks of starlings nest around dwelling houses, they perch on chimney pots. Close relatives of the mynah-bird, they are known to mimic human speech. In the midst of chaos, enmity and the stasis of civil war the starlings chatter loquaciously as they go about their life-affirming business – mating, nesting, hatching, bringing food to their young, fledging, leaving behind their empty nests. The tower is teeming with life: the stares nest in the cracks and crevasses, and inside the tower the Yeats's – W. B., George, their small children Anne, Michael, and a menagerie of pets – are nesting too. The Yeats's nest supports other nests: the stare's empty house becomes home in turn to honeybees. In a time of intense liminality, when 'the key is turned on our uncertainty' and 'no clear facts can be discerned'; when death is frequent and anonymous; houses are being burnt down, and Yeats's own tower, the ancient symbol of power and authority, symbol of the upright man of principle who stands for the name of the Father, has cracks, crevasses, loosening walls and crumbling masonry: this is the moment of Yeats's ritual incantation that we should pay attention to beautiful and eternal home truths. Yeats anticipates a principle later formulated by Bateson, that in times of crisis and liminality especially 'oversimplified ideas will always displace the sophisticated and the vulgar and hateful will always displace the beautiful. And yet the beautiful persists' (Bateson, 2002: 5). What should be done to ameliorate the social pathologies of liminality and stasis, Yeats (and Bateson) suggests, is to take care of the beautiful and help it to persist.

The little beasts, the starlings and honeybees, are twin hero antitheses to the buzzing flies of the marketplace that drive Nietzsche's Zarathustra back to the mountains. The starlings and the honeybees show us how we may live together. Like the flocks of starlings, the honeybees swarm. They communicate; they collaborate. Their hives are miniature miracles of domestic economy and cooperative work. The bees accumulate honey, the food of the gods, which is saved, shared to sustain the hive over the winter. This is Yeats's metaphor for the ideal of a holistic domestic, moral and political economy. The public is on the one hand like Beelzebub's cloud of flies in the marketplace, but it is also, equally, the swarm of honeybees descended from Melissa, the bee-nymph who fed the infant Zeus her honey. Aristaeus, the mortal son of Apollo, a pastoral twin of Hercules, was fed by Hermes on nectar and ambrosia so that he grew to be 'the best', and Aristaeus became the master of wise and useful arts, paradigmatically beekeeping (Graves, 1960). Melissa's honeybees, under the careful husbandry of Aristeaus, showed bestial humans how to build civilization, to communicate with one another, to collaborate, to gather, to store and to share rather than to kill and cannibalize one another.

Honeybees symbolize harmony achieved by virtue of eloquence and intelligence. Bees settled on the mouth of the boy Plato without stinging him, Virgil
tells us. The swarm of bees is the public as *demos* in the historical democratic
age of men: society that retains its potential for renewal even when it is locked
in the morbid stasis of civil war. By this metaphor of birds and honeybees
Yeats, like Joyce, reminds us of the community of interlocutors whose loqua-
ciousness retains a potential for renaissance even as we decline again into
noise, obscurity and darkness. 'The Stare's Nest' and *Finnegans Wake* assert
and celebrate the beauty of the social and its inexhaustible liveliness as a *sui
generis* reality that survives even the eclipse of society by the totalitarian
tyrannies of the Market and the masses.

The rough beast is amongst us now. We are assimilated and possessed by
it. World War III is a post-national, which is to say it is a pre-modern, war.
The war machines of a global plutocracy, banks and hedge funds, are laying
siege to democratic, republican and federal states: debauching currencies by
junking sovereign bonds; raising interest rates; cutting off cash flows; forcing
austerity measures that make democratic legitimation of government increasingly impossible; forcing states to empty their *mundus* and to sell off public
assets to private plutocrats. In Ireland as elsewhere this global war is cutting
swathes of casualties through the poor, the vulnerable, the elderly, children,
and increasingly amongst the middle classes whose lives are now precarious.
At stake in this war is nothing less than a return to pre-modern global neo-
feudalism, a recurrence of a dark age. We are losing this war. What is to be
done?

There are many things that should be done. The ceremony of innocence
has been drowned. 'Come build in the empty house of the stare' is Yeats's
ritual incantation that suggests the form of anamnesis for a new republic. We
are living through a period of extensive and intensive liminality. Limits and
sacred boundaries have been transgressed, deliberately and gratuitously. The
names of the Father are erased in favour of the flux and liquescence of the free
market and global financialization. Like neophytes in a rite of passage that has
gone wrong, while we are suspended in the liminal zone there is at times a
sense of communitas and collective effervescence: we reassure one another
that 'we are all in this together'; that we might recover our lost innocence and
'get back to being ourselves again'; that 'sure it'll all be grand!' We gape at
spectacles of soccer and rugby singing 'The Fields of Athenry' while we wait for
the next painful cut. We live in anti-structure. We are in need of structure.
Rituals and ceremonies re-establish structure. We need a reinvention of ritual
to restructure time and space that have been de-structured.

In the ancient city the moment when the *mundus* was ritually opened so
that the first fruits of each year's harvest were deposited was a time of extreme
danger, for the sacred *mundus* was a hell-mouth and the purpose of the

ceremony was for the goods placed therein be gifted to appease the demons of the underworld –poverty, ignorance and sickness. We must close the hell-mouth by holy rituals of purification, sacrifice and atonement. Neoliberal economists' mantras on low corporate taxes must be recanted, and instead of resisting financial regulation Irish politicians should proclaim taxation as a good word, and their mission in Europe should be as missionaries and evangelists for the regulation of international moneylenders.

The International Financial Services Centre should be shut down in a solemn public ceremony whereby the key is ritually turned on its dark practices. After a thorough ritual purification it should be stripped out and refitted and ceremoniously re-dedicated as a temple to the well-being of public life. It could become the National Children's Hospital. Or it could become an Academy dedicated to governing Hermes's entrepreneurial 'smart economy' by education in civic virtues for a wise society. Such an Academy would take up the challenge of re-imagining and reinvigorating the core ideals of education as the lifelong cultivation of wisdom and civic virtue. Education that enables human flourishing and a healthy body politic means something more than 'skills training'. *Educare* means to cultivate, to lead forth, to draw out from within; and wisdom is derived from *vis* in 'vision' and *dom*, meaning judgment and authority. When we consider the challenges of recovery we realize that it is not just enterprise and innovation in economy and technology that are at issue, but more fundamentally a creative revitalization of our political, cultural and moral institutions. Our individual and collective abilities to be innovative and creative, to adapt to change and to reinvent our society and our economy to face the challenges of recovery and the future, whether in the fields of science and technology, industry and economy, law and politics, culture and the arts will come primarily from vision and the exercise of judgment based on good authority, inspired and guided by the light of higher values and ideals. Ireland's unique contribution to the philosophical discourse of Modernity and to world cultural heritage – Yeats, Joyce, Beckett; more recently Heaney; more historically the Golden Age of saints and scholars; and more remotely anthropological deep truths encoded in mythology and landscape – is brimming with representations of higher values and ideals: good models that could serve as external mediators to be emulated in a virtuous spiral, counteracting the tendency towards schismogenesis, scapegoating and a downward vicious circle.

The foolish giveaway of national resources – oil, gas (and future prospects such as wave and wind energy) – should be taken back and developed responsibly as a collective inheritance so that imaginary debts owed to purported senior bond-holders are used instead to make real bonds with future generations. The National Assets Management Agency should give stewardship of empty houses to Threshold, Focus, Simon Community and St Vincent de

Paul, who would oversee ceremonies and celebrations of the gifting of homes to individuals and communities. Communities should decide what could be done with hotels and commercial premises: some ghost estates could become supported housing and assisted living for the elderly; or become crèches, community centres or youth cafés, so that empty houses become hives of activity. Toxic assets – schemes that cannot be salvaged and sanctified by gifting – should be purified by public sacrificial rituals of demolition, ploughed back into the earth, planted over as groves and gardens, restored to natural wilderness; but a small sample of the most grotesque and barbarous places should be preserved and maintained just as they are, to serve as public memorials that future generations of children visit on school tours to witness their ancestors' collective madness, so that, hopefully, our sins may never be repeated.[4] We could do all, and more, or little or none of these and similar things, but it would have to be a mindful and deliberate practice of public ritual.

Notes

1 American versions are 'Read my lips: No More Taxes' and the Tea Party's acronym, 'Taxed Enough Already'.

2 O'Regan was a local boy who had grown up in the family hotel and catering business in Ennis. He had travelled and trained on the Continent and spoke German and French. Amongst his professional experiences he had catered a banquet for Hitler. O'Regan was a professional host and Master of Ceremonies. Talented, debonair and efficient, a consummate entrepreneur, he took over a drab Dublin club and transformed it overnight. There, Lemass spotted O'Regan's flair, and when Pan Am sea-planes began landing at Foynes Lemass invited O'Regan to manage the catering facilities there. O'Regan rose to the occasion magnificently, and the restaurant at Foynes catered to the jet-set of the times. Hollywood glitterati, millionaires, royalty and politicians were well pleased by the high modern standards combined with traditional Irish hospitality. Irish coffee, a libation specially prepared for the divinities of globalization, was first served at Foynes, and O'Regan invented the concept of 'duty free' shopping for passengers in transit, a concept that he fully developed at Shannon, first as a much larger duty free emporium, then as an international mail order duty free, and ultimately as a tax free industrial zone.

3 By her own admission at first she was faking, but soon, she says, she felt her hand seized by an unseen power.

4 Former Gestapo and Stasi offices in Berlin have been re-dedicated as the offices of children's services, and concentration camps have been preserved as public memorials and sacred places where subsequent generations of schoolchildren are brought on pilgrimage to help ensure that evil is not perpetuated.

9

Conclusion: Omen of a post-republic: the demon child of neoliberalism

Who is the subject of post-republican Ireland? According to Dufour (2007, 2008, 2011) 'the subject who is coming ... after liberalism' – s/he is already amongst us – will be an *a*critical, *a*historical, isolist libertine with narcissistic-psychotic tendencies; a demon child; the ideal-type subject of neoliberal plutocratic authoritarian anarcho-capitalism and the divine market.

The subject is formed within the symbolic order, through being subject to the name of the Father. 'Man is, prior to his birth and beyond his death, caught up in the symbolic chain. ... [T]he subject is the slave of a discourse' (Lacan, 1956, in Dufour, 2008: 155). Neoliberalism's cultural revolution is to disarticulate the symbolic chain, to decompose and dissolve its *points de capiton*, to undermine and erase the 'name(s) of the Father' – the ideals, the authorities, the meaningful and meaning-giving traditions that have formed modern subjects, the 'big Other' to which modern subjects have been beholden and through which modern societies have been solidary and integrated.

The 'name of the Father' is an abstract, transcendental source of authority, a divine *Logos* 'in the name of' which individuals' desires are subordinated and reconciled with one another. As well as the great number and variety of gods in the historical and anthropological record that stand for 'the name of the Father' we may count the Ideal (Plato), Reason (Kant), Society (Durkheim), the superego (Freud), the Nation, the People, the Proletariat, the Party and similar names. All of these are further variations and declensions of the general form whereby the world is ordered and the identities and the actions of individual and collective subjects are made meaningful and justified 'in the name of the Father', the 'big Other'. The mutation that Dufour identifies as specifically post-modern and neoliberal is the de-symbolization of the big Other(s), undermining the strength of the authoritative discourses that have governed society, so that the power of society over the individual wanes. As the names of the Father, the powerful meaning-giving discursive frames that constituted modern society and by virtue of which modern subjects were formed, are erased, there is a generalized condition of liminality and anomie. Dufour echoes Yeats's opening line of 'The Second Coming', 'the falcon cannot hear the falconer', which suggests 'man's separation from every ideal of himself that has enabled him to control his life ... his break with every traditional tie' (Ellmann, 1964: 259).

The breaking of frames, being no longer interpellated by the name of the Father, releases centrifugal pleonexic appetites – greed, ambition and hubris. This can give the appearance of vitality and vigorous growth as the raptor flies free, so much so that the principle of neoliberal political-economic and moral theology becomes 'greed is good'. But this apparent vitality, seen from a different aspect, is like a cancer, proliferating, thriving, metastasizing; an aggressive and deathly form of growth, giving rise to extensive and intensive social pathologies, threatening civilization with sociocide and ecocide. And it is not just a process of de-symbolization that is taking place (de-symbolization occurs at other times of crisis and transition in the history of civilization – the fall of Athens, and also of Rome, and during periods of Renaissance, Reformation and Enlightenment, revolution, and so on): what is characteristic of de-symbolization in the global neoliberal revolution is that a particular process of re-symbolization is taking place too. The new servitude of the liberated in an age of total capitalism (Dufour, 2008) means the reducing and recoding of all values and meanings in terms of monetary value alone.

The weakening of other chains of symbolization and their monetization, so that, increasingly, 'the only nexus remaining between man and man is naked self interest and callous cash payment' (Marx and Engels, 1985: 82), has effects at the level of subject formation and political anthropology. All revolutions set afoot a new man, and the neoliberal revolution also engenders a new subject: no longer the modern Kantian–Marxian–Freudian subject, a critical, historical subject with neurotic tendencies; a thinking subject governed by discourses of Reason; a producing subject who, through experiences of alienation from their product, from their fellow producers, and from their humanity, becomes conscious of their historical situation; an emotional subject whose psyche is formed by suffering the weight of the social, repressing, sublimating and feeling guilty and neurotic. That modern subject is declining, Dufour argues. Evolving instead is a post-modern, neoliberal subject; the acritical, ahistorical individual consumer, 'liberated' from the signifying chains of the symbolic order, the meaningful discursive frames that constitute the social limits that discipline our animal appetites and narcissisms. Neoliberalism's mission is not so much to maintain the disciplinary institutions that cultivate docile bodies than it is to dismantle those institutions and discourses that formed the modern subject, encouraging people to break out of confining frames, to exercise freedom of choice, 'to produce individuals who are supple, insecure, mobile and open to all the market's modes and variations' (Dufour, 2008: 157).

In Ireland our servitude to discourse, our being bound in chains of signification, have been ambivalently subject-creating and subject-constraining. To be Irish is to have belonged to a symbolic order where powerful authorities have been for most of the twentieth century, the nineteenth century, and into a deeper historical background, the names of the Father(s) that define the collective and individual identity: Catholicism and Nationalism are the well-known traditional authoritative discourses within which Irish identity has been formed, and also the various levels of national, regional and local Community that form the matrix of sociation wherein identity is constituted and interpellated.[1]

The recent history of Ireland has seen the erasure of the 'name(s) of the Father(s)' of Catholicism, Nationalism and Community. These erasures have been by turns spectacular, devastating, liberating and unsettling. The history of their erasure is so recent and so prevalent that it hardly needs reiteration; suffice it to point to the thoroughgoing exposure of physical and sexual abuses of children and the Hierarchy's systematic denial and cover-up of abuse in schools, orphanages, convents, hospitals and parishes, extending to hundreds of thousands of cases over many decades, so much so that the traditional moral authority of the Catholic church in Ireland reputedly lies in ruins. Similarly, in parallel and at the same time, the name of the Irish nation, as it has been institutionalized and monopolized by Fianna Fail, 'the Republican Party', the party that was once upon a time described by its leader as not so much a political party as a national movement, the party that has been in government for more than three quarters of the time since independence, has been de-legitimated and brought into disrepute under the leadership of Charles Haughey and Bertie Ahern, revealed by Tribunals to be thoroughly corrupt, so much so that, like Irish Catholicism, it seems to many commentators to be a force that has spent itself. And Community, the dense web of local and extended-familial reciprocal exchanges and mutual connections, shared knowledges, meanings and traditions, a holistic and wholesome taken-for-granted familiar Irish lifeworld – that all of that too has been breaking down by the individualizing and estranging experiences of accelerated modernization. Though perhaps it may turn out that rumours of their deaths have been exaggerated, it is difficult to argue against the general thesis that contemporary Ireland is characterized by the erasure, the weakening, of these three traditional authoritative names of the Father – Catholicism, Nationalism and Community. It is in the lacunae created by this process of de-symbolization of the formerly authoritative names of the Father that the neoliberal revolution has been taking place in Ireland: Catholicism is replaced by materialism, commodity fetishism and the cult of the individual; the Republic is de-symbolized as a historical, national, public, collective identity and re-symbolized as 'Ireland Inc.', a re-privatized corporate enterprise of individual entrepreneurs; and the values of Community are re-coded in terms of economic actors exercising individual rational choices.

Dufour's formulation of de-symbolization and re-symbolization by processes of monetization of all values, of the divinity of the Market (2007), and of the genealogy of 'the subject that is coming' (2011), resonates with Simmel's formulation in the *Philosophy of Money* as a diagnostic of financialization as wealth creation by de-symbolization, specifically in terms of how money liquefies and dissolves all values and meanings and re-codes them in terms of monetary values. In this context of flux and indeterminacy the value of real estate increases as 'home' becomes a meaningful goal in an otherwise endless sequence of purposes that money can serve, a value that can then be leveraged, broken apart, releasing a plenitude of derivative financial products: the Plutonic-Hermetic magic key to wealth creation in the years before the crash. Financialization is the source of the de-symbolization of society, as Simmel shows. 'Money is the frightful leveller, it hollows out the core of things ... money reduces all value to the question of "how much?"' (Simmel, 1964a: 414–415). As a lowest common denominator and at the same time the measure of the highest value, money, Simmel says, comes to occupy the place in the symbolic order of modern secular civilization previously occupied by God. In terms of the genealogy of the modern subject, Simmel argues, the world ruled by the principle of money value as the only value generates greed, avarice, cynicism and a blasé outlook at the level of subjective psychology and ideal-typical personality.

Globalization entails the expansion of limits and the dissolution of boundaries, and the indefiniteness, liquidity and boundlessness of spatial-temporal frames. In the heart of darkness that is the indefinite and unlimited space of the de-symbolized financialized world of globalization a new type of subject is born. The omen of this demon child as ideal-type subject associated with the divinity of the market and neoliberal culture has already been prognosticated by deSade as the Libertine 'isolist' (van den Berg, 2012).

In the amoral world of the Sadean libertine isolist 'all boundaries become unfixed and transgression becomes the only law'. The libertine isolist exists in 'the beyond', a place without boundaries, a place of pure transgression, where Nothing exists. Sadean 'isolism' (from 'isolation') means that libertines cast off the bonds of human relations. They feel no emotion or compassion for their fellow man, instead caring only for themselves and their own pleasure. The libertine isolist is narcissistic to the point of psychosis. In contrast to the morality of the group isolism is based on the *a*moral, *a*historical notion that humans are not connected but are isolated rational choice actors who think only of themselves and their own desires. This demon child is the incarnation of the rough beast of neoliberalism.

Kurtz, the protagonist of Conrad's *Heart of Darkness*, is a prototype of *homo economicus* as Sadean libertine isolist. 'All Europe contributed to the making of Kurtz', Conrad (2009: 54) says. He is Western civilization in short (*'kurtz'* in German means 'short'). Kurtz is purported to be a great man, a 'universal genius' with 'immense plans'. He eloquently expounds on all the ideals of Modernity – development, growth, progress – but 'he had kicked himself loose of the earth' (Conrad, 2009: 72). 'His intelligence was perfectly clear – concentrated, it is true, upon himself with horrible intensity ... images of wealth and fame revolving obsequiously round his inextinguishable gift of noble and lofty expression. My Intended, my station, my career, my ideas' (Conrad, 2009: 74). Kurtz seems a man of reason but he is 'a hollow sham' his 'method is unsound'; 'Mr Kurtz lacked restraint in the gratification of his various lusts, ... there was something wanting in him' (Conrad, 2009: 63). The project of modern civilization that he represents – *laissez faire* economic liberal individualism – falls short: Kurtz is a creature of the modern jungle, an isolist who has gone Beyond; an intrepid modernist explorer, like man as represented by Yeats's falcon, transgression as a way of life has brought him back – or forwards again – to the savagery of a state of Nature. He is diseased; the walking dead; totally amoral. This is the heart of darkness, the horror of nihilism in modern civilization. Conrad's meeting Roger Casement, a man motivated by empathy for the suffering of fellow human beings rather than by the prevailing conceits of abstract reason; a caring man who was appalled by the excesses of predatory imperialism and *laissez faire* capitalism in Africa as in Ireland, was his inspiration for *Heart of Darkness*. The acritical, ahistorical Sadean isolist libertine resembles the zombie as the post-social living dead, incapable of caring for others, even others of its own kind. For de Sade isolism is the human condition *per se*: 'In Nature all creatures struggle only for their own survival and supremacy' (in Hallam, 2012: 45). DeSade here is precisely on the same page as Herbert Spencer, Adam Smith and neoliberalism: 'survival of the fittest'; 'you eat what you kill'; the 'savage god' of Yeats's 'Second Coming'; 'a monstrous ideal of abstract animal power' (Ransom, 1939: 318).

Yeats was a pre-Holocaust fascist sympathizer who diagnosed the social pathologies of modern civilization very well and favoured a Platonic restoration of sober, self-disciplined aristocratic Guardians. In Ireland we now have guardianship by a technocratic elite in the form of the IMF–ECB–EU Troika. Rule by the Platonic guardian technocrats of the Troika turns out to be less an alternative to anarcho-neoliberalism than a variation of authoritarian neoliberalism. The rule of the guardians is characterized not by interpellation of their subjects to a new moral order of elevated and elevating ideals, but of conformity to a stern and austere economic materialism and by a cultivated apathy and indifference to feeling, which, according to Adorno and Horkheimer (1992) is the point where Kant meets deSade as dialectical monstrous twins of Enlightenment. '[Moral] apathy (in the form of rigor),' says Kant, is a necessary presupposition of virtue. De Sade's heroine Juliette, Adorno and Horkheimer argue, is an exemplary subject of Kantian aggressive Enlightenment. 'She favours system and consequence. She is a proficient manipulator of the organ of rational thought and emotional self-control.' Kant's basic proposition, Adorno and Horkheimer remind us, is that virtue is founded on inner freedom, which contains an affirmative commandment for men, which is to bring all their abilities and inclinations under its control (that is, of reason), and therefore under self-control, which prevails over the negative commandment not to be ruled by one's emotions and inclinations because 'unless reason takes the reins of government into its hand, emotions and inclinations will be in control' (Kant, cited in Adorno and Horkheimer, 1992: 95). Like a good Kantian, deSade's Juliette, as she becomes turned away from virtue within human community towards the new freedoms promised by libertine isolism, believes in dispassionate reason, serene calm and stability: 'a murderer's face should display calm and equanimity; try to summon up an extreme degree of callousness so that you feel no pangs of conscience and suffer no remorse' (Adorno and Horkheimer, 1992: 95). Insensibility and indifference are essential to the inner freedom necessary for morality, Kant says. Calmness and decisiveness constitute the strength of virtue. Kurtz and Juliette were omens, fictional prototypes of the subject to come ... after liberalism. Dufour says that the demon child of the neoliberal revolution is now becoming the norm.

The Kantian–Sadean principles embodied by Kurtz and Juliette are the very hallmarks of how the financial crisis is managed by the Troika and by their local Auxiliaries, those who oversee the city on behalf of the Guardians, whom Plato likens to sheepdogs corralling the flock: in other words, the auxiliary post-republican Irish government, its ministers, administrators and managers who are barking at us that their austerity programmes and deep cuts are painful, but necessary, and right.

Caring for the demon child

As we and our children are becoming the demon spawn of the neoliberal revolution we stand in need of a practice of care of the self (Foucault, 1998). For the Greeks 'not to be a slave (of another city, of those who surround you, of one's own passions)' was vitally important. To not become a slave required a 'care of the self', that is, 'the deliberate practice of liberty'. Care of the self entails sustained self-reflection, a systematic effort 'to know oneself, and to improve oneself, to master the appetites that risk engulfing you' (Foucault, 1998: 4–7). The moral problem of modern civilization is how to redeem modernity from perdition by helping us to understand our insatiability so that we are not slaves to our appetites, and to reorient our desires towards higher ideals and the realization of the good life. In *Les Fleurs du Mal* Baudelaire (1988) gives us a precise formulation of the problem of insatiability that is at the heart of the modern experience in terms of *le gout de l'infini*.

'The taste for the infinite' is the source of *les fleurs du mal*. This is represented by Baudelaire's heroines, the lesbian lovers Delphine and Hippolyte of *Femmes damnées*. For Baudelaire's heroines to live authentically they must break out of the conventional symbolic and normative frames within which they are confined. They transgress the sacred limits of the social, they defy traditional morality 'in the name of love' – that is, in pursuit of the ideal, the Good, but thereafter they must live as outsiders. This, for Baudelaire, is the tragedy of Modernity: that transgression of limits, defiance of conventions and destruction of traditions is often done *not* for base and banal motives of profiteering and thrill-seeking, but for the most beautiful and exalted of causes – love, in Baudelaire's famous poem. But whether for profane or for sacred motives, one pays a high price for transgression as a way of life, as Yeats's Fergus discovers when he takes the Druid's magic enabling him to break away from the constraints of his social position and assume any form he desires. King Fergus is burdened and constrained by his role and envies the Druid who transgresses the boundaries between the mundane and supernatural realms. Fergus tracks the Druid all day as he shapeshifts through various forms until he materializes for a moment as 'A thin grey man half lost in gathering night' (Yeats, 1925: 101). The Druid tries to dissuade Fergus, for living in liminality is lonely and frightful, he says: 'Look on my thin grey hair and hollow cheeks / And on these hands that may not lift the sword / This body trembling like a wind-blown reed / No woman's loved me, no man's sought my help' (Yeats, 1925: 101).

But Fergus will not give up on his desire to break free from the constraints of the mundane world and to experience infinity in a world beyond limits.

> [Druid] Take, if you must, this little bag of dreams
> Unloose the cord, and they will wrap you round.
> [Fergus] I see my life go drifting like a river
> From change to change; I have been many things –
> A green drop in the surge, a gleam of light
> Upon a sword, a fir-tree on a hill,
> An old slave grinding at a heavy quern,
> A king sitting upon a chair of gold –
> And all these things were wonderful and great;
> But now I have grown nothing, knowing all.

Ah! Druid, Druid, how great webs of sorrow
Lay hidden in the small slate-coloured thing!

Yeats (1925: 102)

Fergus abdicates the throne, he repudiates the name of the Father in favour of transgression as a way of life, but living in liminality and antistructure means that he 'grows nothing'. Similarly, Baudelaire provides us with a powerful image of modern Hell and the road to perdition in terms of a mirroring of inner and outer abysses. Our desires, appetites and ambitions, when loosened from the constraints of society, are like a volcano, a monster:

> *Brulant comme un volcan, profound comme le vide!*
> *Rein ne rassasiera ce monstre gemissant ... (Baudelaire, 1988: 243)*
> (Boiling like a volcano, as deep as the void! Nothing can assuage this groaning monster ...)

Freed from the normative frames of collective life, modern people who transgress and seek to transcend conventional morality are condemned to wander in the desert like hungry wolves, and, living in disorder and anti-structure, they have to try to make out their own destiny, all the while fleeing from the infinity that they carry within themselves:

> *Loin de peoples vivant, errantes, condamnees*
> *A travers les deserts courez comme les loupes*
> *Faites votre destine, ames desordonnes*
> *Et fuyez l'infini que vous portez en vous.* (Baudelaire, 1988: 243)
> (Far away from living people, strays, damned
> through deserts running like wolves
> make your own destiny, disordered souls
> and flee from the infinity that you carry within yourselves).

The tragedy of modern life is that the pursuit of ideals puts people on a road that may lead to perdition and to Hell; the hell of slavery to the tyranny of insatiable desires that rage from '*l'infini que vous portez en vous*'; 'that which is in you more than yourself' (Lacan, 1981: 263), passion 'provoked by something intangible and intensified by the very impossibility of fulfilment' (Baudelaire, 1988: xv).

The heroic form of the person who manages to 'hold it together' in the face of the excess of modern life proved elusive for Baudelaire himself.[2] Baudelaire's work is a relentless self-reflection on the sources of the perdition of his own moral and physical well-being. Baudelaire's despair at the hopelessness of his own perdition made it increasingly difficult for him to see a good relation to excess; all of modern culture appears in terms of *fleurs du mal.*

James Joyce gives us the aesthetic image of a principled relation to excess that proved elusive to Baudelaire. Whereas Baudelaire was the botanist of the asphalt who identified *le gout de l'infini* as the characteristic *fleur du mal* of modernity, from the mire of modern city life Joyce gives us Leopold Bloom – the flower, an ideal type of flourishing humanity, an aesthetic image representing a care of the self as a deliberate practice of freedom that might be emulated as our uncreated conscience.

Turning Earwicker around

How do we turn around and come back from the 'beyond', from Baudelaire's desert, from the infinities that Fergus releases from the Druid's bag of tricks, from the neolibertine world of transgression represented by Conrad's Kurtz and deSade's Juliette? Our Secular Age, Taylor says, is the age of *eros*, the exemplary subject of which (extrapolated teleologically) is the pleonexic Sadean libertine: *eros* as insatiable and aggressive, transgressive and destructive hedonism breaking out of the discursive moral frames of society under the banner of authentic self-realization. Against this form of life Sorokin and Taylor both seek to reanimate *philia* and *agape*. Sorokin was writing in the wake of the Holocaust and the bomb, in the middle of the cold war, on the brink of MAD – mutually assured destruction; Taylor writes from the midst of our present catastrophes – climate change, global economic convulsions and materialist nihilism. James Joyce, writing from the edge of a world descending into totalitarianism, war and Holocaust, draws his inspirations from more ancient cults.

Amongst the treasure trove of the world's mythologies that inform Joyce's work, in *Finnegans Wake* the rough beast appears in the form of the earwig as a metaphor for the problem of ideology. According to ancient myth, earwigs crawl into sleeping people's ears and lay eggs. The eggs hatch and the insects eat into their hosts' brains, making them stupid and insane (Pliny, 1991: 160). The French call the earwig *perce oreille* ('ear piercer' – Joyce's Pearse O'Reilly/ Earwicker of the *Wake*); the German word is *ohrwurm* (ear worm), and the Russian *ukhovertka* (ear turner). To be the subject of ideology, the dreaming collective subject of modernity, is, as it were, to have 'a bug in your ear', an ear worm, laying eggs, eating your brain, making you a mindless zombie. A variation of this theme is that of poisoning by dropping something in the ear, as in the murder of Hamlet's father, and Hamlet himself being driven insane by poison words dropped into his ears. The earwig in the ear also stands for the slave trapped in the cave, enthralled by the images flickering on the wall.

How does the subject turn around and begin to move towards the light? The traditional remedy for getting the earwig out of one's ear is to shine a light into the ear, so that the earwig, drawn to the light, turns around, and crawls out of the ear by itself.[3] Joyce, like Wittgenstein, wants 'to show the fly the way out of the bottle' by changing the aspect by which things are viewed. *Ulysses* is a work that shines a bright light in our ears in that it is a representation of goodness, truth and beauty in the ordinary life of common humanity as representations of types of persons and their actions to be recognized and emulated, so that 'the mind illuminated by what is highest will lead the spirit to what is best' (Vico, 1999: 136). *Finnegans Wake* develops this theme by celebrating the beauty of the over-determination of the word and the inexhaustibility of language that survives tyranny, war and holocaust and that enables the world to regenerate. Just as the earwig's poisonous egg-words enter the social body through the ear, so too may the good word. The Immaculate Conception is impregnation through the ear – the Annunciation of the Good Word, the divine Idea that grows from the word-seeds dropped in the ears.[4]

In Yeats's (1916b: 77) vision the Magi are stony-faced witnesses to history's unfolding. As Christian civilization becomes exhausted and fades through Enlightenment into modern nihilism, they are unsatisfied but impassive; they make no intervention, they give no guidance as to a divine plan or cosmic order, and yet they are hopeful that there is such, and that it remains to be found again on the bestial floor to which we have fallen.

> Now as at all times I can see in the mind's eye,
> In their stiff, painted clothes, the pale unsatisfied ones
> Appear and disappear in the blue depth of the sky
> With all their ancient faces like rain-beaten stones,
> And all their helms of silver hovering side by side,
> And all their eyes still fixed, hoping to find once more,
> Being by Calvary's turbulence unsatisfied,
> The uncontrollable mystery on the bestial floor.

The riddle of the Sphinx is that it is always internal to us; we cannot evade, avoid or get around it somehow. Yeats (1927) tells us how he 'began to imagine as always at my left side just out of the range of sight, a brazen winged beast which I associated with laughing, ecstatic destruction'. This, he tells us, is the 'rough beast' depicted in 'The Second Coming', a vast image out of *spiritus mundi*, drawn by Yeats from many sources (Yeats, in Foster, 2003: 151, 696 fn41), amongst them Burke's depiction of the Revolution as a monstrous being 'in which the wildest anarchy is combined with the most stern despotism' (Burke, 1999: 6) represented by 'a dog-headed Egyptian demon' (Burke, 1999: 80). How we answer the riddle, whatever we do to respond to Sphinx, Manticore, Pazuzu will remain ambivalent; our actions will have unintended consequences, some of which will be evil. Such is 'the uncontrollable mystery on the bestial floor' (Yeats, 1916b: 77). The point, with Yeats as with Weber, is knowing that to enter politics to fight the real and present evils in the world is to engage with diabolical powers – that evil is inherent and omnipresent and in fighting it we unavoidably become evil. So also, and knowing the danger, we could as well, or as an alternative, emulate Joyce's celebration of the epiphany and the beauty of the Word, even – especially – on the eve of Apocalypse, and take the advice proffered by the intrepid explorer Marco Polo to the Kublai Khan when they met at an axial moment in a previous cycle of historical recurrence, representatives of ascendant Western civilization and a declining Oriental dynasty respectively. Kublai Khan, grasping the predicament of his people on the eve of the fall of his great city said:

'It is all useless, if the last landing place can only be the infernal city, and it is there that, in ever narrowing circles, the current is drawing us.'

And Polo said: 'The inferno of the living is not something that will be; if there is one, it is what is already here, the inferno where we live every day, that we form by being together. There are two ways to escape suffering it. The first is easy for many: accept the inferno and become such a part of it that you can no longer see it. The second is risky and demands constant vigilance and apprehension: seek and learn to recognize who and what, in the midst of the inferno, are not inferno, then make them endure, give them space'. (Calvino, 1997: 165)

Notes

1 Take for example the familiar Irish experience of being introduced to another. The other person immediately begins a process of 'placing' the stranger in a symbolic chain: 'So, you work at the university; you must know so and so in such and such a department? No? Well, you're from Cork; whereabouts? Then maybe you are related to so and so ...' and so on until finally a web of signification is woven to the point at which one's interlocutor declares, with some triumph: 'Now I have you!' For the subject who finds themselves entrammelled in these symbolic chains and webs of signification the experience is both pleasantly familiar – one now 'belongs' – and unpleasantly constraining – one is now 'limited', constrained by the place that one finds oneself placed in the symbolic order by the other.

2 Baudelaire's surrender to excess and vice – alcohol and absinthe, dandyism and fashion, hash and opium, a bohemian life of eroticism and sensuality – severely compromised his health and well-being. Despite a significant inheritance he lived in abject poverty as he had been legally deemed financially incompetent and access to his money was tightly controlled by a lawyer. He suffered ill-health from a combination of poor diet and over-indulgence in drugs and alcohol on the one hand, and, on the other, lacking self-esteem due to penury and artistic under-recognition, he was chronically depressed. To make matters worse he had syphilis, a combination of morbidity that eventually killed him at the age of thirty-eight.

3 Modern medicine occasionally rediscovers this folklore. See, for instance, Fischer (1986).

4 This is the kind of project that Walter Benjamin had in mind with his 'Radio Broadcasts for Children', a series of interventions using the mass media of his time that were so much implicated in the culture industry and in fascist and communist propaganda (Mehlman, 1993).

Bibliography

Ackermann, H. W. and Gauthier, J. (1991) 'The Ways and Nature of the Zombi.' *Journal of American Folklore*, 104(414): 466–494.

Adorno, T. and Horkheimer, M. (1992) [1944] *Dialectic of Enlightenment*. London: Verso.

Agamben, G. (1999) *Potentialities: Collected Essays in Philosophy*. Stanford, CA: Stanford University Press.

Allen, K. (2007) *The Corporate Takeover of Ireland*. Dublin: Irish Academic Press.

Anderson, C. and O'Brien, N. (2006) *Beyond the European Social Model*. London: Open Europe Institute.

Arendt, H. (1955) *Men in Dark Times*. New York, NY: Harcourt & Brace.

Arendt, H. (1990) 'Philosophy and Politics.' *Social Research*, 57(1): 73–103.

Arendt, H. (2006) [1963] *Eichmann in Jerusalem: A Report on the Banality of Evil*. London: Penguin Classics.

Arensberg, C. (1937) *The Irish Countryman: An Anthropological Study*. London: Macmillan.

Arensberg, C. and Kimball, S. T. (1940) *Family and Community in Ireland*. Cambridge, MA: Harvard University Press.

Aristotle (1934) *The Nicomachean Ethics*, translated by D. P. Chase. London and Toronto: J. M. Dent & Sons.

Attridge, D. and Howes, M. (2000) *Semicolonial Joyce*. Cambridge: Cambridge University Press.

Bachelard, G. (1994) *The Poetics of Space*. Boston, MA: Beacon Press.

Balot, R. K. (2001a) *Greed and Injustice in Classical Athens*. Princeton, NJ: Princeton University Press.

Balot, R. K. (2001b) 'Aristotle's Critique of Phaleas: Justice, Equality and Pleonexia.' *Hermes*, 129(1): 32–44.

Barry, T. (1955) *Guerrilla Days in Ireland*. Cork: Mercier Press.

Bateson, G. (1958) *Naven: A Study of the Iatmul People of New Guinea as Revealed through a Study of the 'Naven' Ceremonial*. Stanford, CA: Stanford University Press.

Bateson, G. (1972) *Steps to an Ecology of Mind: Collected Essays in Anthropology, Psychiatry, Evolution, and Epistemology*. Chicago, IL: University of Chicago Press.

Bateson, G. (2002) *Mind and Nature: A Necessary Unity*. New York, NY: Hampton Press.

Baudelaire, C. (1988) [1857] *The Flowers of Evil [Les Fleurs du Mal]*. Oxford: Oxford University Press.

Baudelaire, C. (1999) [1860] *Artificial Paradises*. London: Broadwater.

Baudelaire, C. (2001) [1859] 'The Painter of Modern Life' in *The Painter of Modern Life and Other Essays*. London: Phaidon. 1–41.

Baudrilliard, J. (1987) *The Evil Demon of Images*. Sydney: Power Publications.

Baudrilliard, J. (1988) *The Ecstasy of Communication*. New York, NY: Semiotext(e).

Bauman, Z. (1995) *Life in Fragments: Essays in Postmodern Morality*. London: Blackwell.

Bauman, Z. (2000) *Liquid Modernity*. Cambridge: Polity Press.

Bauman, Z. (2003) *Liquid Love: On the Frailty of Human Bonds*. Cambridge: Polity Press.

Bauman, Z. (2005) *Work, Consumerism and the New Poor*. London: McGraw-Hill.

Beck, U. (1992) *Risk Society: Towards a New Modernity*. London: Sage.

Beck, U. (2000) *What is Globalization?* Cambridge: Polity Press.

Beck, U. and Beck-Gernsheim, E. (1995) *The Normal Chaos of Love*. Cambridge: Polity.

Beck, U. and Beck-Gernsheim, E. (2002) *Individualization*. London: Sage.

Beckett, S. (2006) *The Complete Dramatic Works of Samuel Beckett*. London: Faber & Faber.

Benjamin, W. (1968) 'The Storyteller' in *Illuminations*. New York, NY: Schocken Books. 83–107.

Benjamin, W. (1983) *Charles Baudelaire: A Lyric Poet in the Era of High Capitalism*. London: Verso.

Benjamin, W. (1992a) 'On Some Motifs in Baudelaire' in *Illuminations*. New York, NY: Fontana. 152–196.

Benjamin, W. (1992b) 'Theses on the Philosophy of History' in *Illuminations*. London: Fontana. 253–265.

Benjamin, W. (1997) 'A Berlin Childhood' in *One Way Street*. London: Verso. 293–346.

Benjamin, W. (1999a) *The Arcades Project*. Cambridge, MA: Belknap.

Benjamin, W. (1999b) 'The Task of the Critic' in *Selected Writings Vol. II*. Cambridge, MA: Harvard University Press. 548–549.

Benjamin, W. (1999c) 'Little Tricks of the Trade' in *Selected Writings Vol. II*. Cambridge, MA: Harvard University Press. 728–730.

Benjamin, W. (1999d) 'Paris: Capital of the Nineteenth Century' in *The Arcades Project*. Cambridge, MA: Belknap–Harvard University Press. 14–26.

Berger, J. (1985) *Pig Earth*. London: Chatto & Windus.

Berger, P. (1976) *Pyramids of Sacrifice: Political Ethics and Social Change*. New York, NY: Anchor Books.

Birdwell-Pheasant, D. and Lawrence-Zuniga, D. (eds) (1999) *House Life: Space, Place and Family in Europe*. Oxford: Berg.

Blum, A. (1974) *Theorizing*. London: Heinemann.

Blum, A. and McHugh, P. (1984) *Self-Reflection in the Arts and Sciences*. Atlantic Highlands, NJ: Humanities Press.

Boardman, J., Griffin, J. and Murray, O. (2001). *The Oxford History of the Roman World*. Oxford: Oxford University Press.

Boas, F. (1975) [1909] *Kwakiutl Ethnography*, ed. H. Codere. Chicago, IL: University of Chicago Press.

Boleat, M. (1995) 'The 1985–1993 Housing Market in the UK: An Overview.' *Housing Policy Debate*, 5(3): 253–274.

Bonner, K. (2007). 'A Fry-Up and an Espresso: Bewley's Café and Cosmopolitan Dublin.' *New Hibernia Review*, 11(3): 9–20.

Bourdieu, P. (1999) *Acts of Resistance: Against the Tyranny of the Market*. London: New Press.

Bradford, R. D. S. (1977) *Nelson: The Essential Hero*. New York, NY: Harcourt.

Bright, W. (1993) *A Coyote Reader*. Berkeley, CA: University of California Press.

Brody, H. (1973) *Inniskillane: Change and Decline in Rural Ireland*. London: Norman & Hobhouse.

Browne, V. (2011) 'Growing Inequality Met with General Indifference', available at http://politico.ie/social-issues/8138–our-indifference-to-inequality.html (accessed 12 October 2012).

Burke, E. (1999) [1796] *Letters on a Regicide Peace*. Indianapolis, IN: Liberty Fund Inc.

Callanan, B. (1984) 'The work of Shannon Free Airport Development Company.' Administration, 32(3): 342–360.

Callanan, B. (2000) *Ireland's Shannon Story: Leaders, Visions, and Networks: A Case Study of Local and Regional Development*. Dublin: Irish Academic Press.

Calvino, I. (1997) *Invisible Cities*. London: Vintage.

Carey, J. (2009) 'Compilations of Lore and Legend: *Leabhar na hUidhre* and the books of *Ui Mhaine, Ballymote, Lecan* and *Fermoy*' in B. Cunningham and S. Fitzpatrick (eds), *Treasuries of the Royal Irish Academy Library*. Dublin: Royal Irish Academy. 17–31.

Carroll, N. (1990) *The Philosophy of Horror: or Paradoxes of the Heart*. New York, NY: Routledge.

Central Statistics Office (CSO) (2006) 'EU Survey on Income and Living Conditions' (EU-SILC), available at www.cso.ie/eusilc/statistics.htm (accessed 17 April 2008).

Centre for Public Inquiry (2005) *The Great Corrib Gas Controversy*. Dublin: Centre for Public Inquiry.

Cerny, P., Menz, G. and Soederberg, S. (2005) 'Different Roads to Globalisation: Neoliberalism, the Competition State, and Politics in a More Open World' in S. Soederberg, G. Menz and P. Cerny (eds), *Internalising Globalisation: The Rise of Neoliberalism and the Decline of National Varieties of Capitalism*. Basingstoke: Palgrave. 1–30.

Cixous, H. (1976) *The Laugh of the Medusa*. Chicago, IL: University of Chicago Press.

Cixous, H. (1984) 'Joyce: The (R)use of Writing' in D. Attridge and D. Ferrer (eds), *Post-structuralist Joyce: Essays from the French*. Cambridge: Cambridge University Press.

Cohen, A. (2000) *The Symbolic Construction of Community*. London: Routledge.

Colum, P. (1989) [1907] 'An Old Woman of the Roads' in S. Sternlicht (ed.), *Selected Poems of Padraic Colum*. Syracuse: Syracuse University Press.

Comaroff, J. and Comaroff, J. (eds) (2001) 'Millennial Capitalism: First thoughts on a Second Coming', in *Millennial Capitalism and the Culture of Neoliberalism*. Durham, NC: Duke University Press. 1–56.

Combat Poverty Agency (2006a) *Annual Report*, available at www.cpa.ie/publications/annualreports/2006_AnnualReport.pdf (accessed 15 April 2008).

Combat Poverty Agency (2006b) 'Policy Statement: Promoting Equity in Ireland's Tax System', available at www.cpa.ie/publications/policystatements/2006_PromotingEquityInIrelandsTaxSystem.pdf (accessed 16 April 2008).

Comte-Sponville, A. (2003) *A Short Treatise on the Great Virtues*. London: Vintage.

Conrad, J. (2009) [1899] *Heart of Darkness*. London: Oneworld Classics.

Cooney, G. (2000) *Landscapes of Neolithic Ireland*. London: Routledge.

Corcoran, J. (2009) 'The Nation Faces Ruin as our TDs Squabble.' *Irish Independent*, 22 February.

CORI Justice (2008) 'Taxation: Submission to the Commission on Taxation' in CORI Justice, *Annual Socio-economic Review: Planning for Progress and Fairness: Policies to Ensure Economic Development, Social Equity and Sustainability*, available at www.cori.ie/justice/Specific_Policy_Issues/32–taxation (accessed 30 April 2008).

Coser, L. (1977) *Georg Simmel: Makers of Modern Social Science*. New York, NY: Prentice-Hall.

Cronin, M. (2000) *Across the Lines: Travel, Language, Translation*. Cork: Cork University Press.

Cronin, M. (2010) 'We Are All In This Together?', available at http://politico.ie/country-is-broke/6944–we-are-all-in-this-together.html (accessed 12 October 2012).

Cronin, M. (2012) *The Expanding World: Towards a Politics of Microspection*. Dublin: New Island.

Dames, M. (1992) *Mythic Ireland*. London: Thames & Hudson.

Delanty, G. (2006) 'Modernity and the Escape from Eurocentrism' in G. Delanty (ed.) *Handbook of Contemporary European Social Theory*. London: Routledge. 266–279.

Deleuze, G. and Guattari, F. (1983) *Anti-Oedipus: Capitalism and Schizophrenia*. Minneapolis, MN: University of Minnesota Press.

Department of Finance (2007) 'Budget Financial Statement, 2007' available at www.budget.gov.ie/2007/financialstatement.html (accessed 17 April 2008).

Derrida, J. (1984) 'Two Words for Joyce' in D. Attridge and D. Ferrer (eds), *Post-structuralist Joyce: Essays from the French*. Cambridge: Cambridge University Press. 145–160.

Derrida, J. (1991) *A Derrida Reader: Between the Blinds*. New York, NY: Columbia University Press.

Derrida, J. (1992) *Acts of Literature*, D. Atteridge (ed.), London: Routledge.

deVries, H. and Sullivan, L. E. (2006) *Political Theologies: Public Religions in a Post-Secular* World. New York, NY: Fordham.

Dineen, P. S. (1996) [1934] *Fóclór Gaedilge agus Béarla: An Irish English Dictionary*. Dublin: Dublin Texts Society.

Dodds, E. R. (1964) *The Greeks and the Irrational*. Los Angeles, CA: University of California Press.

Donegan, P. (Sen.) (1961) 'Shannon Free Airport Development Company Limited (Amendment) Bill, 1961.' Parliamentary Debates. Seanad Éireann, 54:3 (August) Office of the Houses of the Oireachtas, Dublin.

Douglas, M. (1966) *Purity and Danger: An Analysis of the Concepts of Pollution and Taboo*. London: Routledge & Kegan Paul.

Douglas, M. (1975) *Implicit Meanings: Essays in Anthropology*. London: Routledge & Kegan Paul.

Dufour, D.-R. (2007) *Le Divin Marché: La Révolution Culturelle Libérale*. Paris: Éditions Denoël.

Dufour, D.-R. (2008) *The Art of Shrinking Heads: On the New Servitude of the Liberated in an Age of Total Capitalism*. Cambridge: Polity Press.

Dufour, D.-R. (2011) *L'Individu Qui Vient ... Après le Libéralisme*. Paris: Éditions Denoël.

Dumouchel, P. (1988) *Violence and Truth: On the Work of René Girard*. London: Athlone Press.

Durkheim, E. (1966) [1897] *Suicide.* New York, NJ: The Free Press.

Durkheim, E. (1974) [1924] *Sociology and Philosophy.* New York, NY: The Free Press.

Durkheim, E. (1995) [1912] *The Elementary Forms of Religious Life.* New York, NY: The Free Press.

Durkheim, E. (1997) [1893] *The Division of Labour in Society.* New York, NY: The Free Press.

Eco, U. (1989) *The Aesthetics of Chaosmos: The Middle Ages of James Joyce.* New York, NY: Harvard University Press.

Eliade, M. (1957) *The Sacred and the Profane: The Nature of Religion.* San Diego, CA: Harcourt Brace.

Elias, N. (1994) *The Civilizing Process.* Oxford: Blackwell.

Eliot, T. S. (1996) [1922] 'The Waste Land' in M. Ferguson, M. J. Salter and J. Stallworthy (eds), *The Norton Anthology of Poetry.* London: Norton. 1236–1248.

Ellmann, R. (1964) *The Identity of Yeats.* London: Faber & Faber.

Ellmann, R. (1977) *The Consciousness of Joyce.* London: Faber & Faber.

Ellmann, R. (1982) *James Joyce.* Oxford: Oxford University Press.

Ellmann, R. (1989) *Yeats: The Man and the Masks.* London: Penguin.

Ellmann, R. (1991) *Four Dubliners.* London: Cardinal.

Erzgraber, W. (1992) 'The Narrative Presentation of Orality in James Joyce's *Finnegans Wake.' Oral Tradition,* 7(1): 150–170.

Fanon, F. (2004) *The Wretched of the Earth.* New York, NY: Grove Press.

Fischer, J. (1986) 'Earwig in the Ear: Bright Light Draws the Insect.' *Western Journal of Medicine,* 145(2) (August): 245.

Fisher, W. R. (1985) 'The Narrative Paradigm: An Elaboration.' *Communications' Monographs,* 54(4): 347–367.

Fisher, W. R. (1987) *Human Communication as a Narration: Toward a Philosophy of Reason, Value, and Action.* Columbia, SC: University of South Carolina Press.

Fleiss, J. P. (1959) 'Political Disorder and Constitutional Form: Thucydides' Critique of Contemporary Politics. '*Journal of Politics,* 21(4): 592–623.

Foster, R. F. (1998) *W. B. Yeats: A Life I. The Apprentice Mage.* Oxford: Oxford University Press.

Foster, R. F. (2001) *The Irish Story: Telling Tales and Making it Up in Ireland.* London: Penguin.

Foster, R. F. (2003) *W. B. Yeats: A Life II. The Arch Poet.* Oxford: Oxford University Press.

Foucault, M. (1982) 'The Subject and Power' in H. Dreyfus and P. Rabinow, (eds), *Michel Foucault: Beyond Structuralism and Hermeneutics.* Chicago, IL: University of Chicago Press. 208–226.

Foucault, M. (1991) *Discipline and Punish: The Birth of the Prison*. London: Penguin.

Foucault, M. (1998) 'The Ethic of the Care of the Self as a Practice of Freedom' in J. Bernauer and D. Rasmussen (eds), *The Final Foucault*. Cambridge, MA: MIT Press. 1–20.

Fraser, N. (2004) 'Recognition, Redistribution and Representation in Capitalist Global Society: An Interview with Nancy Fraser.' *Acta Sociologica*, 47(4): 374–382.

Fraser, N. and Honneth, A. (2003) 'Introduction' in *Redistribution or Recognition? A Political-Philosophical Exchange*. London: Verso. 1–5.

Freud, S. (1961) [1930] *Civilization and its Discontents*. New York, NY: Norton.

Freud, S. (1976) [1900] *The Interpretation of Dreams*. London: Pelican.

Friedman, M. (1953) *Essays in Positive Economics*. Chicago, IL: University of Chicago Press.

Friedman, M. (1962) *Capitalism and Freedom*. Chicago, IL: University of Chicago Press.

Frisby, D. (1998) 'Introduction to Georg Simmel's "On the Sociology of the Family"' *Theory, Culture and Society*, 15(3–4): 277–281.

Frisby, D. (2002) *Georg Simmel*. London: Routledge.

Frye, N. (1977) 'Haunted by Lack of Ghosts' in D. Staines (ed.), *The Canadian Imagination*. Cambridge, MA: Harvard University Press. 22–40

Galbraith, J. K. (1958) *The Affluent Society*. New York, NY: Mariner Books.

Garavan, M., et. al. (2006) *Our Story: The Rossport Five*. Wicklow: Small World Media.

García-Márquez, G. (1998) [1967] *One Hundred Years of Solitude*. New York, NY: Perennial.

Geertz, C. (1993) *The Interpretation of Cultures*. New York, NY: Fontana.

Gibbon, E. (2005) [1776] *The History of the Decline and Fall of the Roman Empire*. London: Penguin.

Giddens, A. (1992) *The Transformation of Intimacy: Sexuality, Love and Eroticism in Modern Societies*. Cambridge: Polity Press.

Gill, R. (1963) 'The 'Corporal Works of Mercy' as a Moral Pattern in Joyce's Ulysses.' *Twentieth Century Literature*, 9(1): 17–21.

Girard, R. (1976) *Desire, Deceit and the Novel: Self and Other in Literary Structure*. Baltimore, MD: Johns Hopkins University Press.

Goldsmith, O. (1996) [1770] 'The Deserted Village' in M. Ferguson, M. J. Salter and J. Stallworthy (eds), (1996) *The Norton Anthology of Poetry*. London: Norton. 627–635.

Goudsblom, J. (1992) 'The Civilizing Process and the Domestication of Fire'. *Journal of World History*, 3(1): 1–12.

Grant, M. (1973) *Roman Myths*. London: Penguin.

Graves, R. (1960) *The Greek Myths Vols. 1 and 2*. London: Penguin.

Gravelle, J. (2010) *Tax Havens: International Tax Avoidance and Evasion*. Washington, DC: Congressional Research Service.

Habermas, J. (1987) *The Theory of Communicative Action: Reason and the Rationalization of Society*. Boston, MA: Beacon Press.

Habermas, J. (1989) *The Theory of Communicative Action: Lifeworld and System: A Critique of Functionalist Reason*. Boston, MA: Beacon Press.

Habermas, J. (1991) *The Structural Transformation of the Public Sphere*. Cambridge, MA: MIT Press.

Habermas, J. (2001) *The Postnational Constellation*. Cambridge: Polity Press.

Hallam, L. A. (2012) *Screening the Marquis de Sade: Pleasure, Pain and the Transgressive Body in Film*. Jefferson, NC: McFarland & Co.

Hansen, M. (2006) 'The Irish Growth Miracle: Can Latvia Replicate?' *Baltic Journal of Economics*, 5(2): 3–15.

Hanson, J. (1998) *Decoding Homes and Houses*. Cambridge: Cambridge University Press.

Haraway, D. (1991) *Simians, Cyborgs and Women: The Reinvention of Nature*. London: Free Association Books.

Harney, M. (2000) *Remarks by Tánaiste, Mary Harney at a Meeting of the American Bar Association in the Law Society of Ireland, Blackhall Place, Dublin on Friday 21st July 2000*. Dublin: Department of Trade & Enterprise.

Harris, M. (1989) *Cows, Pigs, Wars and Witches: The Riddles of Culture*. New York, NY: Vintage Books.

Hart, K. (2004) 'Religion' in J. Reynolds and J. Roffe (eds),*Understanding Derrida*. London: Continuum. 54–62.

Harvey, D. (2003) *The New Imperialism*. Oxford: Oxford University Press.

Harvey, D. (2005) *A Brief History of Neoliberalism*. Oxford: Oxford University Press.

Havell, H. L. (2003) [1914] *Ancient Rome: The Republic*. London: Geddes & Gresset.

Hayek, F. A. (1991) *The Fatal Conceit: The Errors of Socialism*. Chicago, IL: University of Chicago Press.

Heaney, S. (1988) *The Government of the Tongue*. London: Faber & Faber.

Heather, P. (2005) *The Fall of the Roman Empire: A New History*. London: Macmillan.

Hegel, G. W. F. (1977) [1807] *The Phenomenology of Spirit*. Oxford: Oxford University Press.

Heidegger, M. (1977) 'Building, Dwelling, Thinking' in D.F. Kvell (ed.) *Martin Heidegger. Basic Writings*. New York: Harper & Row. 243–264.

Heilbroner, R. (1999) [1953] *The Worldly Philosophers: The Lives, Times and Ideas of the Great Economic Thinkers*. New York, NY: Simon & Schuster.

Hobbes, T. (1985) [1651] Leviathan. London: Penguin.

Holland, T. (2003) *Rubicon: The Triumph and Tragedy of the Roman Republic*. London: Abacus.

Honneth, A. (1996) *The Struggle for Recognition: The Moral Grammar of Social Conflicts*. London: Polity Press.

Honneth, A. and Fraser, N. (2003) *Redistribution or Recognition? A Political–Philosophical Exchange*. London: Verso.

Horvath, A. (2009a) 'Liminality and the Unreal Class of the Image Making Craft: An Essay on Political Alchemy' *International Political Anthropology*, 2(1) May: 53–72.

Horvath, A. (2009b) 'Ekstasis, or the Estranged Sophist in Plato', paper presented at the Fourth Socrates Symposium, 7–9 November, Firenze, Palazzo Guidi.

Horvath, A. and Thomassen, B. (2008) 'Mimetic Errors in Liminal Schizmogenesis: On the Political Anthropology of the Trickster.' *International Political Anthropology*, (i): 3–25.

Hyde, L. (1998) *Trickster Makes this World: Mischief, Myth and Art*. New York, NY: Farrar, Straus & Giroux.

Inglis, D. (2011) 'Putting the Undead to Work: Wade Davis, Haitian Voudou, and the Social Uses of the zombie' in C. M. Moreman and C. J. Rushton (eds) *Race, Oppression and the Zombie*. Jefferson, NC: McFarland. 42–60.

Irish Congress of Trade Unions (2004) *Tax Cuts Did Not Create the Celtic Tiger*, available at www.ictu.ie/publications/fulllist/tax-cuts-did-not-create-celtic-tiger/ (accessed 17 April 2008).

Jameson, F. (1991) *Postmodernism, or the Cultural Logic of Late Capitalism*. Durham, NC: Duke University Press. 1–54.

Jebens, H. (ed.) (2004) *Cargo, Cult and Culture Critique*. Honolulu, HI: University of Hawaii Press.

Jenks, C. (1996) *Childhood*. London: Routledge.

Johnson, D. (2011) 'A Chariot Worth 4.58 million Bondsmaids', available at http://politico.ie/crisisjam/8141–a–chariot–worth–458–million–bondmaids.html (accessed 12 October 2012).

Jones, E. (1974) *Psycho Myth, Psycho History: Essays in Applied Psychoanalysis*. London: Hillstone, 2 vols.

Joyce, J. (1995) [1939] *Finnegans Wake*. London: Picador.

Joyce, J. (1998) [1922] *Ulysses*. Oxford: Oxford University Press.

Joyce, J. (2003) [1916] *A Portrait of the Artist as a Young Man*. London: Penguin.

Joyce, J. (2007) [1914] *Dubliners*. London: Penguin.

Jung, C. (1959) *Memories, Dreams, Reflections*. London: Fontana.

Jung, C. (1972) *Four Archetypes: Mother, Rebirth, Spirit, Trickster*. London: Routledge.

Kamper, A., Macleod, N. and Singh, N. (2005) *The 'Plutonomy' Equity*

*Strategy: Part I 'Plutonomy: Buying Luxury, Explaining Global Imbalance';
part II 'Revisiting Plutonomy: The Rich Getting Richer*. New York, NY:
Citigroup Global Markets Inc.

Kant, I. (2002) [1875] *Groundwork for the Metaphysics of Morals*. Oxford:
Oxford University Press.

Kant, I. (2007) [1790] *Critique of Judgment*. Oxford: Oxford University Press.

Kaufmann, W. (1968) *Nietzsche: Philosopher, Psychologist, Antichrist*. New
York, NY: Vintage.

Kavanagh, P. (1964) 'The Great Hunger' in A. Quinn (ed.) *Patrick Kavanagh
The Collected Poems*. London: W.W. Norton. 34–57.

Keena, C. (2009) 'Poles Look to Replicate the Celtic Tiger.' *Irish Times*, 24 April.

Keohane, K. (2005) 'Trickster's Metempsychosis in the Mythic Age of
Globalization: The Recurrence of the Leprechaun in Irish Political Culture.'
Cultural Politics, 2(1): 257–278.

Keohane, K. and Kuhling, C. (2004) *Collision Culture: Transformations in
Everyday Life in Ireland*. Dublin: The Liffey Press.

Keown, E. and Taffe, C. (eds) (2010) *Irish Modernism: Origins, Contexts,
Publics*. Bern: Peter Lang AG.

Kerenyi, C. (1980) *The Gods of the Greeks*. London: Thames & Hudson.

Kiberd, D. (2000) *Inventing Ireland*. New York, NY: Vintage.

Kiberd, D. (2009) *Ulysses and Us: The Art of Everyday Living*. London: Faber &
Faber.

Kiberd, D. (2001) *Irish Classics*. London: Granta.

Kinsella, T. (2002) *The Táin: From the Irish Epic Táin Bó Cuailnge*. Oxford:
Oxford University Press.

Kirby, P. (2003) 'Globalisation' in B. Fanning, P. Kennedy, G. Kiely and S.
Quin (eds), *Theorising Social Policy*. Dublin: UCD Press. 23–41.

Kirby, P. (2010) *Celtic Tiger in Collapse: Explaining the Weaknesses of the Irish
Model*. London: Palgrave Macmillan.

Kirby, P. (2012) [2009] 'When Banks Cannibalize the State: Responses to
Ireland's Economic Collapse.' *Socialist Register 2012: The Crisis and the Left*,
48: 249–268.

Kirby, P. and Murphy, M. (2008) 'Ireland as a Competition State' in M.
Adshead, P. Kirby and M. Millar (eds), *Contesting the State: Lessons from the
Irish Case*. Manchester: Manchester University Press. 165–185.

Klamer, A. (1983) *Conversations With Economists: New Classical Economists
and Opponents Speak Out on the Current Controversy in Macroeconomics*.
New York, NY: Rowman & Littlefield.

Klien, N. (2007) *The Shock Doctrine: The Rise of Disaster Capitalism*. London:
Penguin.

Knorr Cetina, K. D. and Preda, A. (2007) 'The Temporalization of Financial
Markets: From Network Markets to Flow Markets.' *Theory, Culture and*

Society, 24(7–8): 123–145.

Koth, M. (2004) 'Payment Difficulties of German Home Owners', paper presented to ENHR International Housing Conference, Cambridge University 2–6 July.

Krugman, P. (2007) 'Who was Milton Friedman?' *New York Review of Books*, 54(2): 27–30.

Kuhling, C. and Keohane, K. (2007) *Cosmopolitan Ireland: Globalisation and Quality of Life*. London: Pluto Press.

Lacan, J. (1961) *The Seminar of Jacques Lacan VIII: Transference* (translated by C. Gallagher from un-edited French manuscripts), available online at www.lacaninireland.com (accessed 12 May 2011).

Lacan, J. (1975) *The Seminar of Jacques Lacan Book XXIII: Joyce and the Sinthome*, Seminar I: 18 November (translated by C. Gallagher from un-edited French manuscripts), available at www.lacaninireland.com (accessed 12 May 2011).

Lacan, J. (1976) *The Seminar of Jacques Lacan Book XXIII: Joyce and the Sinthome*, Seminar II: 10 February (translated by C. Gallagher from un-edited French manuscripts), available at www.lacaninireland.com (accessed 12 May 2011).

Lacan, J. (1978) *The Four Fundamental Concepts of Psychoanalysis*. New York, NY: Norton.

Lacan, J. (1994) *Speech and Language in Psychoanalysis*. Baltimore, MD: Johns Hopkins University Press.

Lacan, J. (1999) *The Seminar of Jacques Lacan Book XX: On Feminine Sexuality, the Limits of Love and Knowledge (Encore)*. New York, NY: Norton.

Laclau, E. and Mouffe, C. (1985) *Hegemony and Socialist Strategy*. London: Verso.

Lawrence, P. (1964) *Road Belong Cargo: A Study of the Cargo Movement in the Southern Madang District, New Guinea*. Manchester: Manchester University Press.

Lee, J. J. (1989) *Ireland 1912–1985: Politics and Society*. Cambridge: Cambridge University Press.

Lemass, S. (1947a) *Customs Free Airport Act 1947, Irish Statute Book Number 5 of 1947*. Dublin: Office of the Attorney General.

Lemass, S. (1947b) *Committee on Finance, Customs-Free Airport Bill, 1947– Second Stage. Tuesday, 28 January 1947*. Committee Debates. Dublin: Houses of the Oireachtas.

Leonard, L. (2007) *The Environmental Movement in Ireland*. New York, NY: Springer.

Lernout, G. (1992) *The French Joyce*. Ann Arbor, MI: Michigan University Press.

Littlewood, R. and Douyon, C. (1997) 'Clinical Findings in Three Cases of Zombification.' *The Lancet*, 350(9084): 1094–1096.

McCaughan, M. (2008) *The Price of our Souls: Gas, Shell and Ireland.* Dublin: AFRI.

McDonald, L. G. (2009) *A Colossal Failure of Common Sense: The Inside Story of the Collapse of Lehman Brothers.* New York, NY: Ebury Publishing.

MacKenzie, D. (2008) *Material Markets: How Economic Agents are Constructed.* Oxford: Oxford University Press.

McNally, D. (2012) *Monsters of the Market: Zombies, Vampires and Global Capitalism.* London: Haymarket.

Maddox, B. (1999) *Yeats's Ghosts: The Secret Life of W. B. Yeats.* New York, NY: Harper Collins.

Malinowski, B. (1924) *Argonauts of the Western Pacific.* London: Routledge and Kegan Paul.

Marmot, M. (2004) *The Status Syndrome: How Social Standing Affects Our Health and Longevity.* London: Bloomsbury.

Marx, K. (1992) [1867] *Capital: Volume 1: A Critique of Political Economy.* London: Penguin.

Marx, K. and Engels, F. (1985) [1848] *The Communist Manifesto.* London: Penguin.

Mauss, M (2002) [1925] *The Gift.* London: Routledge.

Mead, M. (1928) *Coming of Age in Samoa.* New York, NY: William Morrow & Co.

Mehlman, J. (1993) *Walter Benjamin for Children: An Essay on his Radio Years.* Chicago, IL: University of Chicago Press.

Merton, R. K. (1938) 'Social Structure and Anomie'. *American Sociological Review'* 3(5): 672–682.

Metscher, P. (2002) *James Connolly and the Reconquest of Ireland.* London: MEP Publications.

Mill, J. S. (1956) [1859] *On Liberty.* Leicester: The Liberal Arts Press.

Mill, J. S. (2008) [1836] 'On the Definition of Political Economy, and on the Method of Investigation Proper to It' in *Essays on Some Unsettled Questions of Political Economy*, London: Serenity Publishers. 105–112.

Millar, M. (2008) 'Social Inclusion and the Welfare State: Who Cares?' in M. Adshead, P. Kirby, and M. Millar (eds), *Contesting the State: Lessons from the Irish Case.* Manchester: Manchester University Press. 100–119.

Miller, T. (1996) 'From City Dreams to the Dreaming Collective: Walter Benjamin's Political Dream Interpretation.' *Philosophy & Social Criticism,* 22(6): 87–111.

Mills, C. W. (1959) *The Sociological Imagination.* London: Oxford University Press.

Mouffe, C. (1988) 'Radical Democracy: Modern or Postmodern?' In A. Ross (ed.), *Universal Abandon? The Politics of Postmodernism.* Minneapolis, MN: University of Minnesota Press. 31–45

Mouffe, C. (2005) *On the Political.* London: Routledge.

Mumford, L. (1989) *The City in History: Its Origins, Its Transformations, and Its Prospects*. New York, NY: Harcourt.

Murphy, R. (2008) 'Ireland "nicking" tax revenue.' *Sunday Business Post*, 14 September, M1.

Murphy Report (2009) *Report by Commission of Investigation into the Handling by Church and State Authorities of Allegations and Suspicions of Child Abuse against Clerics of the Catholic Archdiocese of Dublin*. Dublin: Department of Justice, Equality & Law Reform.

NESF (National Economic and Social Forum) (2006) *Creating a more Inclusive Labour Market*. Dublin: NESF.

Nancy, J.-L. (1991) *The Inoperative Community*. Minneapolis, MN: University of Minnesota Press.

Nietzsche, F. (1986) [1872] *Thus Spoke Zarathustra*. London: Penguin.

Nietzsche, F. (1989) [1886] *Beyond Good and Evil: Prelude to a Philosophy of the Future*. New York, NY: Vintage.

Nietzsche, F. (1995) [1887]. *The Birth of Tragedy*. New York, NY: Dover.

Nikely, A. (2006) 'The Pathogenesis of Greed: Causes and Consequences.' *International Journal of Psychoanalytic Studies*, 3(1): 65–78.

Nozick, R. (1973) *Anarchy, State and Utopia*. New York, NY: Basic Books.

O'Brien, F. (1967) [1939] *At Swim-Two-Birds*. London: Penguin.

O'Brien, N. (ed.) (2006) *Beyond the European Social Model*. London: Open Europe.

O'Carroll, J. P. (1987) 'Strokes, Cute Hoors and Sneaking Regarders: The Influence of Local Culture on Irish Political Style.' *Irish Political Studies*, 2: 77–92.

O'Crualaoich, G. (2003) *The Book of the Cailleach: Stories of the Wise-Woman Healer*. Cork: Cork University Press.

Ó'Dónaill, N. (2010) *Foclóir Gaeilge-Béarla*. Dublin: An Gum.

O'Neill, J. (1975) *Making Sense Together: An Introduction to Wild Sociology*. New York, NY: Harper & Row.

O'Neill, J. (1985) *Five Bodies: The Human Shape of Modern Society* Ithaca, NY: Cornell University Press.

O'Neill, J. (2002) *Incorporating Cultural Theory: Maternity at the Millennium*. New York, NY: SUNY Press.

O'Toole, F. (2009) *Ship of Fools: How Stupidity and Corruption Killed the Celtic Tiger*. London: Faber & Faber.

O'Toole, F. (2010) *Enough is Enough: How to Build a New Republic*. London: Faber & Faber.

Pakenham, V. (1998) *The Big House in Ireland*. London: Cassell and Co.

Pearse, P. H. (2012) [1915] *Oration at the Grave of Jeremiah O'Donovan Rossa*. Dublin: Office of Public Works.

Perrot, M. (1990) *A History of Private Life: From the Fires of Revolution to the*

Great War. A. Goldhammer (trans.), Philippe Aries and Georges Duby (general eds), Cambridge, MA: Harvard University Press.

PHAI (Public Health Alliance Ireland) (2004) *Health in Ireland: An Unequal State*. Dublin: PHAI.

Plato (1892) *The Dialogues of Plato translated into English with Analyses and Introductions by B. Jowett, M.A. in Five Volumes. 3rd edition revised and corrected*. Oxford: Oxford University Press.

Plato (1997) *Republic*. translated by D. J. Vaughan and J. L. Davies. London: Wordsworth Editions.

Pliny the Elder (1991) [77] *Natural History: A Selection*, translated and with an Introduction by J. F. Healy. London: Penguin.

Poe, E. A. (1965) 'The Philosophy of Furniture' in *The Complete Works of Edgar Allen Poe, vol 14*. Michigan: University of Michigan Press.

Poggi, G. (1993) *Money and the Modern Mind: Georg Simmel's* Philosophy of Money. Berkeley, CA: University of California Press.

Price, J. (2001) *Thucydides and Internal War*. Cambridge: Cambridge University Press.

Rabinow, P. and Sullivan, W. M. (1987) *Interpretive Social Science: A Second Look*. Berkeley, CA: University of California Press.

Radin, P. (1972) *The Trickster: A Study in American Indian Mythology*. New York, NY: Schocken Books.

Ransom, J. C. (1939) 'Yeats and his Symbols'. *Kenyon Review*, 1(3): 309–322.

Rawson, E. (1988) 'The Expansion of Rome' in J. Boardman, J. Griffin and O. Murray (eds), *The Oxford History of the Roman World*. Oxford: Oxford University Press. 417–437.

Rostow, W. (1960) *The Stages of Economic Growth: A Non-Communist Manifesto*. Cambridge: Cambridge University Press.

Ryan, Mr. Justice Sean, Judge of the High Court (Chairperson) (2009) *Report of the Commission to Inquire into Child Abuse*. http://www.childabusecommission.ie/ (accessed 15 November 2010).

Rykwert, J. (1998) *The Idea of a Town: The Anthropology of Urban Form in Rome, Italy and the Ancient World*. Cambridge, MA: MIT Press.

Schama, S. (1988) *The Embarrassment of Riches: An Interpretation of Dutch Culture in the Golden Age*. Berkeley, CA: University of California Press.

Schmitt, C. (2006) [1922] *Political Theology: Four Chapters on the Concept of Sovereignty*. Chicago, IL: University of Chicago Press.

Schmitt, C. (2007) [1932] *The Concept of the Political*. Chicago, IL: University of Chicago Press.

Schnuer, G. (2010) *Just Suffering: A Theoretical Engagement with the Demands of Justice*. Unpublished PhD Thesis in Sociology, University of Edinburgh.

Schopenhauer, A. (1966) [1818] *The World as Will and Representation*. London: Dover.

Sennett, R. (1978) *The Fall of Public Man*. London: Penguin.

Sennett, R. (1996) *Flesh and Stone: The Body and the City in Western Civilization*. New York, NY: W. W. Norton.

Sennett, R. (1998) *The Corrosion of Character: The Personal Consequences of Work in the New Capitalism*. New York, NY: Norton.

Serres, M. (1991) *Rome: The Book of Foundations*. Stanford, CA: Stanford University Press.

Share, B. (1992) *Shannon Departures: A Study in Regional Initiatives*. Dublin: Gill & Macmillan.

Shaviro, S. (2002) 'Capitalist Monsters: Children of Production.' *Historical Materialism*, 10: 281–90.

Shelley, M. (1987) [1823] *Frankenstein, or the Modern Prometheus*. London: Marshall Cavendish.

Shell to Sea (2012) *Liquid Assets: Ireland's Oil and Gas Resources and How they could be Managed for the People's Benefit*. Dublin: Shell to Sea.

Sherwood, Y. and Hart, K. (2005) *Derrida and Religion: Other Testaments*. London: Routledge.

Siggins, L. (2010) *Once Upon A Time In The West: The Corrib Gas Controversy*. London: Transworld Publishers.

Simmel, G. (1964a) *Conflict and the Web of Group Affiliations*. New York, NY: The Free Press.

Simmel, G. (1964b) 'The Stranger' in Kurt H. Wolff (ed.), *The Sociology of Georg Simmel*. New York, NY: Free Press. 402–408.

Simmel, G. (1964c) 'The Metropolis and Mental Life' in Kurt H. Wolff (ed.), *The Sociology of Georg Simmel*. New York, NY: The Free Press. 409–424.

Simmel, G. (1964d) 'Types of Social Relationships by Degrees of Reciprocal Knowledge of their Participants: Marriage, in *The Sociology of Georg Simmel*, edited by K. H. Wolff. New York: Free Press. 317–329.

Simmel, G. (1990) [1905] *The Philosophy of Money*, D. Frisby (ed.). London: Routledge.

Simmel, G. (1997a) 'The Sociology of Space' in *Simmel on Culture: Selected Writings*, edited by D. Frisby and M. Featherstone. London: Sage. 137–170.

Simmel, G. (1997b) 'The Conflict of Modern Culture' in *Simmel on Culture: Selected Writings*, edited by D. Frisby and M. Featherstone. London: Sage. 75–90.

Simon, G. (2005) 'Ireland's 'Economic Miracle' and Globalization.' *Journal of the Institute of Economics, Hungarian Academy of Sciences*, 57(1–2): 5–30.

Slater, P. E. (1992) *The Glory of Hera: Greek Mythology and the Greek Family*. Princeton, NJ: Princeton University Press.

Sorokin, P. (1992) [1941] *The Crisis of Our Age*. Oxford: Oneworld Publications.

Sorokin, P. 2002 [1954]. *The Ways and Power of Love: Types, Factors and*

Techniques of Moral Transformation. Philadelphia, PA: Templeton Foundation Press.

Soulsby, J. A. (1965) 'The Shannon Free Airport Scheme: A New Approach to Industrial Development'. *Scottish Geographical Magazine*, 81(2): 104–114.

Starkie, E. (1971) *Baudelaire*. London: Pelican.

Stinson, E. (2011) 'Zombified Capital in the Postcolonial Capital: The Circulation (of Blood) in Sony Labou Tansi's *Parentheses of Blood*' in C. M. Moreman and C. J. Rushton, *Race, Oppression and the Zombie*. Jefferson, NC: McFarland. 77–93.

Stoker, B. (1993) [1897] *Dracula*. Hertfordshire: Wordsworth Classics.

Stoker, B. (2006) [1890] *The Snake's Pass*. Kansas: Valancourt.

Strange, S. (1986) *Casino Capitalism*. Oxford: Basil Blackwell.

Sweeney, V. (2004) *Shannon Airport: A Unique Story of Survival*. Shannon: Treaty Press.

Swift, J. (1996) [1729] *A Modest Proposal for Preventing the Children of Poor People from being a Burthen to their Parents or the Country, and for Making them Beneficial to the Publick*. London: Dover.

Szakolczai, A. (2000) *Reflexive Historical Sociology*. London: Routledge.

Szakolczai, A. (2007) *Sociology, Religion and Grace: A Quest for the Renaissance*. London: Routledge.

Szakolczai, A. (2009a) 'Liminality and Experience: Structuring Transitory Situations and Transformative Events.' *International Political Anthropology*, 2(1): 141–171.

Szakolczai, A. (2009b) 'Sophists: Ancient and Modern', paper presented at the Fourth Socrates Symposium, 7–9 November, Firenze, Palazzo Guidi.

Szakolczai, A. (2013) 'Genealogy' in Byron Kaldis (ed.), *Encyclopedia of Philosophy and the Social Sciences*. Thousand Oaks, CA: Sage 461–462.

Taft, M. (2011) 'Notes from the Front: Commentary on Irish Political Economy', available at http://notesonthefront.typepad.com/politicalecon-omy/2011/11/the-dublin-council-of-trades-unions-march-against-austerit y-tomorrow-12-noon-from-the-garden-of-remembrance-is-taking-pl.html (accessed 12 October 2012).

Taussing, M. (1980) *The Devil and Commodity Fetishism in Latin America*. Chapel Hill, NC: University of North Carolina Press.

Taylor, C. (2007). *A Secular Age*. Cambridge, MA: Harvard University Press.

Think Tank for Action on Social Change (2008) *The Solidarity Factor: Public Perceptions of Unequal Ireland: 2008 TASC Survey Results*. Dublin: TASC.

Thomassen, B. (2013) 'Modernity as Spiritual Disorder: Searching for a Vocabulary of Social Pathologies in the work of Eric Voegelin' in K. Keohane and A. Petersen (eds), *The Social Pathologies of Contemporary Civilization*. London: Ashgate. 43–59.

Time (1963) 'Lifting the Green Curtain.' *Time Magazine*, 82(2): 30–39.

Titmuss, R. (1970) *The Gift Relationship: From Human Blood to Social Policy.* London: Allen & Unwin.

Trinh T. Minh-ha (1985) 'Naked Spaces: Living is Round' (135 mins, color). Produced by Jean-Paul Broudier, Berkeley: University of California Berkeley.

Turner, V. (1967) 'Betwixt and Between: The Liminal Period in *Rites de Passage*', in *The Forest of Symbols.* New York, NY: Cornell University Press. 93–111.

Turner, V. (1969) *The Ritual Process.* Chicago, IL: Aldine.

Tusing, A. Dale, and Wren, M. A. (2006) *How Ireland Cares: The Case for Health Care Reform.* Dublin: New Island.

van-Boheemen-Saaf, C. (1999) *Joyce, Derrida, Lacan and the Trauma of History.* Cambridge: Cambridge University Press.

van den Berg, B. (2012) 'Depression: Resisting Ultraliberalism?' in *The Social Pathologies of Contemporary Civilization,* ed. A. Petersen and K. Keohane. London: Ashgate.

van-Gennip, A. (1964) [1909] *The Rites of Passage.* Chicago, IL: University of Chicago Press.

Veblen, T. (1994) *The Theory of the Leisure Class.* New York, NY: Dover.

Verene, D. P. (2003) *Knowledge of Things Human and Divine: Vico's New Science and Finnegans Wake.* New Haven, CT: Yale University Press.

Vickery, A. (2009) *Behind Closed Doors: At Home in Georgian England.* New Haven, CT: Yale University Press.

Vico, G. (1999) [1744] *New Science.* London: Penguin.

Virilio, P. (1995) *The Art of the Motor.* Minneapolis, MN: University of Minnesota Press.

Weber, M. (1958) *The Protestant Ethic and the Spirit of Capitalism.* New York, NY: Charles Scribner's Sons.

Weber, M. (1988) *Max Weber: A Biography.* Piscataway, NJ: Transaction Publishers.

Weber, M. (1997) *The Theory of Social Economic Organization.* New York, NY: The Free Press.

Weber, M. (1978a) 'Politics as a Vocation', in *Weber: Selections in Translation,* ed. W. Runciman. Cambridge: Cambridge University Press. 212–225.

Weber, M. (1978b). 'Household, Enterprise and *Oikos*' in *Economy and Society* ed. G. Roth and C. Wittich. Berkeley, CA: University of California Press. 370–384.

Whelan, B. (2000) *Ireland and the Marshall Plan, 1947–57.* Dublin: Four Courts Press.

Wilkinson, R. (2005) *The Impact of Inequality: How to Make Sick Societies Healthier.* London: Routledge.

Wittgenstein, L. (1994) [1958] *Philosophical Investigations.* London: Blackwell.

Worsley, P. (1987) *Trumpet Shall Sound: A study of Cargo Cults in Melanesia.* New York, NY: Schocken.

Wren, M. A. (2003) *Unhealthy State: Anatomy of a Sick Society.* Dublin: New Island.

Wren, M. A. and Tussing, D. (2005) *The Health Report.* Dublin: Beyond the Pale.

Yeats, W. B. (1934) *Wheels and Butterflies.* London: Macmillan.

Yeats, W. B. (1916a) 'September 1913' in *Responsibilities and Other Poems.* New York, NY: Macmillan. 32–33.

Yeats, W. B. (1916b). 'The Magi' in *Responsibilities and Other Poems.* New York, NY: Macmillan. 77.

Yeats, W. B. (1920a) 'The Second Coming' in *Michael Robartes and the Dancer.* Dublin: The Cuala Press. 10–11.

Yeats, W. B. (1920b) 'Easter 1916' in *Michael Robartes and the Dancer.* Dublin: The Cuala Press. 4.

Yeats, W. B. (1925) 'Fergus and the Druid' in *Early Poems and Stories.* London: Macmillan. 101–103.

Yeats, W. B. (1927) *The Resurrection.* Dublin: Adelphi.

Yeats, W. B. (1928) The Stare's nest by my window / Meditations in Time of Civil War, in *The Tower.* London: Macmillan. 26–27.

Yeats, W. B. (1996) *The Collected Poetry of W. B. Yeats,* edited by R. B. Finneran. New York, NY: Simon & Schuster.

Yeats, W. B. (2003) [1918] *Irish Fairy and Folk Tales.* New York, NY: Random House.

Zelizer, V. (1981) 'The Price and Value of Children: The Case of Children's Insurance.' *American Journal of Sociology,* 86(5): 1036–1056.

Žižek, S. (1990) 'Eastern Europe's Republics of Gilead.' *New Left Review,* 183 (October): 50–63.

Žižek, S. (2010) *Living in the End Times.* London: Verso.

Zizler, M. (1997) *The Social Meaning of Money.* Princeton, NJ: Princeton University Press.

Index

Adorno, Theodor, and Max Horkheimer 1, 92, 100, 163
agape xii, 83, 109–22, 166
anamnesis 142–57
anarchy 13, 14, 22, 35, 93, 136, 167
Aquinas, Thomas 116
Arendt, Hannah 76, 84, 110, 119
Arensberg, Conrad M., and Solon T. Kimball 145–6
Aristotle 78, 107, 110, 126–8
austerity 11–12, 28, 92, 96, 137, 155, 163

Bateson, Gregory 29, 57, 58, 79, 145, 154
Baudelaire, Charles 112, 164–6, 168n
Baudrillard, Jean 42
Bauman, Zygmunt 42, 75, 108–9
beauty x–xiii, 20–1, 48, 110, 112–13, 116, 119, 122, 155, 167–8
Beckett, Samuel 26, 144, 156
Benjamin, Walter 19, 20, 24, 51, 52, 69, 74, 100, 169n
Bourdieu, Pierre 64, 65
Brigid/St. Brigid 22

Cailleach 74–8, 82, 85n
Calvino, Italo 168
capitalism 9, 40, 42
cargo cult 143–52
Celtic Tiger xiv, 1, 9, 23, 26–30, 64, 70, 76, 85n, 86n
Christianity xi, 5, 10
Cold War 28

Colum, Padraic 25
communism 13, 29, 35
conceit ix
Conrad, Joseph 37, 49, 162, 166
consumerism 14, 25, 27
corporate republic 4
Corrib gas 72–5, 85n
Cronin, Michael 11, 85n
Cyclops 96–7

dark age 4, 12–14, 52, 74, 76, 83, 113, 119–20, 155
de Sade, Marquis 161–3, 166
democracy 11, 13
demon / demonic xi, xii, 2, 23, 139, 149, 151, 167
Derrida, Jacques 99, 100, 106n
dictator/tyrant 88, 94–102, 105n, 107n, 121, 127, 129–31, 136–8
Dracula 5, 13
    see also vampire
Dufour, Dany-Robert 158–63
Durkheim, Émile x, xiii, 1, 26, 102, 104n, 110, 111, 128, 158

ECB 9, 11
economics x, xiv, xv, 2, 3, 25, 27, 28, 31, 36, 39, 46–8, 89–92, 96
    see also oikos
Elias, Norbert ix, 49n
Ellmann, Richard 103, 105n, 120, 153, 159
empiricism ix–xi

Engels, Friedrich 159
Enlightenment ix, xi, 5, 11, 13
equality 11, 35
eros 107, 109–19, 166
EU 11, 12, 29, 31, 52–66, 96, 152
evil xii, 24, 25, 101, 107

fair trade 69–86
fascism 29, 30
Fianna Fáil 72, 76, 160
financialization 156, 161
Finnegans Wake 15n, 100, 103, 121
Foucault, Michel 4, 140, 163–4
foundations xiv, 33, 51–66, 74–7, 83
Frankenstein 13
Freud, Sigmund 49n, 100, 109, 158
Friedman, Milton 28, 31, 36, 76, 89–91,
    93, 104n, 132

Geertz, Clifford 145
ghost estates 25–7, 31–2
ghosts 19–27
Giddens, Anthony 108–9
gift 19, 24, 30–5, 48, 50n, 53, 55, 57,
    64–6, 74–9, 84
Girard, René 44, 50n, 80, 81
Goldman-Sachs 4
Graves, Robert 3, 22, 154
Greece 4, 30

Habermas, Jürgen 42, 64, 132
Haiti 10–11, 16n
Hayek, Friedrich 76, 90–1, 93, 132
Heaney, Seamus 83
Hegel, Georg Wilhelm Friedrich 54
Heidegger, Martin 19, 33, 34
Hermes 3, 14, 23–5, 31–2, 75, 127, 142,
    154, 156
Hestia/Vesta 22–5, 30, 31, 35, 52–8, 66n,
    74, 78
historicism ix, xi
Hobbes, Thomas 81, 90
Holocaust 29, 52, 105n, 166
Honneth, Axel 54
Horvath, Agnes 46, 50n, 85n

house/home/dwelling xiv, 19, 20, 24–7,
    31–59, 65–6, 78, 82

Idea/Ideal x, xi–xiii, 12, 24, 41, 65, 110,
    113, 158, 167
IFSC 66, 152, 156
IMF 4, 9, 11
individualization xv, 1, 14, 26, 27–8,
    48–9, 92–4, 108–10, 113, 117, 160

Jameson, Fredric 42
Joyce, James xiii, 1, 12–13, 14n, 15n, 21,
    83, 94–5, 100–3, 105n, 106n,
    114–21, 155–6, 166–8
Jung, Carl xii, 19, 20

Kant, Immanuel xii, xiii, 21, 33, 37–9,
    94, 158, 163
Kavanagh, Patrick 25–6
Keynes, John Maynard 76
Kiberd, Declan 15n, 117
Kinsella, Thomas 81–2, 85n
Kirby, Peadar 9
Klein, Naomi 2
Krugman, Paul 89–90

Lacan, Jacques 5, 15n, 26, 44, 50n, 106n,
    119, 158, 165
Laclau, Ernesto 84
Lemass, Seán 146–9, 152, 157
Leprechaun 148–50, 152
liminality xii, xiv–xv, 1, 2, 10, 22–4, 36,
    42, 71, 81, 94, 109, 115, 129, 138,
    142, 145, 150, 153–5, 159, 164, 165
love 40, 46, 48–9, 50n, 83, 92, 107–13,
    118, 164
    see also eros; philia; agape

Malinowski, Bronisław 145
Market ix, 2, 4, 9, 12–14, 23–4, 27–9, 31,
    35–8, 42, 45–9, 65–87, 89–103, 108,
    113, 118, 130, 132, 138–9, 142, 148,
    155–6, 158, 161
Marx, Karl 1, 9, 13, 25, 36, 159
materialism 25, 27

Mauss, Marcel 30, 79, 84, 145
Mead, Margaret 145
Mill, John Stuart 90–2, 104n
Mills, C. Wright x
modernity ix, 1, 11–12, 35
money 37–8, 44, 46–7, 49n, 127, 134, 135, 161
monsters xii, 1–16, 138–9
mortgage xiv, 36–7, 43–8
Mouffe, Chantal 58, 84, 128
myth 9, 14, 52–3, 69, 77, 95, 100, 144, 166

name of the father 97–9, 106n, 119, 154–5, 158–60, 165
neo-feudalism 4
neoliberalism 1–2, 14, 27, 35–7, 42
neo-nationalism 14
Nietzsche, Friedrich xii, 1, 5, 89, 95, 105n, 154
nihilism 24, 27, 37, 39, 41, 54, 55, 89, 94–5, 111, 119–20, 131, 162, 166–7
Nozick, Robert 2, 90, 93, 104n, 132

O'Brien, Flann 150
oikos xiv, 31, 39, 41, 44–8, 78
    see also economics
O'Neill, John 15n, 74
O'Regan, Brendan 148, 152
O'Toole, Fintan 84n

paganism 22
patricians and plebeians 12–13, 57–8
Pearse, Pádraig 7–8, 15n
Persephone 3
philia, philanthropy 109–10, 112–15, 117–19, 152, 166
Plato xv, 46, 50n, 78, 99, 107, 110–11, 120–2, 126, 129–40, 141n, 155, 158, 163
pleonexia xv, 76–7
Pluto 3
plutonomy 2–4, 11, 130
political theology 2, 27, 87–91, 93–5, 97, 99, 100, 103, 104n, 125, 159

possession 2, 24, 25, 38, 117, 139
precarity 2, 4, 11, 43, 48

Radin, Paul xii, 27
rationality ix, xi, 52
real estate 3, 25, 26, 38–40, 42, 44, 45, 161
Reason xi–xiii, 7, 11, 51, 93–4, 100, 102, 121, 158–9
recurrence 1, 4, 12, 13, 15n, 27, 28, 75–6, 77–82, 88, 95, 109, 133, 155, 168
Rome 4, 50n, 51–66, 83, 85n
rough beast 1, 2, 4, 8, 14, 24, 25, 27, 88, 96, 103, 117, 120, 139, 155, 162, 166–7
Rykwert, Joseph 151

schismogenesis 29–30, 54, 55, 57, 58, 74, 79–81, 85n, 156
Schmitt, Carl 87–99, 103, 104n, 105n, 106n
Schopenhauer, Arthur 21
Second Coming, The xiv, 1, 2, 13–14, 22, 83, 139, 144, 152, 154, 159, 162, 167
Sennett, Richard 48, 50n, 51
Serres, Michel 52, 76, 85n
Shannon 142, 143, 146–9, 151–2, 157n
Shell to Sea 69–74
Simmel, Georg 24, 35–44, 47–8, 49n, 50n, 83, 161
slavery 10–11, 16n
Smith, Adam 91
Socrates 50n, 84, 95, 110–21, 126, 130–2
sophist, sophistry 23, 45–8, 50n, 131, 133
Sorokin, Pitrim 112–13, 120, 166
sovereignty 14, 25, 75, 78, 96, 99
Szakolczai, Arpad 42, 46, 81, 144–5

Táin Bó Cuailnge 75–82
tax, tax free zone xv, 9, 11–12, 14, 23, 29, 32, 60–6, 72, 73, 93, 134, 142, 144, 146–9, 151–2, 156, 157n

Taylor, Charles 108, 111–13, 118–20, 166
Thatcher, Margaret 26–7, 76
theology 88–106, 159
Titmuss, Richard 31
totalitarianism 30
Treaty of Rome 52–4, 60
Trickster xii, 2, 20, 23–4, 27, 31–2
Troika 11, 14, 59–60, 88–9, 96, 99, 103, 162–3

Ulysses 95, 117–19
unconscious 5, 19–32
Utopia 65, 93, 102, 130

value x, 24, 30–1, 35–49, 50n, 93, 95, 104n, 112, 159, 161

vampire 7–9, 28
Vico, Giambattista, ix, xiii, 1, 12–14, 34, 53–8, 97, 99, 116, 167

Wall Street Crash 29
Weber, Max x, xii, 1, 26, 35–44, 50n, 63, 89, 105n, 140n, 146, 149, 167
Wittgenstein, Ludwig ix, 167
World War II 29, 112, 143, 150

Yeats, William Butler xiii, xiv, 1, 7, 13, 22–5, 81–3, 96, 139, 145, 152–67

Žižek, Slavoj 30
zombie 9–14, 25–6, 162, 166